IBM® Personal Computer
Upgrade Guide

IBM® Personal Computer Upgrade Guide

Tom Badgett
Corey Sandler
Jim Terry

HOWARD W. SAMS & COMPANY
Macmillan Computer Publishing

FIRST EDITION
FIRST PRINTING—1990

International Standard Book Number: 0-672-22723-1
Library of Congress Catalog Card Number: 90-61250

Acquisitions and Development Editor: *James Rounds*
Manuscript Editor: *James M. Moore*
Indexer: *Hilary Adams*
Production: *Brad Chinn, Sally Copenhaver, Tami Hughes, Bill Hurley, Charles Hutchinson, Jodi Jensen, Jennifer Matthews, Dennis Sheehan, Bruce Steed, Mary Beth Wakefield, Nora Westlake*
Composition: *Cromer Graphics*

Printed in the United States of America

Trademark Acknowledgments
All terms mentioned in this book that are known to be trademarks or service marks are listed below. In addition, terms suspected of being trademarks or service marks have been appropriately capitalized. Howard W. Sams & Company cannot attest to the accuracy of this information. Use of a term in this book should not be regarded as affecting the validity of any trademark or service mark.

PostScript is a registered trademark of Adobe Systems, Incorporated.

LaserWriter is a registered trademark of Apple Computer, Inc.

Framework is a registered trademark of Ashton-Tate.

Unix is a registered trademark of AT&T.

Commodore is a registered trademark of Commodore Electronics Limited.

FastBack Plus is a registered trademark of Fifth Generation Systems.

SpinRite is a trademark of Gibson Research Corporation.

HP and LaserJet are registered trademarks of Hewlett-Packard.

Intel is a trademark of Intel Corporation.

DOS, PC-DOS, VGA, and XT are trademarks and AT, IBM, IBM PC, OS/2, PC/XT, and Selectric are registered trademarks of International Business Machines Corporation.

1-2-3, Lotus, and Symphony are registered trademarks of Lotus Development Corp.

Mace Utilities is a registered trademark of Paul Mace Software, Inc.

Microsoft, MS-DOS, and Xenix are registered trademarks of Microsoft Corporation.

Multisync is a trademark of NEC America, Inc.

The Norton Utilities is a trademark of Peter Norton Computing, Inc.

WordPerfect is a registered trademark of WordPerfect Corporation.

*This book is lovingly dedicated to
Libby, Helen, James, and Will
for long-suffering and forebearance.*

Contents

Acknowledgments

The authors note with thanks the contributions of some of the people and companies who helped with this book.

Thanks to Tracy Smith at Waterside Productions for her capable agentry, to Howard W. Sams & Company for publishing the book, and to Jim Rounds at Sams for being so helpful and flexible during the writing of this book.

Thanks to our families for their understanding and cooperation. Any vocation you pursue at home—but perhaps writing more than some—is a group effort.

We also wish to acknowledge the valuable assistance provided by a number of major hardware and software companies.

This book was researched and prepared using equipment and software that included the following:

CompuAdd 316S computer, a 16-MHz 80386SX computer with 110 megabyte hard disk. CompuAdd Corp., 12303 Technology Boulevard, Austin, TX 78727; (800) 627-1967.

InSet software for image capture and conversion. Inset Systems, 71 Commerce Drive, Brookfield, CT 06804; (800) 828-8088, (203) 775-5866.

Lanlink Version 5.0, serial network for printer and file sharing. The Software Link, Inc., 3577 Parkway Lane, Atlanta, GA 30092; (404) 448-5465.

NEC Silentwriter LC-890 PostScript LED printer. NEC Information Systems, Inc., 1414 Massachusetts Avenue, Foxboro, MA 01719; (508) 264-8000.

Swan 386/20 computer. A 20-MHz 80386 microprocessor with 0 wait state memory, shadow BIOS, and 150-megabyte hard drive. Tussey Computer Products, 3075 Research Drive, State College, PA 16801; (800) 468-9044.

WordPerfect Version 5.1 word-processing software. WordPerfect Corporation, 1555 N. Technology Way, Orem, UT 84057; (801) 227 4288.

Preface

One of the strengths of the modern personal computer is its chameleon-like ability to change its personality with a change of software. One moment, with the use of a capable word processor, the PC is a sophisticated writing assistant. The next moment, it is an ultraprecise accountant juggling your financial numbers in an electronic spreadsheet, and just a few seconds later it can transport you around the world with a communications program.

But often overlooked is the hardware side: a PC is very much like a child's Transformer toy. Twist it on its side to become a database server; change its video card to switch from monochrome numbers to full-color graphics; pull out its floppy-disk drive and replace it with a gigantic Winchester...the list goes on.

IBM revolutionized the computing world nearly ten years ago with the introduction of its Personal Computer. Other companies had offered machines in this class for several years before that, but when the biggest name in computing gave its blessing to the concept, the desktop computer market was on its way. The familiar "PC" moniker now applies to almost any personal-sized computer.

It was significant that IBM endorsed personal computing, and it was significant that individuals could purchase so much computing power for such a reasonable price. But, the most important aspect of IBM's 1981 announcement was the open architecture of the hardware and the PC-DOS operating system.

IBM published technical specifications of the PC's bus architecture and told software developers how to access the DOS features they needed for applications design. For the first time in the personal computer industry, users began to have a choice of suppliers.

Over the years, IBM has enhanced the original design, and third-party developers have designed their own versions of these machines. Indeed, the popular "AT" bus architecture has a life beyond its progenitor, forming the basis for many 80386 and 80486 high-end machines.

Not only has this progression been good for purchasers of new machines, it has enhanced the value of existing units. Because much of the very latest expansion hardware is still compatible with earlier computers, it is easier to add new features to a machine you already have.

If you need more power than add-on boards and peripherals can provide, you can replace the entire motherboard with a faster, more capable design, and still use many of the peripherials and expansion boards you already have. You can plan a staged expansion that replaces your existing hardware over a period of months or years.

Because of the spread of PC-clone retailers, you can hire someone to help you design and build your system upgrade; but the nature of the hardware is such that even if you don't have very much computer experience, you can probably easily handle the job yourself.

If you've never delved under the covers of your PC, that may sound like an outrageous claim, but the information in this book can change your mind. It is true that today's desktop computers are powerful, complicated, and expensive. But the complicated parts of a computer are well contained, isolated in the chips and the circuit boards, and in the software that make it what it is.

From the user perspective, PC components are basically nonthreatening, even innocuous, building blocks. Consider another example. You maybe wouldn't think of mounting a tire on a wheel and balancing the wheel yourself. This takes specialized equipment and experience the average driver doesn't have. However, most of us are comfortable putting on a spare if the tire develops a flat.

What about the telephone? Maybe you wouldn't disassemble an instrument, but you probably wouldn't hesitate to plug in an answering machine or install a cordless telephone on your system.

With today's PC designs, upgrading a machine is very little different from changing a tire or adding telephone equipment. You work with the basic building blocks, adding or subtracting components as necessary. There is no need for you to work with complex components, and little requirement for you to understand how the building blocks function. You only need to know generally what each component does, and decide which ones you need. Then it is just a matter of some fairly simple remove-and-replace operations to upgrade your machine.

That's what this book is about, upgrading your existing PC platform with peripherals and expansion cards. We even show you how to start with a bare case and build a new system from scratch. And the best news is, you can do it! With just a little attention to how you plan to use your computer in the future, and a little research to find the products you need, you can greatly expand your PC with only a screwdriver.

So let's get busy. You're already on your way to a better, faster, more capable PC.

TOM BADGETT
COREY SANDLER
JIM TERRY

Chapter 1

Should You Upgrade or Buy?

Fom the early days of the IBM era, back in 1981, the PC has been ready for upgrades. The early IBM PC came with a motherboard and five expansion slots. All the slots weren't occupied, so there was room for an upgrade. This arrangement has become known as an *open configuration*. Contrast that with the way some other types of PCs have been designed; with them there's little if any room for expansion, and users are actively discouraged from tampering with the inside of the computer.

Since that rather humble beginning by IBM, many engineers have spent a tremendous amount of time designing and redesigning expansion cards, motherboards, data storage devices (floppy diskette drives, hard drives, and tape drives to name a few), and power supplies to fit inside a PC case with a little room left over. All this effort is directed at allowing you, the user, to upgrade your system whenever you want.

That makes you sound pretty important. In fact, you are! A rather large industry has developed with the express purpose of making it easy for you to configure your PC in ways that were only wild dreams five years ago. Today you can put a card in your PC that will let it communicate with other PCs at 9600 bits of information per second; five years ago, a rate of 300 *baud* (bits per second) was common and 1200 baud was state of-the-art for PCs.

That's impressive, but what about fax? Facsimile machines have swept businesses by storm. This ubiquitous transceiver technology links desktops and telephones around the world. You can even order your lunch-time pizza by fax. And now you can expand your PC with a fax card so that your memos never have to make it to hard copy in your office to appear on someone's desk 2000 miles away. Other cards will help you scan documents directly into your computer so that no one has to retype them.

You're looking in this book for upgrade information. That means you think you're on the verge of taking the plunge. One or more of your PCs is getting old, not quite taking care of business anymore. Some of your troops may have been grumbling for a long time about having to deal with such ancient systems. So let's look at upgrades. What do you have to gain and lose by performing an upgrade? In some companies, there are two pots of money, one for new equipment and the other for maintaining and upgrading old equipment. Frequently the latter pot is much easier to dip into. In that case, even if an upgrade is dead even or slightly unfavorable from a cost standpoint, going with an upgrade will probably get you the higher-performance systems you need more quickly.

This looks like a gain.

What about the losses? You could lose time. If you just buy an off-the-shelf PC, someone else has made all the decisions about components and compatibility. When you do your own upgrade, you have to make those decisions yourself. Don't panic! We'll lead you through such issues. They're really not such a big deal.

Upgrade Advantages Uncovered

Potential advantages come in two basic forms: money and flexibility. In many instances, it will cost less to upgrade compared to buying a new system. Flexibility relates to both incremental upgrades and component choices. Let's look at these ideas in a bit more detail.

Money

It's quite true that any upgrade from an 8088-based PC to an 80286-based system that costs less than $1500 is a good deal. You'd be hard pressed to buy a new stripped-down 80286 system for much less than that. You can find low prices on new systems, but you have to be very cautious when comparing costs for an upgrade with prices for new units. Frequently, very low prices are advertised for new units that don't have system memory, hard drives, or monitors. Your PC already has all those and it's ready to work now.

Do you have to spend all your money now? Not really. You can work an upgrade like taffy candy—pull it out as far as you want. In fact, upgrades really look good when you stretch them out over several months. All the costs don't arrive at once, and you have a functioning PC all along. You don't have to wait around until a large block of money becomes available. In fact, with some forethought, you can fix the one or two major problems in your PC first so that you get a better performing machine during the entire process. So you wind up looking good; no one fought for a large lump sum, and performance was improved.

Flexibility

Flexibility is nice for a gymnast, but how does it apply to an upgrade? For one thing, you get time to make incremental changes as well as the opportunity to shop around for bargains. With an upgrade, you have a chance to make small changes to see what works best with your PCs and users.

You shouldn't lose sight of who it is that will be using the upgraded PC. After all, the purpose of an upgrade is to improve performance of the PC-and-user combination. You're on the losing end of the deal if users can't figure out how to take the new system through its paces or are too intimidated to try to work with it.

What about getting parts from several different sources? That works fine for an upgrade. You can hunt around to find the best deals on the components you need. There are industry standards for most components and interfaces (the rules for how components talk to each other). Since most manufacturers are working hard to maintain compatibility with the existing standards, you can pick and choose. Most suppliers of new PCs do just that. They don't get their components from a single source. And most especially, they don't make all the components themselves.

Do you always agree with the people you work with? Of course not; they don't understand the problem, or maybe they just have a different set of priorities. Why should it be different with people who set up new PCs? They have their own agendas. They're working to maximize their profit. That's not bad, but it may work against giving you the best system for your needs. To get the very best system for you, you have to pick the components that suit your set of problems. Generally, you can accomplish that best by performing an upgrade. That way, you're not stuck with a system that is optimal for maximizing profits at Megacolossal Computer Industries, but doesn't really do the job for you.

You also have to be careful to put together systems that are tailored to each of your users. Don't use a brush that paints with too broad strokes. Not everyone needs or even wants the latest and greatest in technology. When you have the best of anything, curious visitors start appearing. They assume that the user is an expert and begin a barrage of questions. This isn't good for productivity and sometimes upsets the users, especially during rather trying days of becoming acclimated to the system. Some of this type of activity can be avoided by upgrades. Superficially, the system looks the same. A casual observer isn't likely to notice much more than a change from a monochrome to a color monitor. You still have the same old box sitting on the desk.

Disadvantages

Of course, there are some disadvantages to upgrading a PC. An important disadvantage is that someone has to do the work and it's likely to be you. You may not see that as a disadvantage. You may be looking forward to getting your hands inside the PC. (Personally we don't see it as a disadvantage.) There is a strong sense of accomplishment associated with doing a job that others think is tough. We'll try to make the tough parts easier for you.

Another disadvantage is debugging. It seems that there is a corollary to Murphy's Law that says, "Nothing new works right the first time you turn it on." With an upgrade you are taking some of the bite out of the corollary. You're using a proven design. You know the PC used to work. If worse comes to worst, you can always put it back the way it was. That's a real advantage of the modular way PCs are built.

Okay, you may have to do a little debugging. In later chapters, we discuss many of the common mistakes and how to correct them (we encourage you to avoid them). We also discuss recovering from real hardware problems as well as the more common operator errors. In reality, PCs are hardy beasts. Most of the problems associated with them are user problems and not hardware problems.

Save the Body

Is it really worth it to keep an old PC case? After all it's gotten dirty and gunked up with coffee and doughnuts and maybe even more than just a little cigarette smoke. Wouldn't a shiny, new PC look great? Of course it would. So if appearance is a concern, take a little liquid cleanser to the top of the case after you have removed it. Don't spray liquids on any electrical equipment while it is energized. As far as the effects on the inside of the case, short work with a vacuum cleaner and a rag will take care of the inroads of noxious smoke. DON'T poke around inside the case while the system is plugged in. Always turn it off and then unplug it. And, of course, use care in cleaning any boards and other electrical components. Hint: Instead of trying to vacuum lint and other debris out of the inside of a computer case, use the blowing end of the machine with a crevice tool. This will direct a small, powerful stream of air inside the case, dislodging most of stuff that has accumulated inside without requiring you to touch any of the components with a vacuum wand.

How about expansion boards? Can you really put the ones you want in the case you have? The answer here takes a couple of twists. First, there are upgrade motherboards that will fit in your case, and they have either seven or eight expansion slots. That should give you enough room, if the rear panel of your case supports that many expansion boards. The older PC cases have room for only five expansion boards.

Another way to get more performance in less room is to use multifunction boards. In the early days, you had to buy separate boards for every function. That's no longer true.

There are circumstances in which replacing the case makes sense. If the case is physically damaged, replace it. If you need more hard drives or floppy disks than the old case will hold, replace it. If you need more expansion slots than the rear panel of your existing case supports, replace the case. Otherwise, don't bother. The old case probably is quite adequate.

New cases are available for less than $100. If you're going to buy a new case, why not just get a new computer? Certainly that's a possibility, but when you do that you lose the flexibility that comes with the upgrade process.

What's in This Book

This book is arranged into nine chapters, five appendixes, and an index. Our position is that a detailed index containing cross references is important for any book. It is a must for a book like this that is to be used as a reference rather than being read from cover to cover once and then placed on a shelf.

Chapter 1 is a general introduction to upgrading PCs and the kinds of questions and issues associated with upgrades.

Chapter 2 discusses the peripheral equipment available for upgrading your PC. Printers are noticeably absent from Chapter 2; they get their own chapter, Chapter 5, where we discuss specific types and upgrades for them.

Chapter 3 gives you an idea of the interaction between software and hardware upgrade decisions. The kind of hardware upgrade you perform affects the kinds of software you can run, and the reverse is also true.

Chapter 4 takes you in detail through two examples—an 8088-to-80286 switch and an 80286-to-80386 upgrade.

Chapter 5 discusses printer upgrades.

Chapter 6 takes you through the testing process. Once you've assembled your PC, you need to test it to see if it is working properly and to determine just how much you increased the system performance.

Chapter 7 provides you with the information you'll need if you decide to go one step beyond an upgrade and build a PC from scratch.

In Chapters 8 and 9, you'll be introduced to the upgrading strategy. You'll find out why you need to develop a strategy and how your strategy relates to the ultimate system performance and cost. Cost is revisited in the latter chapter with a more detailed analysis of costs associated with an upgrade strategy.

Appendix A covers converting numbers among various number bases.

Appendix B provides a list of manufacturers of printers and printer products.

Appendix C discusses some general safety considerations you should observe when working with your PC. There isn't anything particularly dangerous about a personal computer, but there are some common-sense precautions you should remember to ensure your personal safety and the safety of your hardware.

Appendix D provides a brief list of manufacturers and suppliers of the type of equipment we discuss in this book.

Appendix E offers some hardware troubleshooting hints to help you debug a recalcitrant system.

The cross-referenced index will help you to find the topics of interest as you progress with your PC upgrade.

Chapter 2

Upgrading Peripherals

Your initial personal-computer purchase was a complex decision, with a lot of factors to consider. Changing components or upgrading peripherals could follow as a close second for difficulty.

After some great deliberation, and in all respects some sleepless nights, that first step was decided upon, and your investment was made. Your PC was configured for solutions to problems or to reach goals based on conditions as they then existed. By now, the rules have changed; it's time to add more power, increase storage capacity, expand RAM, or try a new product just for the heck of it. That's the purpose of this chapter, to rewrite the rules to help you win in today's upgrade game.

Computer peripherals include a variety of products. New and exciting advances are made every day, and it is almost impossible to keep up with them all, so don't even try. This chapter will give you a good place to start, however. Here are some of the topics that will be discussed:

1. Hard-disk drives
2. Floppy-disk drives
3. Monitors
4. Memory
5. Fax-communication adapters
6. Mice and joysticks
7. Modems

Hard-Disk Drives

Hard-disk drives have become an everyday word in the PC world, but buying your first one or upgrading what you have to something with more speed and capacity still can be a difficult process. It truly is a decision that will impact every aspect of your PC operations. Not too long ago, a hard disk on a PC was a rare luxury. In the early days, the first PC hard drives were big, bulky conglomerations of metal, magnetic platters, circuit boards, and even their own power supplies. More often than not, the entire hard-drive unit occupied more space than the PC. In that time, this fantastic state-of-the-art storage device usually provided an unheard of 5 megabytes of secondary storage that set the computer industry on its way to a new era.

While the basic principle of a hard disk has remained unchanged from these early days of washing-machine-sized drives, today's hard-disk drive bears about the same relation to its forebears in terms of technology that a jumbo jet does to a Piper Cub. Over the past decade, the hard disk has come from disks the size of a phonograph record to 8-inch platters to 5.25-inch disks to 3.5-inch devices. In the next year, expect to see 2-inch devices hit the market. As the size has gone down, the capacity has gone up, and the speed of transfer of information to and from the disk has grown spectacularly.

So, too, the reliability of hard-disk drives has improved. The quality of the magnetic coating on the platters is better than before, and the design and longevity of the read/write heads has dramatically improved. One of the measures of reliability is *mean time between failures*; ratings here have doubled and quadrupled in just the past few years.

Hard-Drive Components

All hard drives consist of a few basic components:

- Rigid disks coated with magnetic media for data storage
- Read/write heads, usually one per surface
- A motor and mechanical elements to move the heads
- An electronic interface between the heads and the computer interface
- A computer interface/controller
- One or more cables between the drive and computer

Remember that not many years ago, a 5.25-inch platter typically stored about 5 megabytes of data. With newer technology, a 3.5-inch platter can hold 40 megabytes of data. While the drives are getting smaller in size, the medium has gotten more dense and more reliable.

Up until the past few years, each platter was coated with an oxide material, generally iron oxide. This process is still used today for some drives; however, a new process called *plating* produces a more reliable medium that also is more durable. A plated disk is coated with a fine metal compound derived from a process called *sputtering*. The plated medium is thinner, and the plating process produces surfaces more uniformly smooth than the oxide process. This allows denser data storage and reduces the number of platters and their size. This new type of plated drive is also more resistant to data loss.

Most of the progressive manufacturers of magnetic media have been reducing the number of platters derived from the oxide process and are instead manufacturing plated products. This process is more expensive, but it is typically found in faster drives with capacities of more than 40 megabytes. As of the writing of this book, a new industry push is taking place, and the new goal of media manufacturers is to pack as much as 80 megabytes on a single platter.

New methods of storing the data also have been developed to take advantage of denser storage capacities. Traditionally, data was stored by a process called *modified frequency modulation (MFM)*. This procedure stores data on the medium one bit at a time. While MFM is a simple and fairly reliable process, the way data is stored on the medium is relatively inefficient. A more efficient encoding technique is referred to as *run-length limited (RLL)*. This method stores data in a more dense fashion, allowing a savings of up to 50% in medium space.

Another important aspect of hard-drive technology is the speed at which data can be found or accessed. Performance in some CAD, data-base, or spreadsheet applications can be affected directly by hard-disk read/write speed.

One factor that directly impacts performance is the head positioning technique used. Today, two common types of positioning methods are found, stepper motors and voice-coil positioners. A stepper motor uses a notched disk to move the read/write head in fixed increments, or steps, across the disk surface. A voice-coil mechanism uses wire coils that act as an electromagnet to move the head very fast in precise increments.

The main difference between the two head-positioning processes is speed. The best access time that a stepper motor can achieve is about 28 ms, compared to access times of 18 ms and lower for voice-coil positioners. One other good aspect about a voice-coil positioner is automatic parking of the heads. This prevents the sensitive read/write head from bouncing on the surface of the medium if the computer is bumped or moved.

Most of the time, data is physically stored on both sides of a drive platter, with one read/write head per side. A drive with three platters, and conforming to this storage type, would have six read/write heads, one for each surface. With this configuration, the servo information (on-drive data that tells the drive where information is stored and how to read and write it) is written with the data. This approach is called an *embedded servo*.

Another common control method is a *dedicated servo*. This method reserves one entire platter to store the servo information and employs a special kind of read/write head to access the information. A dedicated-servo design allows a faster way to locate information, while the embedded servo can provide more accurate data seeking when extreme conditions are encountered.

Another important factor is the *disk interleave*. Interleave is the addressing scheme that is assigned to the physical surface during the low-level format process. Each sector on the platter is given a number that is used as an address. This address controls how each is read. A drive with an interleave of three, for example, would be accessed as follows: The first sector would be read, the next two would be skipped, the next one read, the next two skipped, and so on.

The reason for skipping some sectors during a write and read is the time required for the drive controller to transfer the information and for the CPU to store the data read into memory. When this process is finished for the data read, the CPU issues another read command to the next addressed sector. While these instructions are being exchanged, the platters are spinning at 3600 revolutions per minute, so if the CPU and controller can't keep up, the data can't be read contiguously without waiting for the platter to make an additional revolution.

Interleaving eliminates some of this wait time. Some drive and controller combinations have an interleave of 1:1, which means they are fast enough to transfer data at disk speed. They are the fastest hard-disk subsystems available and provide the best overall performance. Typically, these are available only in machines that have an 80286 or higher-speed processor.

The hard part in upgrading your hard drive is deciding which drive is right for your specific needs. Major points to consider are:

1. Speed—How fast your new hard drive can provide the data needed will have a direct effect on your performance and level of patience (or impatience). In today's market, there is no reason to accept any seek time of more that 40 ms.

2. Size Limitations—The physical space available to install the hard drive is a factor. However, with a little custom work, you should be able to find room for a high-capacity hard-disk drive in just about any machine. New hard drives are available in 3.5-inch form factors only 0.78 inch tall. Even if you have to mount the drive in an unusual position or location, that's OK because you don't have to access it as you do a floppy drive. Just make sure you don't interfere with other boards or devices, and try not to disrupt air flow unnecessarily.

3. Capacity—Storage capacity is the main reason to add or upgrade the hard drive. Don't cut yourself short. A good rule of thumb is to plan all your storage needs for the next three years. After arriving at that factor, double it. That should provide the current capacity you need and give some growing room. In any case, you probably shouldn't consider anything less than 40 megabytes. Some 30-megabyte drives have caused more than their share of maintenance problems, and the cost differential between a 20-megabyte and a 40-megabyte drive is very small.

4. Power requirements—Power consumption should be a factor only for users with old IBM PC's or some early PC compatibles. These older models tend to have a 65-watt power supply. This could create problems that may or may not be traceable to the power supply. These problems should only

occur with a combination of other adapter cards installed in the system. To determine if a problem is related to power, the easiest way to find out would be to remove one or two of the adapter cards with the heaviest power requirements. The first choice would be a network-communication adapter card. Next would come fully populated multifunction memory-expansion cards. Last would be serial and parallel cards, for the power they draw is minimal. If you do have problems and need to replace your power supply, install a 150-watt or higher unit. That is a power supply you will not outgrow.

With all the vendors in the hard-drive arena, picking one would be like picking a number out of a hat. No matter what model or vendor you choose, a hard drive is a mechanical object. You probably will have at least one problem with it in the future. But that is why adequate backup procedures must be designed. With that in mind, here are some general suggestions to help you select a hard-drive upgrade.

For a PC, PC/XT, or compatibles based on the 8086 or 8088 processor:

Capacity: 40 megabytes

Random-Access Seek Time: 40 milliseconds

Data-Transfer Rate: 5 megabits per second

For an IBM PC/AT or compatible based on the 80286 processor:

Capacity: 50 megabytes

Random-Access Seek Time: 28 milliseconds

Data-Transfer Rate: 7 megabits per second

For 80386- or 80486-based machines:

Capacity: 80 megabytes

Random-Access Seek Time: 15 milliseconds

Data-Transfer Rate: 10 megabits per second

Remember, these are only suggestions, not requirements.

Interface Options

As you add a new or upgraded hard drive, there are several controller options to consider. Older systems generally use some form of the ST-506 or ST-412 controller system. This was the de facto standard for PC hard-disk controllers up until now. Today, controllers with better performance and more flexibility are available. Many AT-class and 80386-based machines today use *ESDI (Enhanced Small Device Interface)* interfaces or some form of IDE interface.

The *intelligent drive interface*, sometimes called *imbedded drive elec-tronics* or *intelligent drive electronics (IDE)*, gives manufacturers of hard drives more room for maneuvering in drive design because virtually all of the control-ler electronics are contained in the drive subsystem itself. Only a minimal data-transfer interface is contained in a plug-in board or motherboard-based interface.

Most new motherboards include a 40-pin connector that attaches directly to an IDE hard-drive subsystem. You can also purchase small plug-in interface boards for an older motherboard to let you install an IDE drive. The benefits of IDE include better performance and more flexibility in selecting hard-drive expansion.

ESDI

The ESDI is a quasi-IDE standard that moves the encode-decode functions off the bus-level controller and onto a board that is an integral part of the drive itself. It was developed by a group of drive manufacturers to achieve higher performance. Unfortunately, there are many implementations of ESDI, a situa-tion that can produce incompatibilities among interfaces and hard drives. When you buy an ESDI drive, purchase the vendor's matching interface card as well, or select a package put together by a reputable reseller. This will ensure full compatibility and maximum performance.

SCSI

The *SCSI (Small Computer System Interface)*, often pronounced "skuzzy," is a relatively high-speed I/O bus that recently began moving down from worksta-tion platforms to PCs. There are many advantages to using SCSI hard drives in your system, and a few disadvantages.

The most obvious disadvantage is that SCSI is not the interface you find in packaged PC/AT-class systems. These dual controllers usually contain a floppy-disk and a hard-disk interface on a single board. If you already have a machine with this combined controller installed and then decide to add a SCSI drive, you will have to replace the controller as well. There aren't as many SCSI controllers to choose from as with other interfaces, nor do all manufacturers of PC-class drives have SCSI models.

In addition, many PC users report incompatibilities between SCSI drives and existing software, especially Microsoft Windows based applications.

Although SCSI is a high-speed I/O bus that can provide excellent disk performance, it requires a separate bus-level interface card. If your PC mother-board already contains one of the new 40-pin intelligent drive interfaces, you'll be paying extra for the convenience of SCSI, but if performance and flexibility are high on your list of needs, SCSI is probably worth the price.

In addition, SCSI lets you do some things you can't do with conventional interfaces. It supports multiple devices, including disk drives, tapes, CD ROMs, network interfaces, printers, plotters, or about any other I/O device.

A single SCSI interface usually can support up to seven devices attached in daisy-chain fashion. Also, SCSI offloads some of the I/O tasks usually performed by the CPU. This can result in better I/O performance and reduced load on the central processor.

Two SCSI designations currently are seen, SCSI and the newer SCSI-2, which includes ANSI extensions that increase bandwidth to a 16- or 32-bit bus and raise data-transfer rates to as high as 40 Mbps. Standards work on SCSI-3 already is underway. The enhanced performance, increasing acceptance, and broad base of existing installations portend a strong future for this intelligent interface in the micro world.

Monitors

Upgrading monitors could be one of the most costly moves you will make. The most important thing about monitors and their quality of display is the resolution as it is represented in *pixels*. Pixels are the small pinpoints of light (or dark) that are combined to make up images. If you look closely at your existing monitor, you can actually see pixels, unless your monitor is of very high resolution.

Resolution is expressed using a standard system, usually in the form A × B. The first number (A) represents the number of pixels that make up one horizontal row, and the second number (B) represents the number of pixels that make up one vertical column. Resolutions of various monitors are summarized in Table 2–1.

Table 2–1.   Characteristics of Monitors

Monitor Type	Resolution	Number of Colors
Monochrome	720 × 350 Graphics 640 × 200 Text	Green, Amber, or White
Color—CGA	320 × 200	One
Color—EGA	640 × 350	16
VGA	640 × 480	16
	528 × 480	256
Super VGA	800 × 600	256
Multisync	1280 × 1024 (Maximum)	16
	1024 × 768	256

Depending on how long ago you bought your present monitor, things could have changed quite drastically. The comparison below shows the different types of monitors and what they are typically called in the industry today.

Monochrome

The monochrome monitor, sometimes referred to as an *MGA (Monochrome Graphics Adapter)*, is the least expensive monitor type. This monitor generally has a green or amber screen, or the newer "Paper White" display. The resolution on MGA monitors is better than that of standard color graphics (CGA) monitors.

Monochrome monitors usually require a monochrome adapter card. (Some computers have this function built into the motherboard.) Possible options for the adapter card include graphics support and, more often than not, a Centronics parallel printer port. For graphics support, you'll probably want to stay with Hercules compatible, which seems to have become a popular industry standard.

Practical applications that this type of monitor would be ideal for include word processing, electronic spreadsheet processing, and even some types of graphics processing that require only one color processing. A monochrome monitor can be purchased for as little as $69, and monochrome adapter cards start at around $50. Be sure of your vendor, because generally you get what you pay for.

CGA Color

The *CGA (Color Graphics Adapter)* is the least expensive color monitor available. This type originally was configured and released with IBM's initial entry into the personal computer world with the very first IBM PC. The IBM version of the color adapter card had no printer port, so that was an extra-cost option. Later adapter cards included a printer port, and some even had a serial-port option also.

The Hercules color-graphics adapter board used a half slot and included a printer port, as well as some advanced graphics support, while still maintaining compatibility with the original IBM color adapter.

The CGA monitor enjoyed and still enjoys a heavy part of the market share for color display devices, though that is declining. The popularity CGA monitors still enjoy can be attributed primarily to cost, because the resolution of these monitors for text, numerical, or graphic material falls short of the accepted business-presentations standards of today.

If budget is the question in upgrading, then for your specific application, CGA could be the correct answer. It performs well in a game atmosphere, but for business applications, you will quickly tire of the low resolution. A good-quality monochrome display is a better choice for low-budget business applications.

Prices of CGA-compatible color monitors begin under $200. You can pick up a color-graphics interface with a printer port for less than $50.

EGA

The next step up from CGA is *EGA,* or *Extended Graphics Adapter*. This monitor was developed to fill the gap left by the CGA's lack of resolution; to provide added features to some of the software packages developed to use graphics; and also just to provide acceptable resolution to the everyday user who wanted color, couldn't afford one of the specialized, higher resolution monitors, and wasn't satisfied with monochrome any longer. The EGA adapter cards vary by vendor, but generally all have on-board memory. This allows the higher-resolution screens to be processed into video memory and images to be modified faster.

Some offer a printer-port feature and even use only half-card technology. When upgrading, if you can afford the bigger price tag, choosing the EGA configuration over the CGA should be a no brainer. The increase in readability and ability to display graphics is truly apparent; EGA will do everything that CGA will do, only it does it better.

Special video drivers are available today that will allow you to increase the number of rows and columns that can be viewed on the screen, because of the increase in resolution. In packages like 1-2-3 or Symphony from Lotus, more of the spreadsheet is available, and the only modification needed is to add the video driver to the selections already provided by Lotus. Your spreadsheets are still compatible with other systems that run the Lotus package without modification in any form. The video capability of the other system is controlled by the components of that system. Displayed text for word-processing applications is much more crisp and easy on the eyes. Graphic presentations are markedly improved.

The choice should be obvious; EGA is a much better display method than CGA and is an easy decision to make. Popular EGA monitors can be purchased at prices that start under $300, and EGA adapter cards should be readily available for well under $100.

VGA

Originally developed and released with the IBM PS/2, *VGA (Video Graphics Array)* once again improved upon video-display quality. This entry was really a logical progression in video technology that started with CGA, moved to EGA, and then continued to VGA.

This display provides excellent quality in text and is exceptional in graphics. It is available on most machines today, but it is more expensive than EGA. If you have an IBM PS/2, no adapter card is needed to switch from monochrome to color. If you are adding VGA capability, expect to pay from under $350 to as much as $800 for the monitor, and from about $125 for the very low-end, 8-bit cards to $300 or more for high-end VGA adapter cards.

Super VGA

Super VGA is the next generation of monitors. This relatively new monitor type improves on the already good performance of VGA. The Super VGA provides a video quality that is truly picture perfect. Super VGA is obviously more expensive than the rest of the video types mentioned, but it is the best, too. Any application that you want to process would be acceptable on the Super VGA.

Multisync

With all of the different types of video monitors on the market today, many have been omitted from this summary. There are hundreds of specialty adapters and monitors, and to get into them would not be practical. One type of monitor that is popular and has seen quite a bit of advertising is referred to as *Multisync*. Multisync monitors work on about any video adapter, up to the level of resolution that is provided with the specific Multisync monitor that is purchased. The video scan rate and resolution are matched with those of the video card that drives the monitor. Multisync is a good all-around choice because it will work with a variety of video adapters without replacing the monitor, until the maximum resolution of the monitor itself is reached.

Floppy-Disk Drives

While hard-disk drives supply a tremendous amount of capacity, it's pretty inconvenient to disassemble your machine and take your hard drive to work with you. Floppy drives fill the need for transportable data nicely. While they have been around for awhile, they have improved over the years.

Floppy-disk drives got their name from the fact that the data storage medium is very flexible and it flops when you shake it. When it was originally developed, the floppy was 8 inches in diameter, stored data on one side, and provided a capacity of over 100,000 bytes.

Improvements have been made over the years, and the 8-inch drive is a dead or dying beast. As with the technology of the hard drive, the floppy drive and its medium are getting better. The size of the drive and the diameter of the floppy are getting smaller, and the medium is getting denser.

Types of Floppy-Disk Drives

The 5.25-inch drive was the standard for a good while, supported by virtually all of the personal-computer manufacturers. At first, the 5.25-inch drive used only one side of the diskette, but now it uses both sides to achieve a higher storage capacity. Three basic storage capacities are common for the 5.25-inch floppy drive:

Single sided, double density with a capacity of 180 kilobytes (180K)

Double sided, double density with a capacity of 360 kilobytes (360K)

Double sided, high or quad density with a capacity of 1200 kilobytes (1200K)

Typically, the single-sided drives are found in only the earliest IBM personal computers. Double-sided, double-density drives are normally found in IBM personal computers with two floppy drives, the IBM PC/XT or compatible that is based on the 8086 or 8088 processor.

The double-sided, high-density drives are standard in the IBM PC/AT and most compatible AT or 80286-based machine lines. Early 1.2-Mbyte drives had trouble reading and writing 360K media, so some AT-class machines also include a double-sided, double-density drive. Now, 1.2-Mbyte drives are more flexible and forgiving, and the number of 360K drives is declining, so you almost never see both 360K and 1.2-Mbyte drives in the same machine.

The current popular size in the floppy-diskette world is 3.5 inches. This drive was developed originally for portable computers, but it has moved aggressively onto the desktop. The 3.5-inch drive is the primary drive in the IBM PS/2 line. For IBM and compatibles, this drive has two different formats:

Double-sided, 1-megabyte capacity, which yields a formatted capacity of 760K

Double-sided, 2-megabyte capacity, which yields a formatted capacity of 1.44 megabytes (1.44M)

Most computers with 3.5-inch drives are configured with the higher-capacity units. The lower-capacity drives normally come with a marking on the floppy-release button that states the lower capacity of the drive so that it is easier to distinguish between the two drive types.

Newer technology is coming, and the 2-inch drive should be the next wave. However, as this book is written, only a very small number of packaged systems include 2-inch drives. How widely and how soon they will move into the mainstream is difficult to predict.

Next, let's explore the upgrade possibilities for computers using these drives. For IBM, your internal BIOS will determine what drives you can use without the addition of a different floppy-disk controller card. When your computer was made, a ROM chip was installed that had all of the basic input/ output instruction set encoded into it. This instruction set supplies the computer with the intelligence it needs to talk to the outside world of peripherals.

On the older PCs, the capacity and density of the drives being used today just weren't available. Therefore, the BIOS doesn't know what to do with some of the peripherals in today's market. If your BIOS is older that those released in the last version of PCs in 1988, then it's a good idea to pay the price and upgrade your BIOS. If you own an IBM, you aren't limited to an IBM BIOS. Most of the BIOS ROMs used in clones today will function properly in the older IBM PCs.

Floppy-Disk-Drive Upgrades

Adding a 3.5-inch drive to a system that already has a 5.25-inch drive can be an interesting experience. Always purchase the drive with 1.44-megabyte capacity; it can read and write the 760K format. Note that some early 1.44-megabyte drives did a poor job of using 760K diskettes, but newer units get along pretty well.

If your BIOS will support the 1.44-megabyte format, then install the drive as the instructions specify, and you'll be on the way. If you get some bad luck and your BIOS just can't support the 1.44-megabyte drive, then you will have some choices to make.

The first and least expensive choice would be to do nothing. In most cases, you will still have the capacity to read and write 760K formatted data. If this is true, your computer will in all probability not be able to format a 3.5-inch disk with the standard DOS format program.

You may be able to get around the problem with a third-party software program such as PCTools Deluxe. With this program, you put an already formatted and valid diskette in the drive and ask for a directory of the diskette. After your request has been completed, take out the good diskette, and put the unformatted diskette in the drive. Execute the format program, and watch as the tracks are addressed. If you can accept and use the lower density drive, then you are all set.

If you really want to address the full 1.44 megabytes of storage capacity, then the second step needs to be taken. First, do some research to determine if your specific PC or compatible will support the 1.44-megabyte drive with the addition of an up-to-date BIOS. If the answer is no, then you can try to find a version of a compatible BIOS from a different manufacturer and solve your dilemma or settle for the reduced capacity of a 760K drive.

If no other BIOS is available and the 1.44-megabyte capacity is a must, then your only other alternative would be to replace the motherboard in the computer that you are trying to attach the new drive to, or get a complete new system. Either way will be an expensive path to take.

We have enjoyed very good results with 760K drives installed in old, original 64K-motherboard PC-class machines, even though the ROM BIOS does not recognize this new class of drive. Simply remove the old 360K drive, use a mounting kit to install the 3.5-inch drive in its place, and hook the new drive up to the floppy controller with 3.5-inch-drive cables.

You won't be able to format the drive at 760K, but you can successfully read and write 760K diskettes formatted on another machine. If you must format a 3.5-inch diskette on this cobbled up machine, you will get 360K capacity—but it is a way to get 3.5-inch storage on an old machine, giving you a way to exchange data with a laptop or newer desktop unit.

Adding a 5.25-inch drive to a system that is configured with only a 3.5-inch drive is a very popular option. For the most part, if the system you want to modify is not a PS/2, then the addition should be easy. Just purchase the 5.25-inch drive kit that fits your needs, and install it into the system as the installation guide specifies. If you have a PS/2, then a kit that specifically addresses the problem of adding the larger sized drive will have to be purchased.

Memory

Memory is doubtless the hottest upgrade for today's computer systems. One of our first microcomputers was supplied with 16K of standard memory. That seemed terrific for that day, but the sales person was convincing in his argument that the extra $800 required to bump that up to a mammoth 48K would be a golden investment. And, he was right. That was then. Just booting a PC now takes more memory than it took to run that entire early system, even with sophisticated business software.

The IBM PC was born with 64K of memory, all on the motherboard. This amount was even expandable to 256K. Now the standard configuration on most entry-level computer systems is one megabyte (1024K).

Even with the growth in memory up to that level, sometimes it just isn't enough. The new IBM operating system, formally called Operating System/2 version 1.1, or OS/2 for short, requires an advertised minimum memory configuration of 3 megabytes of RAM and 20 megabytes of fixed disk storage, and that's just the start. If other application programs are needed, then in some cases more RAM is required.

That's more to the top end of the spectrum. For users with more modest requirements, 640K of memory still should be considered the minimum.

Memory is commonly found in three different chip formats. These formats are most often referred to by their capacity, such as 64-kilobit chips, 256-kilobit chips, and 1-megabit chips. As with most other aspects of the computer industry, the price of the chips is directly related to the amount of data that can be stored. Some average prices are:

64K bank of 9 chips: $18 and up

256K bank of 9 chips: $22 and up

1024K bank of 9 chips: $80 and up

There actually can be a broad range of chip prices, depending on the access times required. The *access time* of the data, or the rate at which the bit configuration can be transferred, is measured in *nanoseconds (ns)*. A nanosecond is one billionth of a second. The lower the rating, the faster the chip can read and write data. Table 2–2 represents some high and low chip speeds for each group.

Table 2–2.   Typical Memory-Chip Speeds

Type	Slow	Fast
64K	250 ns	60 ns
256K	250 ns	50 ns
1024K	200 ns	40 ns

The most popular operating system of the 1980's and early 1990's is the *Disk Operating System,* or *DOS* for short. It has a limitation of 640K of active, addressable, regular (conventional) memory. Two other segments of memory are *expanded* and *extended*. These two memory types need to be defined in detail because both are important memory areas, and each has a very special function.

Expanded memory is memory above 640K that specially written DOS application programs (such as Lotus 1-2-3 release 2, Symphony release 1.1, and Framework III) can address and use. These programs use this expanded memory in segments called *pages*. Your computer accesses these pages through a *window*, 64 kilobytes at a time.

If you use DOS application programs, you'll probably want to use expanded memory (rather than extended) with your system. You can use expanded memory with DOS versions 3.0 and greater. You can't use expanded memory with OS/2 or Xenix.

Extended memory is memory above 1024K (one megabyte) and less than 16,384K (16 megabytes) that only Xenix, Vdisk, and specially written programs such as AutoCad and Lotus 1-2-3 version 3 can use. You can't use extended memory to run DOS application programs (such as Lotus 1-2-3 versions 1a-2.2). Extended memory is sometimes referred to as *expansion memory* by some computer manufacturers.

The OS/2 operating system takes advantage of and uses extended memory only. You can't use extended memory to run DOS application programs because extended memory is outside the range that DOS manages. For the older IBM PC, XT, and compatible computers, extended memory can't be used for any reason.

A newer type of memory hardware is increasingly popular in high end PCs. Called *SIMMs (Single In-line Memory Modules)*, these memory modules usually store data 9-bits wide. They are inserted on the motherboard or memory expansion board and are popular in two configurations, 256K and 1024K.

If you are purchasing a brand new computer system, current standard memory configurations should start at 512K and go up from that point. The most commonly advertised configuration is 1 megabyte. If you are planning an upgrade for an existing system, then you have a gang of options to consider. Upgrading a personal computer from 256K to the maximum available regular memory that is addressable by DOS, or 640K, is the most common.

When this feature is added, other features can be added at the same time without much additional cost. Memory-expansion cards are available today in many forms. A bare-bones memory card can be purchased, and you can add more memory as you need it. You get the benefit that the added memory brings, and sometimes that is all that is needed.

At other times, multifunction memory cards are added. Multifunction memory cards provide many features, all built into one compact adapter card. The most common features found on multifunction memory cards are (1) the memory, (2) a Centronics parallel printer port, (3) an RS-232 serial communication port, (4) a joystick adapter port, (5) a perpetual clock/calendar, and (6) the software to make it all work.

The multifunction card is a good option for those who have run out of expansion slots in the main bay of the computer system and can replace a feature card of one type with a multifunction memory card that can provide much needed additional memory as well as a host of other functions.

The memory card described here will generally work only with PCs, PC/XTs, and the line of compatibles. Different memory cards are required for PS/2-type machines, as well as machines that use the 80386 or 80486 as the central processing unit (CPU). Vendor products vary, but pricing is fairly consistent, with a bare-bones memory-expansion board starting at around $65. Multifunction memory adapters with 384K of memory already installed start at around $160 and go up from that point.

Memory requirements are different for systems based on the 80286, 80386, or 80486 CPU. These computer systems are based on a 16-bit or greater bus structure that allows more memory to be addressed. For this reason, the memory adapter has to be purchased specifically for the bus structure with which it is to be used. Some computer systems, the IBM PS/2 line for example, require certain features on the adapter that could cause that specific memory card to be used uniquely on that computer system.

Modems

Modems are devices that allow the transmission of data from computer to computer over normal or dedicated telephone lines. The modem takes a digital signal, converts it to analog pulses, and sends the analog pulses on their way over the telephone network to a computer waiting for the signal at the other end of the line. The name "modem" was coined from the full name "modulator/demodulator."

Modems are classified or rated by the speed at which data is sent or received. Currently, the most common way to classify a modem is to express its speed in bits per second (bps), sometimes referred to as the *baud rate*. Other types of classifications would include capabilities such as synchronous, asynchronous, RS-232, RS-422, V.35, ASCII, EBCDIC, and many more names, types, and descriptions. The types addressed here will be limited to asynchronous modems that connect to the personal computer via an RS-232 serial connection, or that install inside the machine via the standard expansion bus.

First, some terminology: *Asynchronous* as defined and used in this text means the communication of data bits is one way at a time. That is, while two people share data over a communication link, only one of them can send data, and the other answers. The term *RS-232* refers to an industry standard for computer communications. This standard uses a transmit connection, a receive connection, ground, and up to 20 or so additional connections. Usually, however, only three to six serial connections are needed for most RS-232 links.

Modems sometimes use the *clear to send (CTS)* and *request to send (RTS)* lines, which act as traffic controllers. One signals the other, indicating that it is OK to send data, and the other would allow the data to be sent.

Standard modem serial connections include a 25-pin DB-25 connector and a smaller, 9-pin DB-9 jack. External modems generally use the 25-pin female connector, and computer serial cards can have either a 25-pin male, 25-pin female, or 9-pin male connector.

There are advantages and disadvantages to both internal and external modems. It's impossible to say which one is best for your application. The newest internal modems are much smaller than their predecessors, and they offer higher speed, error correction, and other features. The internal modem offers the advantage that it is self-contained inside your machine, eliminating external cables and desktop clutter. The internal device also is slightly cheaper than a similar external model because you don't have to pay for a case, cables, and power supply.

Among the disadvantages to internal designs, however, are the lack of portability, the fact that they require an internal slot that you might need for other devices (especially in older PC platforms), and the fact that they use up an available serial-port address.

External modems usually are supplied in a box smaller than this book. Older designs are considerably larger, while the newest products fit in the palm of your hand and may be battery powered. The unit includes a power on/off switch, two jacks for modular telephone connectors, and a communications port, usually a DB-25 connector. The modular telephone jack is normally referred to as an *RJ-11 connector*.

A useful feature with external modems is the use of LED indicators to show some of the user options that are established when the modem is configured or other LED indicators that reflect the current status of the modem and also show if a connection is made with another modem, if data is being transmitted, or that a successful connection has been made and is in use.

External modems generally cost more than internal designs, but they can be carried easily from computer to computer, and the LED indicators available on some models may be useful.

Speed is another consideration when adding or upgrading a modem. Speed is the one item that adds to the cost of the modem more than any other factor today. With early serial communications devices, a crisp 110 bps was just terrific. The next step up made 300-bps modems the standard. They almost tripled the speed of the original entries into the modem market and, yes, increased in price as well. Later, the 1200-bps modem became the most popular. This new entry was priced higher as well, but caused a problem never encountered in the modem market before: What about all of the 300-baud modems on the market? To answer this demand by users, the modem manufacturers designed a modem that would function at either the newer 1200-baud rate or, for compatibility with the slower modems, function at 300 baud. This type of modem is referred to in publications as 300/1200.

The 1200-baud modem is the most popular and has enjoyed a dominant role for the past seven years or so, but that view is rapidly changing. The 2400-baud modem is now a very affordable option. Most of the more prevalent 2400-baud modems also function with 1200- and 300-baud systems.

And now, the next generation is raising modem performance even more. The availability of 4800- and 9600-baud modems at an affordable price is just around the corner. In fact, we probably won't really see a viable 4800-bps modem market. The technology is bypassing this interim step in favor of 9600-bps units that adhere to national and international standards.

Price points vary, but you can find 2400-bps modems from as little as $70 for internal, half-card devices or around $90 for external units. When you add error correction, security features, or other extras, the price of this basic modem can rise to several hundred dollars. The 9600-bps market seems to be hovering between $700 and $1000 today with fairly rapid declines probable.

Even faster 19.2-kbps modems are working their way down to the PC marketplace, but their performance on voice-grade lines is not consistent. The actual throughput generally is less than the maximum specification, but that, too, is improving.

The Facts on Fax

Facsimile, or *fax* as it's commonly called, is becoming a necessity in today's business market. Not having a fax machine or some type of fax capability is almost unheard of. In many instances, it is cheaper to send a document by fax than through the mail, when you consider paper and postage costs and the time required to print and post the letter. It also is a lot faster and provides assured delivery.

Sending a fax to a local destination has no real cost associated with it, except for the time it takes to send it, which should amount to only a few seconds. The basic principle of fax is not a new technology, but some of the current developments in PC technology have improved fax speed and quality.

Fax Boards

First, let's look at what fax consists of and what it really does. Facsimile is a method by which an image in electronic form is transmitted, most commonly over telephone lines, and reconstructed at the receiving point. There are now two ways in which the document can originate. One is by scanning the original much like making a copy of it. The second is by obtaining the digital signal of the document directly from a file generated with a word-processing program and routing the signal through a fax adapter card that can be installed in your own personal computer.

One drawback to using a PC for a fax machine is that you also will require a scanning device of some type if there is a frequent need for "faxing" original documents. The stand alone fax machines are probably still the best choice for many. The newer ones are much simpler to use, operate, and share. They have a built-in scanner, and they can even provide a direct copy of any normal-sized document.

On the other side, PC fax cards provide features that you can't find on even the most expensive dedicated fax machines. Probably the most important feature is the better image quality provided. This alone is important, considering the popularity and volume of faxed documents.

There are two different and distinct classes of fax boards, those with a 4800-bps rate or below and those with a 9600-bps rate. The older 4800 bps sometimes meant that, for all practical purposes, your PC was tied up while you were busy sending the faxed documents. Even when your fax program ran in background and you could run other programs in foreground, performance was still slow at best.

The older boards also limited which files you could fax and the level that text characters could be translated. As with most other developments, support for the newer scanners and video styles lagged behind. The new breed of fax boards have solved a lot of the problems associated with the older boards.

Because the new boards use on-board processors and dedicated RAM, overhead from background operations is almost nonexistent. New translation capabilities and support for most scanners and video styles are also a result of the power of the newer boards.

Support for the standard group III, or *G3* as it is commonly referred to in the industry, is for the most part a given in today's market. As fax boards take on a more and more important role in today's business world, you'll start to see them used in larger numbers.

Selecting a Fax Card

The following are some important features that you might look for when making a fax-card purchase:

Support for high-resolution fax, typically 198 × 198 dots per inch, should be provided. This allows for the transmission of *halftones,* which transfer pictures in a much clearer mode. Text is recreated in a much sharper format, too. This option has its price, usually slower transmission because of the increased density, and maybe a slightly higher initial cost.

Support for standard-resolution fax, typically 198 × 99 dots per inch, should also be provided. This is the industry standard. Almost all faxes use this mode.

Conversion of ASCII files to fax format is necessary, done on the fly if possible, but available even if it is a separate operation. If you are concerned about phone charges, then you may want to do the conversion off-line, before you make the connection. While on-the-fly conversions are generally quite fast and don't use up space on your hard or floppy drive, they do add time to the call.

The ability to convert a large variety of PC-format files into fax format should be a major concern. Most fax cards can automatically convert batches of ASCII files, but some of the newer ones can even convert some of the popular word-processing formats (in text only).

Support for graphics file formats also is nice. Look for a conversion from bit-map to fax format and back (especially a couple of key formats such as PCX and TIFF). With these, you can transmit special fonts and graphics from almost any desktop publishing or graphics program.

Background operation is a must. This allows the use of the PC in the foreground mode while faxing is handled in a transparent mode. Using your system while faxes are being sent might not sound like a big thing, but if you send a lot of faxes, you'll be wasting a lot of your own computing time.

Automatic receiving of incoming documents should be provided.

Try to find out what printers are supported and how many. The more the better. One bad situation would be to purchase a new fax card and then find that your printer is not supported.

Some vendors of PC fax boards supply software that allows inclusion of graphics, logos, and signatures. These tools, coupled with a scanner and some basic scanner utilities, allow you to send almost any kind of faxed transmission you can ever dream of.

Newer software should provide at least some of the following utilities and features:

- Mailing-list support
- Scheduled fax transfers
- Automatic redial
- Automatic logging
- Polling
- Automatic printing
- Automatic cover-page inclusion

A critical hardware feature would be the inclusion of an independent fax-card processor chip and RAM. This would allow transparent background usage.

The newest standard fax boards are ones with a 9600-bps rate. These typically are priced from $600 up. The other category of fax boards has a rate of 4800 bps. These are generally priced at less than $500. Some are even available for as little as $250.

Pointing Devices

There are a number of keyboard alternatives available to today's PC user, from joysticks and mice to touch screens and scanners. Certainly one or more of these innovations will find its way into your upgraded PC configuration.

Mice

Before the age of computers, mice were hairy little rodents that caused people to yell in fear, made elephants cringe, and gave cats something to do in their spare time. A new breed of mouse has been born of the computer age. The electronic mouse acts as an input or pointing device for use with computer systems. Computer mice fall into two categories. One type of mouse uses a small roller ball to sense the direction in which it is being moved. The other uses LED technology along with a gridded reflective surface to indicate direction of movement.

Most mice let you move a cursor around on the screen to create graphics, specify points for data entry, rearrange text, and select menu commands. Mouse devices require either a serial communication port, a dedicated mouse input port, or a dedicated mouse controller card to allow data to be transferred into the computer system.

A mouse device has somewhere on its surface one or more *clicker* keys that have predefined meanings or that can be defined by the user. Some mice are dumb, some are intelligent. Dumb mice only let you move the cursor around on the screen and use the clicker keys as they have been defined. Intelligent mice are programmable. This means that you can combine special features of the mouse with keyboard-based applications to generate the most efficient use of your time and energy.

Mouse input devices are most handy when used in conjunction with electronic-spreadsheet programs. Using the mouse to move around on the screen is a great deal faster than using the keyboard arrows. As newer software has been developing, new types of graphically illustrated menu systems and environments have emerged. Pull-down or pop-up menus have become the norm, and a mouse pointing device makes moving around these a breeze. Windows make using a mouse almost mandatory. Moving around on the display and choosing options by using the mouse adds speed to the chore.

Most vendors include some type of graphic software in the purchase. These software packages include functions from menu makers to a very popular area today of graphic generation or drawing. Drawing and including graphics on letters and presentations is becoming widely used and very popular in the business world today. Desktop publishing applications and some word processing programs will allow graphic work created using your graphic software to be included in documents and presentations.

Joysticks

Can you believe it? Someone developed a joystick to be used on a business computer system. It's terrific, isn't it?

Well, for some it's a way of life, but for others it's merely another nuisance. Joysticks are used for input to games. No other use is intended. More and more games are being developed for the IBM PC and compatible line, and the joystick is an important part. Joysticks are attached to the personal computer by means of a special port that is included on many multifunction memory adapters. Simply plug your joystick in, configure your games to allow use of the joystick, and you are ready to go.

One quick note: Joysticks that are used with IBM personal computers and compatibles are of a special kind and generally can't be used with any other computer such as Apple or Commodore.

Chapter 3

Upgrading Software

Software is the driving force behind your computer hardware. It gives your PC its personality, manages data, and controls the hardware. As you upgrade your PC hardware, you also need to consider the many opportunities that upgrading affords for moving up to enhanced software.

Should you change operating-system software when you move from an 8088 to an 80286 machine? What about an 80386 upgrade? Should that necessarily mean new system software? Will enhanced hardware let you do more with your existing software? When should you move up to new software versions?

We will discuss these and other issues surrounding software for upgraded PCs in this chapter. The general areas we will discuss include operating systems, utilities, languages, and applications, such as word processing, data bases, or spreadsheets.

Operating-System Upgrades

There has been a reasonably organized progression from DOS 2.1 through 4.01. Strange as it seems now, DOS versions before 2.0 did not support hard-disk drives, and even in 2.1 the level of support for large or complicated disk directories was not very strong.

Network support and better subdirectory management were added with DOS 3.0, and improvements have continued. With DOS 4.01, expanded and extended memory are supported, a user interface shell has been added, and the capability of handling disk volumes larger than 32 megabytes is included.

For comparison purposes, Table 3–1 provides a listing of the major DOS commands for DOS 3.1, 3.3, and 4.01. NOTE: DOS 4.01 is the current version (as of this writing) from Microsoft. The original release of this upgraded operating system, 4.0, contained some operational bugs that have since been corrected. If you are upgrading from an earlier version of DOS, make sure you get version 4.01 or later, not the original 4.0 release. As we discuss the latest releases of DOS in this book, we will use DOS 4.0 to mean the latest version of the 4.xx operating system, whether it is 4.01 or a later release.

Table 3–1. Comparison of Recent DOS Versions

DOS 3.1	DOS 3.3	DOS 4.01
Append	Append	Append
Assign	Assign	Assign
Attrib	Attrib	Attrib
Backup	Backup	Backup
Break	Break	Break
	Chcp	Chcp
Chdir(Cd)	Chdir(Cd)	Chdir(Cd)
Chkdsk	Chkdsk	Chkdsk
Cls	Cls	Cls
Command	Command	Command
	Comp	Comp
Copy	Copy	Copy
Ctty	Ctty	Ctty
Date	Date	Date
Del(Erase)	Del(Erase)	Del(Erase)
Dir	Dir	Dir
Diskcomp	Diskcomp	Diskcomp
Diskcopy	Diskcopy	Diskcopy
		Dosshell
Exe2bin	Exe2bin	
Exit	Exit	Exit
	Fastopen	Fastopen
	Fdisk	Fdisk
Find	Find	Find
Format	Format	Format
	Graftabl	Graftabl
Graphics	Graphics	Graphics
Join	Join	Join
	Keyb	Keyb
Label	Label	Label
		Mem

Mkdir(Md)	Mkdir(Md)	Mkdir(Md)
Mode	Mode	Mode
More	More	More
	Nlsfunc	Nlsfunc
Path	Path	Path
Print	Print	Print
Prompt	Prompt	Prompt
Recover	Recover	Recover
Ren(Rename)	Ren(Rename)	Ren(Rename)
Replace	Replace	Replace
Restore	Restore	Restore
Rmdir(Rd)	Rmdir(Rd)	Rmdir(Rd)
	Select	Select
Set	Set	Set
Share	Share	Share
Sort	Sort	Sort
Subst	Subst	Subst
Sys	Sys	Sys
Time	Time	Time
Tree	Tree	Tree
Type	Type	Type
Ver	Ver	Ver
Verify	Verify	Verify
Vol	Vol	Vol
Xcopy	Xcopy	Xcopy

Ten new commands were introduced in between versions 3.1 and 3.3. Only two new commands were added in DOS 4.01, but the number of ways to configure your computer was increased dramatically.

If you already have an earlier version of DOS, you can stay with it, but in most cases you can't purchase an early DOS version. Microsoft has stopped shipment of DOS 3.3, for example. If you purchase a new operating system, it will be DOS 4.0 unless you can find a vendor with an inventory of DOS 3.3. You may be able to get DOS 3.3 at a reduced price from that vendor, and if you are upgrading from DOS 2.x and you don't need very large disk volumes or the new user interface, this could be a good choice if the price is low enough.

However, you can buy DOS 4.01 for about $100 from mail-order houses and local discounters. That's nearly twice what earlier versions sold for, but inflation and enhanced functionality more than make up the difference.

Even if you don't upgrade your hardware and you are using a hard disk, you should consider upgrading your DOS. In Version 2.1, for example, you can use hard-disk subdirectories, but you can't run a program from another directory. In addition, later versions of DOS contain utilities that offer more features. The XCOPY command alone almost makes the price of an upgrade worthwhile. This new copy utility lets you copy only files that have been changed since the last copy, for example, and you can automatically create and copy subdirectories.

There is little doubt that most users upgrading from 2.x to 3.3 or 4.01 will experience a real increase in power and flexibility. However, these new operating systems require more disk space and more memory, which means you may have to add RAM, at the very least, if your applications already use every byte of available space with your old version of DOS.

File Organization

While you are upgrading your hardware, you should also evaluate how you are using hard-disk space. If you are adding a hard disk for the first time, or you are upgrading because you ran out of room, use the DOS TREE command or other utility to print your directory structure. Then spend some time studying use patterns to find out if you are using the most efficient storage method.

We find that many inexperienced hard-disk users tend to dump everything into one huge directory. That's a little like putting your papers in a file cabinet without separating them into file folders. You have the information in the file cabinet, but retrieving it requires looking through lots of unrelated material. You are placing the same constraint on your operating system if you aren't using subdirectories.

Of course, it is possible to get carried away with a good thing. If you construct subdirectories more than about three levels deep, you are making life more difficult than necessary.

This is certainly an instance where software and hardware decisions are coupled. The decision to implement a more organized file structure almost forces you to move from an all floppy-diskette system to a system with one or more hard disks. The converse is also true. Purchasing and installing a hard disk makes it incumbent upon you to organize your files better. If you don't, you aren't getting the most bang for your bucks.

Working With Floppies

If you have been working with PCs for very long, you probably have seen one or more floppy diskettes go bad. That is, you find that you can't get your data back from the diskette. Where did the data go? That's a question that can have several answers. It's possible that the diskette itself got damaged through mishandling or that it was shipped with a flaw in its magnetic material. It also is possible that your diskette drive has developed a problem. Your diskette has a recording medium made up of a plastic base that is coated with a magnetic medium. It's possible that during manufacture or afterward a small portion of the magnetic coating has been corrupted so that it will no longer retain data.

There are two DOS routines that check the diskette surface for problems. FORMAT checks out a diskette when you first put it into service, and CHKDSK does its job whenever you wish. Diskettes that are only marginally bad when you first format them may go through the FORMAT routine without problems. Later, the disk may not allow you to record or read back data.

It is good practice to use CHKDSK routinely. If any bad sectors show up whenever you test your diskettes, copy all the data you want to preserve to another diskette, and put the suspect one in the trash. Diskettes are too inexpensive to allow one to cost you hours of labor trying to resurrect corrupted data.

Your diskette drive, like any mechanical product, is subject to wear with use. It is possible that the read/write-head alignment will change with time. When this happens, you cannot read diskettes that you made several months ago. If you have a two floppy system, or another computer with a diskette drive, it may be possible to read the old diskettes in a drive that did not create them.

There is no software fix for this particular problem. CHKDSK is absolutely no help to you. You cannot check a disk that you're unable to read. The most realistic approach is to find another machine that will read your diskettes and salvage as much as you can.

After the smoke has cleared, you would be well advised to replace the off-kilter drive. While some alignment problems can be corrected, the diskette drive has become almost a disposable item. It probably will cost very little more to install a new drive than to get the old one fixed. Diskette drives are easy to install, and with a new drive you are assured the electronics and all mechanical features are up to specifications.

Backing up Data

The best single way to preserve your files, whether they are on a hard disk or floppy, is to back them up. Make copies of all the material that you intend to keep. If you are using a floppy only system, you should have at least two copies of any programs or data you intend to keep.

With a hard disk, the most common approach to backup is to copy files onto several floppy diskettes. Unfortunately, backing up a large hard disk with the DOS COPY command can take an hour or more, and you can't copy to a floppy any files that are larger than the size of the diskette. This limits you to 360-kbyte, 1.2-Mbyte, or 1.44-Mbyte files.

The DOS BACKUP utility is designed to help avoid some of the more common problems you'll encounter during a backup session. One of the standard problems is not enough formatted diskettes. BACKUP can format them as required. You only need to keep it supplied with raw material. Note also that BACKUP compresses the files. You won't need 25 megabytes of floppy-diskette storage space to back up 25 megabytes of files.

After the initial backup, a switch can be set so that only the files that have been changed will be overwritten. This can reduce the time that you have to devote to this procedure.

You can use the DOS RESTORE to retrieve data you have backed up. RESTORE from DOS 3.3 is compatible with all earlier versions of BACKUP.

With DOS 3.3, a new version of the utility BACKUP is provided to help make the file-preservation process more palatable. However, the DOS 3.3 BACKUP is not compatible with DOS 3.2 and earlier versions of RESTORE.

The wisest backup routine involves copying everything from your hard disk (or make backup disks of all floppies) at least four times a year, six to 12 times a year if the volume of data is great. Also, you must remember to make immediate backup copies of any new applications you add. Then on a daily basis you can back up only the material that has changed during the day.

The best way to ensure that your data is current and guarded against hardware failure or vandalism is to establish a rigid backup routine, then follow it religiously. Some companies make software backup the first job of the morning. This is good practice if you are using a network and your backup software requires that all users be off the network to conduct a backup. This lets people work as late into the night as they wish, but no one can get on the system the next morning until backups are complete. Usually one person is responsible for this task, but in a company without a central data-processing staff, you could assign floating teams to handle backup chores on a rotating basis.

You should maintain at least two copies of backup material, one on-site where the computers are used and one in a safe location away from where the computers are located. With tape or removable disk backup, it is fairly easy to make an extra copy and charge someone with carrying it away from the site each day.

Many hard-disk users prefer third-party programs to the DOS BACKUP/RESTORE utilities. One of the most popular programs is PC Fullbak + from Westlake Data in Austin, TX. This low-cost utility uses a Lotus-style horizontal menu to select such parameters as hard-disk directory, type of diskette drive to be used, and recording density to use. The PC Fullbak + program can compress 720K of data onto a 360K diskette. Many hard-disk suppliers provide this program free. It is a single file that takes up less than 37K of storage.

Another popular program is Fastback Plus from Fifth Generation Systems. This offers many of the same features as PC Fullbak + and also is available for a reasonable cost. If you depend heavily on hard-disk data and need to back up and restore information regularly, it is wise to go beyond the utilities provided with DOS. Discuss your needs with your computer dealer.

Data security in the form of regular backups is no light matter. It takes only one bad experience that involves hours—or even days or weeks—in lost time recreating data to make you a backup believer. The best course is not to let it happen in the first place.

DOS and Memory

Early DOS machines had only 64 kilobytes of RAM. This was soon increased to 256 kilobytes and then on to 512 kilobytes. With the last bank of memory filled, the well equipped PC had 640 kilobytes, a ten-fold increase from the early machines. The advertisements then suggested that you weren't at the peak unless you had 1 megabyte of high-speed memory. Now it's not unusual to see ads for 8 and 16 megabytes of installed RAM.

Prior to DOS 4.0, the memory DOS made available to application programs was only the first 640 kilobytes; DOS itself was constrained to stay within the first 1 megabyte of memory. In fact, memory-hungry programmers and users have had to resort to circumventing DOS to get enough space.

The frustrations of having to buy your operating system and then having to buy yet another piece of software to do what you want to do has almost ended. "Almost" is the operational word here. The DOS 4.0 system supports both Lotus Intel Microsoft (LIM) version 4.0 expanded memory and extended memory. There is, however, a small problem. Using the DOS 4.0 expanded memory manager makes it impossible to use other software conforming to LIM version 4.0 for expanded memory. This not-so minor glitch has been addressed in revision 4.01. If you purchased DOS 4.0 shortly after it was released, check with your dealer about getting the corrected version.

Extended Versus Expanded Memory

All memory isn't created equal. There's conventional memory that all DOS versions know about, and then there's memory beyond that. Figure 3–1 shows a map of PC memory.

There is considerable confusion regarding extended memory and expanded memory; even some computer publications have carried incorrect information about this memory division. The most common mistake seems to be getting the definitions reversed. Running a close second is the mistaken idea that they are equivalent.

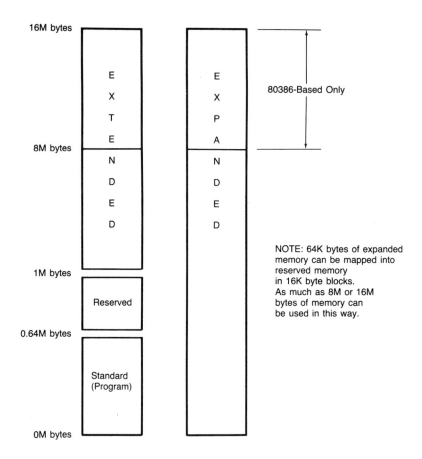

Figure 3–1.   PC memory map.

A large amount of this confusion arises because the same physical locations (RAM chips) can be either extended or expanded memory (but not both). The way the add-in memory card is configured determines the memory type. Once you have decided that a given chip will be part of expanded memory, it will remain expanded memory until the memory board is set up again. You can't swap back and forth between extended and expanded memory as easily as you swap between two application programs. It's worth noting that DOS 4.0 is working to make the swapping task easier. It still requires a reconfiguration at the DOS level, however.

Lotus, Intel, and Microsoft (LIM) got together several years ago to develop a standard for accessing memory beyond the 1 megabyte DOS boundary. This standard has been largely accepted by the microcomputer industry. The LIM standard is now in version 4.0 (LIM 4.0), and it is the basis for the operation of *expanded memory*. In this incarnation, expanded memory can reach out as far as 32 megabytes. Extensions to the standard have been implemented by several vendors.

Expanded memory requires a manager. This is a program that keeps track of the physical location of your data. This is necessary because DOS versions before version 4.0 don't know anything about data above 1 megabyte. The manager also moves copies of your data into DOS space at address D0000 (832K).

The expanded-memory manager handles (maps) data in 16-kilobyte pages. When DOS requests data from a logical address, the manager checks to see if that corresponds to a physical address it controls. If it does, then the manager copies the 16-kilobyte page containing the requested physical address to address D0000. The manager also gives DOS the position (*offset*) in the page for the data it requested. Up to 64 kilobytes of expanded memory at a time can be mapped for DOS access.

This extra memory handling enables DOS to operate as if it could address very large chunks of memory for data storage such as program segments or graphics screens. In addition, *Enhanced Expanded Memory (EEM)* can be used for program execution, giving the CPU up to 64K more of available RAM.

This *mappable* expanded memory can reside anywhere the memory manufacturer determines. The DOS only uses a 64K block of this RAM when it is mapped into a segment of addressable memory between 640K and 1024K. Enhanced expanded memory, now provided by some memory manufacturers, has more capability than standard expanded memory. You can use up to 1 megabyte at a time, for one thing, and it is more flexible in its addressing.

Note that to use expanded memory with an 80286-based PC you must have a separate memory board configured for this application. If you are using an 80386- or 80486-based machine, however, all you need is memory-management software to set up expanded memory.

The process of switching or addressing expanded memory is relatively slow because it requires the expanded-memory manager to intercept a DOS request, find the data, put it where DOS can find it, and then let DOS know it's there. All this takes time (clock cycles). It's slower than having DOS access the data directly.

Expanded memory is the only way 8088- and 8086-based PCs have to go beyond 640 kilobytes. For 80286, 80386, and 80486 machines, there is also *extended memory*. Extended memory is memory above 640 kilobytes that can be addressed by Intel microprocessors (CPUs) operating in the protected mode. This memory is not available to 8088 and 8086 CPUs because they don't have a protected mode.

However, extended memory can only be used as data storage, to hold very large spreadsheets, for example, or as a RAM disk. You can't use extended memory to increase the size of your executable program. Different applications require different types of memory. You can probably set your system up to have some of both. Many new memory-expansion boards can be configured to provide both expanded and extended memory simultaneously. You probably will have to set switches or run special software to access the available RAM in this way.

In principle, protected mode can address extended memory out to 4 gigabytes (2 to the 32nd power). This is a 32-bit address space for the 80386 and 80486 machines. For 80286 machines, the address space is 24 bits. This limits addressable memory to 16 megabytes (2 to the 24th power).

However, DOS is not set up to function with the CPU in the protected mode. To use this memory-addressing mode, you must have an operating system that functions in the protected mode, for example, OS/2, Unix, or one of the DOS extenders. We'll discuss these alternate operating systems later.

Partition Size Limitations

To be able to access disk volumes in excess of 32 megabytes, the way DOS organizes information on the hard disk has been changed. Since the early days of DOS, the smallest piece of disk organization has been the sector which contained 512 bytes. Versions of DOS prior to 4.0 used two bytes (16 bits) to specify the location of a sector. The sectors were numbered sequentially. This means that the maximum partition size was (2 to the 16th power times 512) bytes, or 32 megabytes. Version 4.0 of DOS uses 4 bytes to specify the sector location. Thus for DOS 4.0, the maximum partition size is (2 to the 32nd power times 512) bytes, or 2048 gigabytes (remember that 1 gigabyte = 1024 megabytes). This clearly allows for DOS partitions that far exceed the size of the largest hard disks available today. Such large partitions make directory management even more important.

DOS 4.0—A Warning

With DOS 4.0, the possible size of a disk partition has been increased. The size is now essentially unlimited (it can be bigger than any hard-disk volumes now available). However, not all programs written before DOS 4.0 can be used safely. Pay special attention to programs that perform specialized tasks such as reordering your disk files to improve performance. Always make a backup copy of all your files before you try any reordering.

Several of the commercial hard-disk and file-management utilities sort files by any of several parameters or rearrange files to regain space and improve access speed. Included in this category are Norton Utilities, Mace, PCTools, Fast Trax, Disk Technician, SpinRite, and Disk Organizer. The most recent versions of these utilities are probably safe to use with all DOS versions.

So the only time you have to worry is when you've made the decision to upgrade to DOS 4.0. At that time, you need to check your disk utilities. If you are not certain just how old the utilities are, you should check with the technical-support organization at the software house to be certain that using them with DOS 4.0 won't disrupt your hard disk.

Operating Systems and Memory Requirements

You don't have to worry that DOS will eat up all your available disk and memory space. While the resident and stored size have increased with each new DOS version, there is still plenty of room for your applications. The most space-hungry version, DOS 4.0, requires roughly only 80 kilobytes of RAM and 800 kilobytes of disk space.

DOS Extenders

There are *DOS extenders*, operating systems designed to behave very much like DOS while allowing application programs to execute in the protected mode on '286 and '386 machines. Included in this category are DOS 16M from Rational Systems, 386/DOS Extender from Phar Lap, and OS/286 and OS/386 from A.I. Architects.

This is not the operating system for the casual DOS user. Applications have to be specially tailored to work with these DOS extenders. But when they work properly, they let you do some really neat tricks: for example, big, fat terminate and stay resident (TSR) utilities can occupy extended memory with just a small (about 9-kilobyte) piece sitting in conventional memory. Lotus 1-2-3 uses DOS 16/M with their Release 3.0 to get very high-speed access to at least 1 megabyte of RAM.

There are two important points of concern regarding DOS extenders: They will not run on 8088 or 8086 machines, and they use extended, not expanded, memory. If you want to run programs that use the extenders, at the minimum you must have a '286 machine with 1 megabyte of RAM. In addition, you will probably have to give up any expanded memory you have while the DOS extender is operating. This means that you'll have to construct a special AUTO-EXEC.BAT file to use with the extender applications.

OS/2

The primary contender with DOS for your operating-systems dollars is IBM's OS/2. This is a true multitasking operating system designed to allow more than one program to run at the same time. The computer resources are shared among the executing programs. With this system, you can be running your favorite word processor putting together a presentation while your database program is in the background churning out the numbers for your charts. Alternatively, you can be using your communications package to contact the home-office main frame while a spreadsheet in the background is updating the quarterly report that must be submitted in ten minutes.

However, OS/2 is not limited to two tasks at a time. In theory, you can run as many programs as you have memory and disk space to accommodate. Each standard DOS application that you run can have its own 640-kilobyte partition. In practice, there are two limitations on the number of programs running: (1) your ability to juggle the inputs and outputs and (2) your willingness to tolerate the inevitable slowdown that occurs when several routines are requesting the services of the slower system resources. The latter limitation is not new. Users of main-frame computers have been experiencing it for years.

The size and speed of your hard disk is a concern because OS/2 can use it as slow memory. You aren't limited to running your programs in the RAM installed in your computer. Empty hard-disk space used by the operating system is called *virtual memory*. Up to 2 gigabytes (1 gigabyte = 1024 megabytes) of virtual memory can be addressed by OS/2.

With so much potential for addressing virtual memory, extremely large applications can be run on your PC if you have the hard disk space to support them. However, running programs in virtual memory is slower than if it all could be done in RAM. The actual program execution occurs in RAM with pieces of code and data being swapped in and out from the hard disk as they are needed. The rate at which your hard disk can access and transmit data is a limiting factor on program execution time.

Making the transition from DOS to OS/2 is very attractive if you have the right resources. To take best advantage of this operating system, your '386-class computer should be equipped with at least 4 megabytes of high-speed memory and one or more high-speed hard-disk drives with at least 50 megabytes of empty space available to OS/2.

The primary disadvantage of OS/2 today is the limited number of programs that are written to take advantage of its features. Developers are working to bring out more, but, for the immediate future, you are likely be limited to running DOS programs in their own partitions.

Unix and Xenix

Unix and PC-specific subsets of it such as Xenix are very powerful multitasking operating systems that have migrated down to microcomputers from large main frames and minicomputers. Among those available are Santa Cruz Operations (SCO) Unix, Interactive Unix, AT&T Unix, and the previously mentioned Xenix from Microsoft. There are literally thousands of programs written to run under these systems.

Best performance from Unix is obtained on '386 machines with at least 4 megabytes of RAM. In addition, you need at least a 70 megabyte hard disk to hold both DOS and Unix with a modest number of small applications. You'll need DOS to set up a boot partition. If you intend to get into Unix and its multitude of applications programs in a serious fashion, you will need a large hard disk, at least 150 megabytes, and 6 to 10 megabytes of RAM.

Utilities

Utilities are programs that perform specific functions that make it easier for you to work with your computer. The functions cover a broad range of possibilities:

- Carefully wiping out your files according to Department of Defense standards
- Rearranging the files on your hard-disk drive to reduce access time
- Searching your disk space for a particular string of characters
- Installing disk caches
- Installing print spoolers
- Changing file attributes
- Speeding up your keyboard
- Searching your disk for bad spots
- Backing up your data
- Recovering deleted files

The list goes on and on. Life with your PC can be made easier with the choice of an appropriate set of utilities.

Utilities generally are inexpensive relative to the services they can perform for you. Recovering an accidentally deleted file that has the project you just spent the last four days scrambling to complete can repay the small cost very quickly.

Most utilities are not particularly memory hungry. They usually can be stuffed into 256 kilobytes with a little room left over. Since most typical PCs today have 640 kilobytes or more, there probably is lots of room available for the utilities to do their jobs.

These utilities typically come with very slick menus and windowing features. Some of them can be called up from the command line or by a special key combination called *hot keys* from within your application program.

The more popular utilities are available from mail-order distributors. You can expect to pay less than list price—usually $50-$100—for software you obtain from these sources. Some of the more popular utilities are:

Norton Advanced Utilities 4.5

Mace Utilities 5.0

Mace Gold 1.0

Super PC-Kwik 3.3

PC-Kwik Power Pak 1.3

The number following the software name is the version number. The digit in the units place gives the major revision number, and the decimal digit gives the update or bug-correction edition. Not every publisher sticks to this numbering scheme, but most do.

The only problem that you are likely to experience with any of the more popular utilities is incompatibility of older versions with DOS 4.0. The software and version listed above should work quite well with any DOS version.

Utilities From the Public Domain

Public-domain software is just what the name implies, software that is not copyrighted. It is available from a number of sources. Many suppliers can be found in the back of computer magazines. In a recent issue of one magazine were:

Softshoppe, Inc., of Ann Arbor, MI

The Software Labs, of Los Angeles, CA

Share Net, of Oklahoma City, OK

Best Bits & Bytes, of Van Nuys, CA

California Freeware, of Palmdale, CA

BIG BYTE Software, of Arlington, TX

People's Choice, of Memphis, TN

Contech, of Tarzana, CA

Bright Futures, Inc., of East Windsor, CT

The charge for public-domain software is in the range of $2 to $4 per diskette. You are paying the supplier for making the copy and maintaining a library of software that has been checked for the current source of much talk and concern, the computer virus. One of the prominent suppliers listed above is California Freeware in Palmdale, California. A quick tour through the utilities section of their catalog produces:

AT Utilities—utilities for AT-class machines

Best Utilities—40 assorted utilities

Diagnostics—system-performance utilities

Hard Drive Utils/1,2,&3—just what the name implies

Except where specifically noted, these utilities are written to run on all PC platforms. The programs are said to be compatible with all DOS versions from 2.1 on up. The same caveat applied to commercial utilities applies here. Any software that rearranges your hard disk must be used with care, or you can have big problems. Before you use any such software, make certain that you have backed up your hard disk recently. And, before you buy, ask about the vintage of the software. Very old utilities may not be compatible with DOS 4.0. The California Freeware catalog does not give an indication of the age of their utilities.

Public-domain software can also be obtained from any of the numerous PC bulletin boards maintained around the country. Virtually every moderately sized city has at least one bulletin board. For a nominal connection charge and an hourly use fee, you can transfer (download) as much material as you choose from their library.

The system operators generally do a very good job of protecting you from the computer weirdos who attempt to propagate viruses. However, if you do elect to use public-domain software, you should take precautions such as keeping a write-protected version of your operating system and maintaining backup copies of any materials you would be very miserable without if a virus should strike your computer.

Shareware

Shareware is an alternative distribution channel for commercially prepared software. You are free to share it with your coworkers. But, if they want the documentation and a channel to the upgrades that will surely be coming, they must send in the registration fee that is noted prominently whenever you use the program.

Frequently, distributors of public-domain software also distribute shareware. Sales of the latter are likely to be a major source of revenue for them. Their advertisements can be found in most computer magazines. The list of suppliers given above under Utilities from the Public Domain is valid for shareware, too.

California Freeware also carries an extensive line of shareware. Another stroll through their utilities section reveals:

ALT V1.16s—memory-resident super collection

Fansi Console V2.00—replacement screen driver

Fastcopy V2.0—copying and formatting utilities

List V6.2A—outstanding replacement for DOS TYPE

Pkpak V3.61 & Arcmaster V2.41—archiving and dearchiving program (very fast)

Ram Test V3.0—memory-diagnostic program

It's likely that the most recent versions of shareware will be able to handle DOS 4.0 without problems. It is wise, however, to ask questions about compatibility before putting out money for a product that may cause you problems. As with any software, be certain to have a recent backup before doing any rearranging of your hard disk.

Application Programs

You probably have a favorite application program that you use at least several times a week, a word processor, a database manager, or a spreadsheet. We'll address how upgrades to some of the more prominent programs in these categories can influence your hardware decisions.

Lotus 1-2-3

Lotus 1-2-3 released two new versions in 1989, Release 2.2 and Release 3.0. Release 2.2 is a straightforward upgrade in the series of spreadsheet routines that have been coming from Lotus Development Company. It has a very nice presentation package built into it as well as an assortment of other new features. It does not require any changes to your hardware. If you can run any of the earlier releases, you can run Release 2.2.

Release 3.0 introduces three-dimensional spreadsheets, methods for linking one spreadsheet to one or more additional sheets, quick graphs, and stringent memory requirements. The last item mentioned can be a real problem. If you have an 8088 machine, you can't run Release 3.0 at all. Lotus uses a DOS extender to access extended memory. The requirement is that you have at least 1 megabyte of RAM, and it must be configured as extended memory.

Further, the 1 megabyte must be configured as 640 kilobytes on the motherboard and 384 kilobytes on an add-in board or the motherboard, depending on how your machine is configured. It cannot be arranged as 512 kilobytes and 512 kilobytes, as you may have it if you have an early model IBM PC/AT or a very close clone. Release 3.0 is also a problem for some of the '386 machines that use a RAM shadowing technique to speed up BIOS calls when the shadowing is implemented in hardware rather than software. One manufacturer's computers affected by this are the CompuAdd 386 machines. Rumor has it that Lotus is working to fix the shadowing problem, but it isn't fixed as of this writing.

You may already have quite a bit of additional memory (beyond 640 kilobytes) that is set up as expanded memory. It is possible to configure your memory with most add-in boards to support both extended and expanded memory. However, if you are a serious spreadsheet user, you probably want to stuff huge ones into memory. That would mean assigning all your extra RAM as extended memory to satisfy Lotus. This is clearly a point where a trade off decision must be made—Lotus 3.0 with 3D spreadsheets and lots of extended memory or Lotus 2.2 and keep your expanded memory.

Lotus is certainly a popular spreadsheet program. If you want to stay with it, go with Release 2.2; the new features make the upgrade worthwhile. The hardware configuring that must be done to accommodate Release 3.0 is rather restrictive. Stay away from it if you are unwilling to dedicate your extra RAM to Lotus. On the other hand, if you need the flexibility offered by true 3D spreadsheets—256 separate sheets stacked logically on top of each other—then Release 3.0 may be worth the hardware upgrade required.

dBase IV

If you are familiar with the previous version, dBase III Plus, you will notice some differences in the new version. When you enter dBase IV, it's through a windowing system that isolates you from the dBase command line. This may be of no concern if you are a first-time user, but we're talking about upgrades. Most users choose to become at least modestly proficient with dBase as a programming tool simply because that's how it's designed to be used.

You move from a novice stumbling around in a specific database to a reasonably accomplished dBase programmer creating your own custom databases and modifying ones you inherit from others. When you've moved into the second category of users, you frequently want to issue commands from the "dot prompt," as dBase literature calls it. With dBase IV, there appears to be no one-step method to get to the dot prompt.

Most experienced users of a programming product expect that they will be able to begin working with the upgraded product as soon as they strip the shrink wrap off the box and load up the software. While you probably won't require a massive new training program, the new windowing environment of dBase IV does cause you to pause. In addition, some users may be initially uncomfortable with the report generator.

Additionally, dBase, because of its strengths and popularity, is used by a number of third-party developers as part of their products. An annoying feature of dBase IV that shows up in those applications is that the function keys bounce, or give you more than one signal for each keystroke. This is not apparent when you are using only dBase IV, but it shows up clearly in third party programs. It has been reported that a similar problem occurred with the introduction of dBase III and was cured in the first update of that software. Perhaps this will happen again with an update to dBase IV.

The memory requirement for dBase IV is 640 kilobytes of RAM and maybe 3 megabytes of empty disk space. It clearly isn't the program to move up to if you still have an all-floppy-disk system.

WordPerfect 5.1

WordPerfect 5.1 is a very sophisticated product with a fairly well written instruction manual, but you'll probably need a lot of support if you move beyond basic word-processing features.

Once you become accustomed to the changes, WordPerfect 5.1 is as easy to use as any of the earlier versions. WordPerfect changed the designations for several keys with the introduction of Version 5.0. That's something they have not done before. New ones were added in earlier versions, but locations and names weren't changed. In fact, the relocation and consolidation are appropriate. Related document-formatting actions that were spread across three keys can be accessed from a single key using the new menu system. It does take a bit of getting used to, but it's not difficult and the change makes sense. With version 5.1, the user interface has been improved, giving you access to menus, mouse support, and other desirable features that make learning WordPerfect easier, and that help you access all of the power of this versatile and flexible word processor.

A very useful feature of 5.1 is the document preview that is reached through the print menu. Since many users have access to printers that support proportional type, it is necessary to look at what you have done to be certain that what you can't see won't mess up your output. Since WordPerfect lacks a true WYSIWYG (what you see is what you get) display, the print preview is truly a necessity for proportionally spaced fonts. It is also necessary if you are to use the graphics features of version 5.1, since graphics images don't appear on your screen at all in other than the preview screen.

WordPerfect continues to be usable by the entire range of PC users from 8088 floppy-diskette-based machines to 80386 machines with hundreds of megabytes of storage space. Version 5.1 requires 256 kilobytes of RAM. About half that space is used by the executable program, WP.EXE, and the rest is used for DOS and data. WordPerfect will use as much of the 640 kilobytes of conventional memory space as you have.

The upgrade from an earlier version to 5.1 is worthwhile. You don't have to make hardware-upgrade decisions. It supports both monochrome and color graphics adapters. An update for WordPerfect 5.0 has already been issued. If you currently use 5.0 or are planning to buy it, you should check with Word-Perfect Corporation to be certain that you have the most recent version.

Chapter Summary

Software is the personality module for your computer hardware and, at the system level, it controls every function of the entire system. As you consider hardware improvements, you must coordinate system and application software upgrades as part of the overall plan. Use the guidelines in this chapter as a starting point for software changes; then use your own experience and individual applications needs to develop a well rounded, upgraded hardware and software system.

Chapter 4

Real-World Scenarios:
Step-by-Step Makeovers

Theres a line that's used fairly often in the movies and on TV, "Talk's cheap." The concept applies to computer upgrades as well as detective shows. It's easy to tell you what you need to do to upgrade your computer in general terms.

Rather than spend a lot of time talking upgrades to death, let's look at two specific upgrades in some detail. We'll illustrate the steps to take to perform these upgrades. We're not going to tell you which screw to turn next. That level of detail is outside the scope of this book. Additionally, it's usually pretty obvious.

Fortunately for us, the entire family of PCs was designed to be upgraded. The design with plug-in expansion boards and bays for data-handling devices—hard-disk drives, floppy-diskette drives, and tape drives to name a few—was purposely done to promote upgrades. The system could have been put together much more compactly if space rather than upgrading were the constraint . A lot of engineers have spent much of their time designing PCs so that it will be possible for you to upgrade them. And it's not a job for the Mission Impossible team. You can do it.

We'll examine an upgrade from an 8088-based IBM PC/XT or close clone to an 80286-based machine. This is the upgrade that is frequently done to make an old, poorly functioning PC work well as an entry-level system. You keep the old box (case), but that's about all.

In the second example, we'll walk you through the upgrade of an 80286-based IBM PC/AT or close clone to an 80386-based system. This upgrade will take a marginal performer and remake it into a real powerhouse. You keep a few more components than you did with the 8088-to-80286 upgrade, but not many more.

In later chapters, we'll suggest ways for you to decide how massive your upgrade needs to be (do you really need to replace all the components?). We'll also help you analyze what components make sense from both functional and cost perspectives to satisfy your current and future requirements.

Generic Requirements

There's a set of ideas and equipment that is right for any upgrade. You have to have the right tools and components, and you should observe good safety and construction practices.

The Right Tool at the Right Time

You won't need very many tools to take apart and reassemble your system. You can probably do the entire job with nine tools (Figure 4–1):

- Two flat-blade screwdrivers—one medium and one small.
- Two Phillips-head screwdrivers—one medium and one small.
- Two nut drivers—one 1/4″ and one 3/16″.
- One pair of needle-nose pliers.
- One IC (integrated-circuit) insertion tool.
- One IC removal tool (in case you do it wrong the first time).

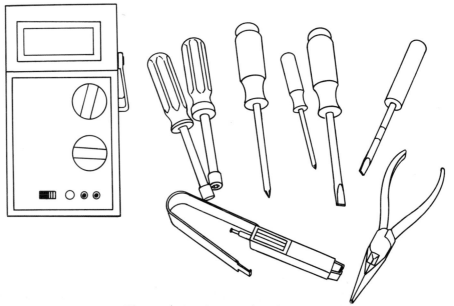

Figure 4–1. Suggested tools.

In addition, it wouldn't hurt to have an inexpensive multimeter for continuity checks.

Collect the Parts

Before you start assembly, make a checklist. Write down all the pieces that you need for the system. Check off each component as you locate it. Place them together on a large flat work space. If the component arrived in protective foam or a plastic bag, leave it protected until you're ready to install it.

Be certain that you have all the pieces it's going to take for your system. Check the list for completeness, and then look over the components for obvious flaws such as broken connectors, missing cables, or wrong number of chips. Now is the time to correct any problems before you get heavily involved in assembling the system.

Stay Safe

Safety is always important. It's doubly important during any operations involving electricity. You need to practice personal safety, and you need to employ practices that will keep your components safe. Don't expose them to static discharges. Refer to Appendix C for information about safe operations with and around electrical equipment.

Keep It Clean and Neat

Good construction practices are simply an extension of common sense to the job you're doing. Be aware that you should:

- Keep the work area clear of anything not involved in system assembly.
- Have the necessary tools where you can get to them easily.
- Locate the parts that you're going to use, and position them near the work area.

8088 to 80286

We assume that the current PC is an IBM PC/XT or clone with a 10-Mbyte full-height hard-disk drive, a full-height 360-kbyte floppy-diskette drive, a color monitor and color graphics adapter (CGA), a serial port, and a separate parallel port. Such a machine is likely to have a 135- or 150-watt power supply. We recommend upgrading to a 200-watt power supply to support larger hard-disk drive(s), additional memory, and more expansion cards.

Replacement Parts, 80286

To give you a better real-world feel for the upgrade, we are including part numbers and prices for the suggested components in Table 4–1. We have taken the components and prices from the 1990 Jameco Electronics catalog. Jameco is a mail-order supplier located in Belmont, CA. Their 24-Hour Order Hotline can be reached at (415) 592-8097.

Table 4–1.   Typical Component List, XT-to-AT Upgrade

Part No.	Description	Cost
JE3010	16-MHz Motherboard (XT Footprint)	$299.95
JE1032	200-Watt Power Supply	$89.95
51100P-10	36 × 100-ns 1-Mbyte × 1 RAM Chips (4 Mbytes RAM)	$466.20
JE1065	I/O Card for AT	$59.95
356KU	Toshiba 3.5″ 1.44-Mbyte Internal Floppy-Disk Drive	$109.95
FD55G	Teac 5.25″ 1.2-Mbyte Internal Floppy-Disk Drive	$119.95
1006VMM2	16-bit MFM 286/386 Hard-Disk Controller— Supports 1:1 Interleave	$169.95
M3085	Miniscribe 70-Mbyte (20-ms) Half-Height Hard Drive	$599.95
JE1016	101-Key Enhanced Keyboard	$69.95
TM5156	Casper 14″ VGA Monitor	$399.95
JE1057	Jameco 8/16-Bit VGA Card	$249.95
	TOTAL PRICE	$3235.65

Out With the Old, XT

In this section, we'll guide you through the 8088-to-80286 upgrade process. We will discuss the selection and decision processes in other chapters. There is a preferred sequence to both assembly and disassembly. We'll take you through a sequence that will require a minimum amount of reworking. It's certainly possible to perform either the removal or installation of components in a different order, but other event sequences may require more effort or even give you skinned knuckles. (The solder side of a printed-circuit board has many sharp points.)

Remove All Electrical Power, XT

Flip the switch to turn off the system. Unplug the system power cord from the 120-volt receptacle. Disconnect the system power cord from the back of the system unit. Store the power cord for future use.

Unplug the Keyboard, XT

Trace the keyboard cord to the back of the unit (Figure 4–2). Unplug the keyboard by pulling on the plug, not on the cord itself. Place the keyboard assembly in your surplus parts pile.

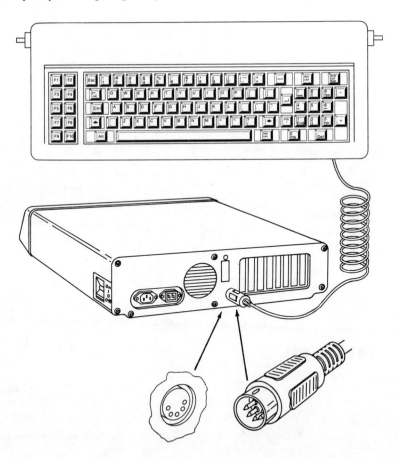

Figure 4–2. The PC/XT keyboard plugs into the back of the case.

Disconnect the Monitor, XT

The monitor has two cords that must be disconnected—a power cord and a signal cord, as shown in Figure 4–3. First, turn off the monitor. Second, remove the monitor power cord from the 120 volt receptacle (probably the switched receptacle on the back of the system case). Finally, unplug the signal cord; you may have to use a screwdriver to loosen two screws holding the connector in place. Put the monitor and cords in your salvage pile.

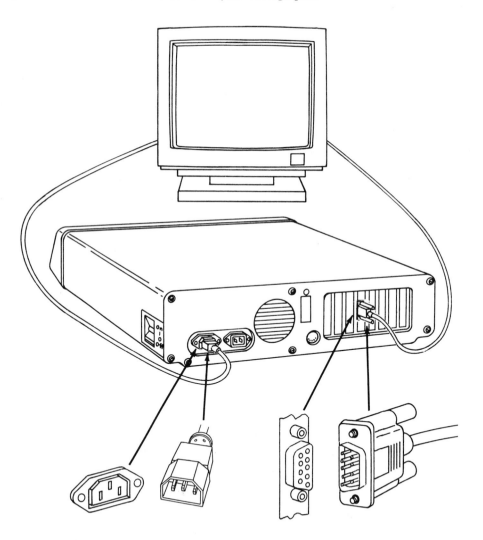

Figure 4–3.   The monitor has two cords to disconnect.

Pull the Printer, XT

The printer has two cords that must be unplugged, a power cord and a signal cord. First, turn off the printer. Second, unplug the power from the 120-volt receptacle. Third, unplug the signal cord from the back of the system unit (Figure 4–4); you may have to loosen two screws holding the connector in place. Finally, flip back the latches and unplug the signal cable from the printer. These spring-like latches can be troublesome, mainly because they are a little delicate and a little sharp. To release them, grip each one, one at a time, firmly between your thumb and forefinger, and squeeze to release the tension; then swing the latch away from the plug. Put the printer, the printer power cord, and the printer signal cable out of the way until the upgrade is completed.

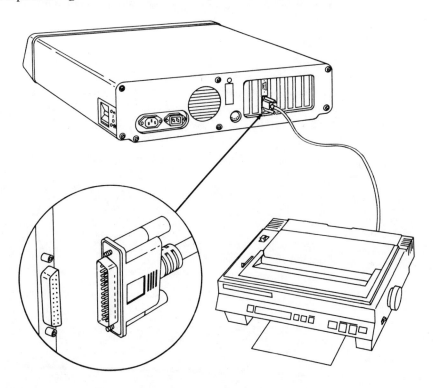

Figure 4–4. Unplug the printer cables.

Open the Box, XT

Unscrew, remove, and save the five screws holding the top of the system case (box) in place (Figure 4–5). Pull the top forward until it stops, and then lift the rear of the top up and back to remove. Store the top for future reassembly.

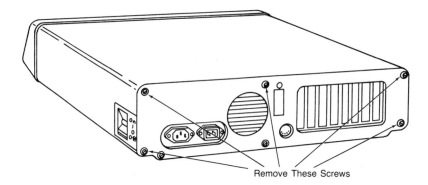

Figure 4–5. Remove five screws that hold the PC/XT case on.

Lift the Cards, XT

Remove each of the expansion cards (printed circuit boards) from the sockets (bus) on the motherboard. See Figure 4–6. First, carefully remove any connectors from the expansion cards. Second, remove the screws holding the metal tabs in place. Retain the screws for attaching other cards. Finally, remove the

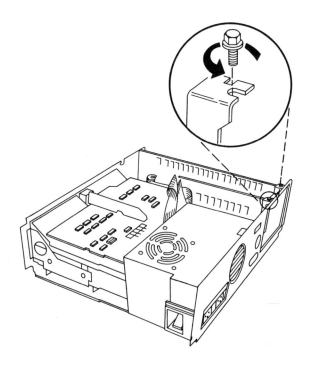

Figure 4–6. Remove all expansion cards from the motherboard.

cards with a rocking motion. Try not to twist the cards from side to side; rather, pull up alternately on one end, then the other. Be careful where you grip the cards as you pull them out. There may be delicate components toward the top of one side of the boards. If you mash them or break them off as you remove the board, you will render it useless. Store the removed cards in your salvage pile.

Floppy-Diskette Drive, XT

Refer to Figure 4–7. First, check the bottom of the case for any screws holding the floppy drive. Remove them and keep the screw(s) from the bottom separate; they may be shorter than the rest. When you install a drive, using a screw that is too long can damage the drive. Second, remove any other screws holding the drive. Third, slide the drive out of the chassis slightly, and disconnect the power and signal cables. Finally, remove the drive. Store the 360-kbyte floppy-diskette drive in your salvage pile.

Hard Drive, XT

Refer to Figure 4–8. First, check the bottom of the case for any screws holding the hard drive. Keep any screws from the bottom separate; they may be shorter than the rest. If you install a drive with a screw that is too long, you may damage the drive. Second, remove any other screws holding the drive. Third, slide the drive out of the bay slightly and disconnect the data, control, and power cables from the back (inside) of the hard drive. Finally, remove the drive. Store the 10-Mbyte hard-disk drive in your salvage pile.

Pull the Power Supply, XT

Refer to Figure 4–9. First, remove the screws holding the power supply to the back of the case. Second, unplug the power connection to the motherboard. Note that on most power supplies this is a two-piece connector. Grab the connectors; don't pull on the cables. Third, slide the power supply toward the front of the case enough to disengage the tabs on the bottom of the case. Finally, remove the power supply. Put the power supply in your salvage pile.

Move Out the Motherboard, XT

Refer to Figure 4–10. First, remove any remaining electrical connectors from the motherboard. Second, remove all screws holding it. Third, slide the motherboard slightly away from where the power supply was; you are trying to disengage plastic standoffs from their slots. Finally, remove the motherboard. Very carefully put the motherboard in your salvage pile.

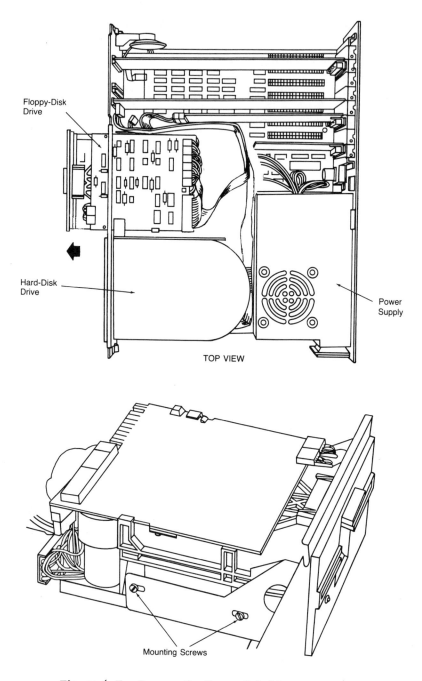

Floppy-Disk
Drive

Hard-Disk
Drive

Power
Supply

TOP VIEW

Mounting Screws

Figure 4–7.   Remove the floppy-disk drive.

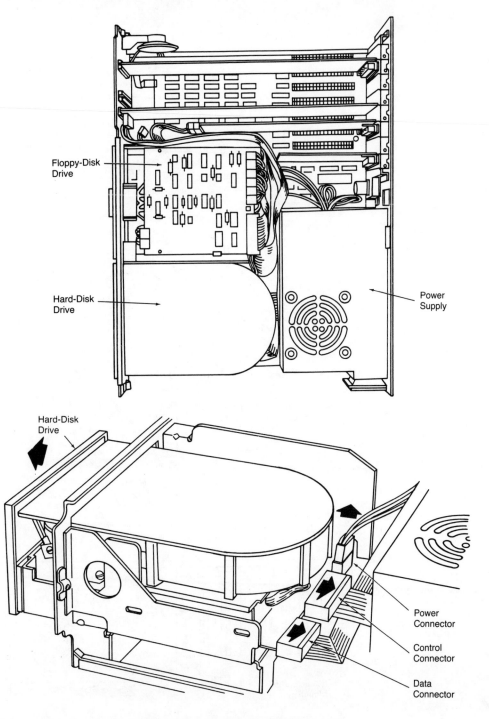

Figure 4-8. Remove the hard drive.

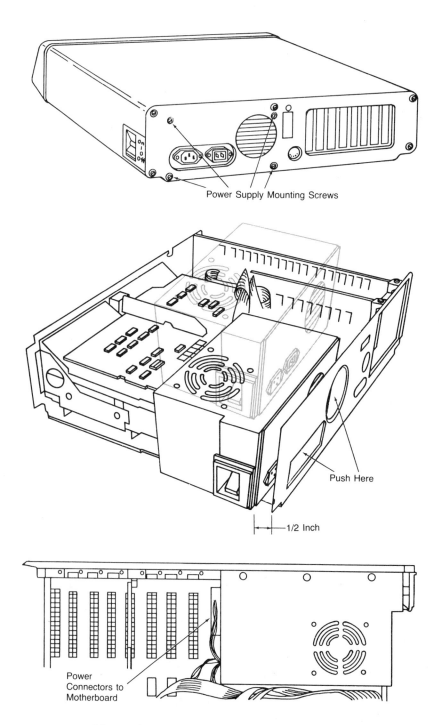

Power Supply Mounting Screws

Push Here

1/2 Inch

Power
Connectors to
Motherboard

Figure 4–9.   Remove the power supply.

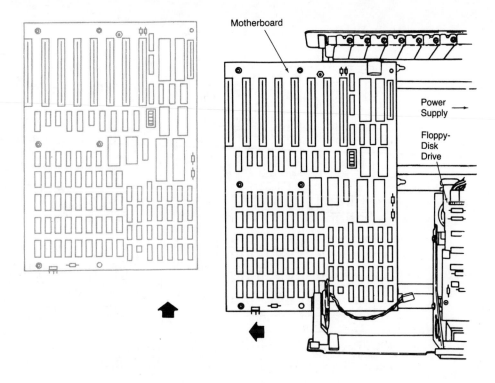

Figure 4–10. Remove the motherboard.

Halfway, XT

That's it. Now you should have an empty case staring at you. Reversing the process with your new components will complete the hand-tools portion of your upgrade.

In With the New

You can now begin the rebuilding process by inserting new components that you have selected for your upgrade.

Add Memory, XT

Now is a good time to add the 4 megabytes of RAM to your motherboard. (See Figure 4–11.) Make a stack of a couple of pieces of cardboard, and place the motherboard on top. This will help to keep you from cracking the motherboard during the chip insertion process.

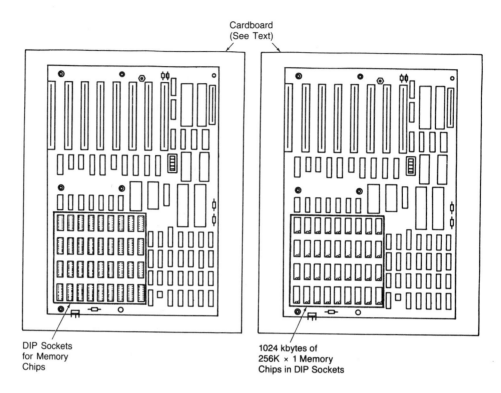

Cardboard
(See Text)

DIP Sockets
for Memory
Chips

1024 kbytes of
256K × 1 Memory
Chips in DIP Sockets

Figure 4–11.   Place the motherboard on cardboard.

Chips can be damaged by the discharge of static electricity from you to them. While you're inserting the chips, keep grounding yourself by touching the grounding strips around the edge of the motherboard before you pick up a chip. Using a ground strap is a good idea (Figure 4–12). Don't touch the legs of the chips.

Chips can also be damaged by breaking off their legs. As a general rule, you can bend and straighten a leg one time. Bend it more than that, and it will probably break. Once a leg is broken, the chip must be replaced. To help avoid bending legs, you should use a chip-insertion tool. These can be obtained at a local electronics store such as Radio Shack for under five dollars.

Each of the chips should have a U-shaped notch that you align with a similar notch in the chip socket. See Figure 4–13. Consult the documentation that came with your motherboard to be certain that you are installing them correctly. If you apply power to a chip that is installed backward, you are likely to damage it. Check the orientation of each chip before and after insertion. Check them all one more time after you've installed the motherboard.

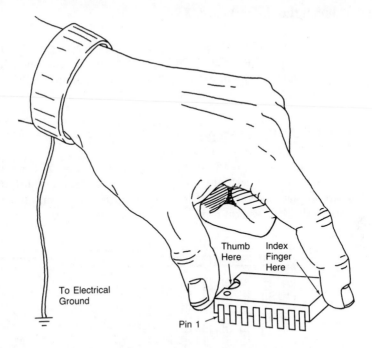

Figure 4–12. Handle the chips properly.

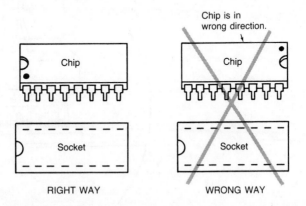

Figure 4–13. Orient the chips properly.

Mount the Motherboard, XT

Position each plastic standoff over the large end of its slot, and slide the motherboard into place. Using the screws you removed from the old motherboard, attach the motherboard to the case. Remember that the multipin slots should be positioned toward the back of the case.

Install the Power Supply, XT

Refer to Figure 4–14. Place the power supply in the case as shown in the drawings provided with the power supply. Make certain the tabs at the bottom are in place correctly before fastening the power supply to the back of the case with the screws you removed from the old supply.

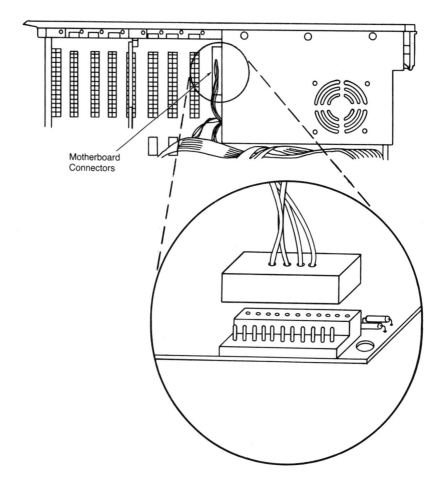

Motherboard
Connectors

continued

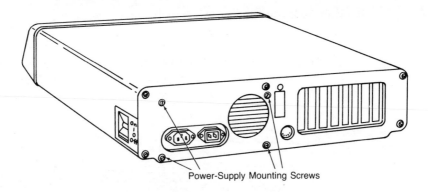

Power-Supply Mounting Screws

Figure 4–14.   Install the power supply.

Plug in the connectors that provide power for the motherboard. In most instances, the connectors are labelled P4 and P5. Connector P4 should be located closer to the back of the case. Most, if not all, manufacturers supply connectors with locating pins to prevent you from hooking up the power incorrectly. Don't force them.

Mount the Disk Drives, XT

Refer to Figure 4–15. Install the floppy-disk drives in the open bay. Mount the hard drive immediately to the right of the floppy drive.

The specified drive is a half-height device; the one you took out was a full-height drive. Use the extra half-height cover provided with the hard drive to block off the upper portion of the hard-drive bay. You need to block the opening to assure proper air flow through your system. Secure the drives with the screws provided. Don't forget; short screws must be used to attach the drives to the bottom of the case.

Connect the power, control, and data cables to the hard-disk drive. Connect the power and signal cables and ground wire to the floppy-diskette drives. Consult your documentation for the location of the terminating resistor. It must be removed from the floppy drive that will be the B: drive in your system. The A: drive must retain its terminating resistor. By convention, the 1.2-MByte, 5.25-inch drive usually is installed as the A: drive, and the 3.5-inch drive is configured as the B: drive. If you do a lot of work with laptop machines, or you simply prefer the smaller format for most of your work, you can just as easily install the 3.5-inch drive as the primary, or bootable A: drive.

Install the I/O Card, XT

See Figure 4–16. Plug the I/O card into the 8-bit slot adjacent to the power supply. (An 8-bit slot has only a 62-pin connector.) Be certain to insert the card with a rocking motion until it is well seated. Fasten the metal tab with the screw you retained.

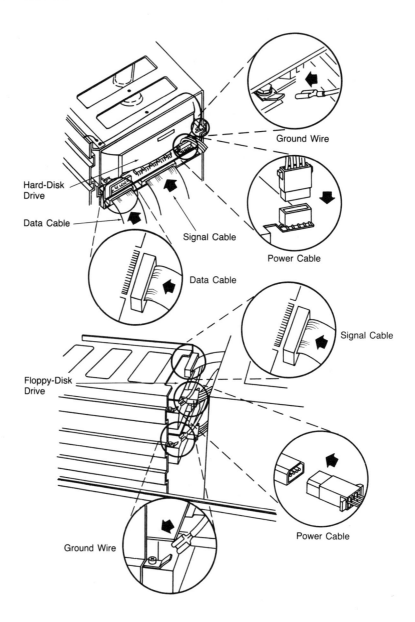

Hard-Disk Drive

Data Cable

Ground Wire

Signal Cable

Power Cable

Data Cable

Signal Cable

Floppy-Disk Drive

Power Cable

Ground Wire

Figure 4–15. Mount the disk drives.

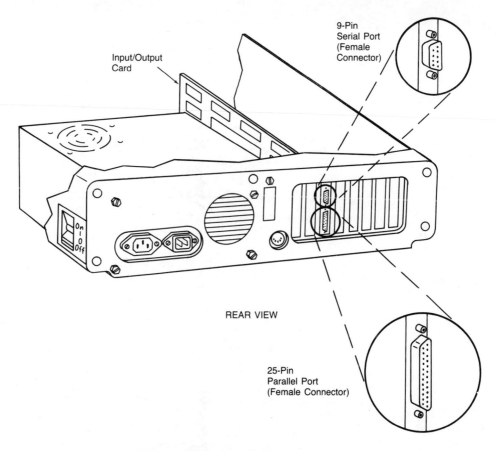

Input/Output
Card

9-Pin
Serial Port
(Female
Connector)

REAR VIEW

25-Pin
Parallel Port
(Female Connector)

Figure 4–16.   Install the I/O card.

Install the Disk Controller Card, XT

Refer to Figure 4–17. Insert the controller card into the 16-bit slot closest to the disk drives. (A 16-bit slot has a 62-pin connector and a 36-pin connector.) Be certain to insert the card with a rocking motion until it is well seated. Fasten the metal tab with the screw that you retained. Plug the connectors into the correct locations as shown in the documentation for the controller card.

Install the Video Card, XT

Refer to Figure 4–18. Plug the video card into the 16-bit slot that is one over from the slot containing the disk controller card. Be certain to insert the card with a rocking motion until it is well seated. Fasten the metal tab with the screw you retained.

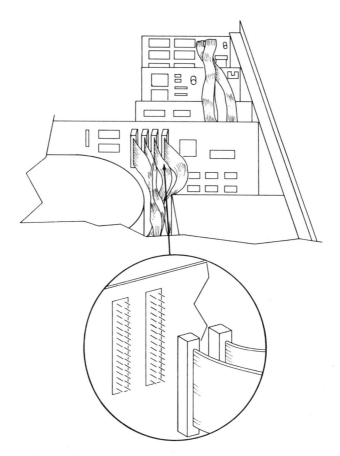

Figure 4–17.   Install the disk controller card.

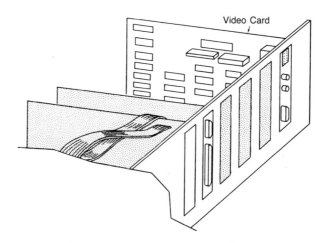

Figure 4–18.   Install the display adapter.

Block the Holes, XT

Be certain that there are no open slots at the back of the case. There must be a metal plate covering each unused expansion slot position. Your PC won't cool properly if a plate is left off, and the possibility of excessive RF (radio-frequency) radiation that could interfere with radio or TV reception is much greater with holes in the case.

Close the Box, XT

Replace the cover. Place it in the track and slide it back as far as it will go. Secure it with the screws you retained.

Install the Keyboard, XT

Plug the keyboard into the outlet provided at the back of the system unit. See Figure 4–19.

Install the Video Monitor, XT

Plug the monitor video connector into the receptacle provided on the back of the video card. (See Figure 4–19.) Plug in the power cord for the monitor. Note that most high-end monitors are not equipped with power plugs that can attach to the switched outlet on the rear of your computer chassis. This is for a very good reason: VGA and some EGA monitors draw more power than these switched sockets can provide. Check the power requirement of your new monitor, and compare it with the available power output on the switched outlet. If the monitor draws more current than the socket provides, don't plug the monitor into the computer socket. Use a wall outlet instead.

Hook Up the Printer, XT

Connect the printer cable to the parallel receptacle provided on the I/O board (Figure 4–19) and to the receptacle with spring clips on the printer (Figure 4–20). Plug the printer power cord into a source of 120 volts ac (alternating current).

Check It All One More Time, XT

Review all your connections. Make sure that all the boards are seated well. Using gentle pressure, check to see that the memory chips are securely in their sockets. Check the memory chips to be certain that all have the correct orientation.

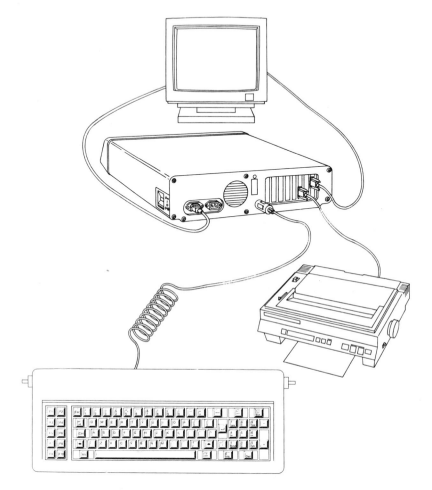

Figure 4–19.   Install the keyboard, monitor, and printer.

Try It Out

Set up your disk drives according to the information that came with the controller and the drives. Your controller and CPU will support 1:1 interleave. Partition your hard drive using DOS FDISK or a similar third-party product. Perform a high-level DOS format, eg., FORMAT C: /S /V. This will put the system files on C: and prompt you for a volume label.

Go through the testing procedures detailed in Chapter 6.

Run some benchmarks of your own. Test your new system by running software that you normally use. Time how long it takes to perform some time-consuming operations on the new system. Is the new system faster than PCs you've been using? Probably so, by a large margin.

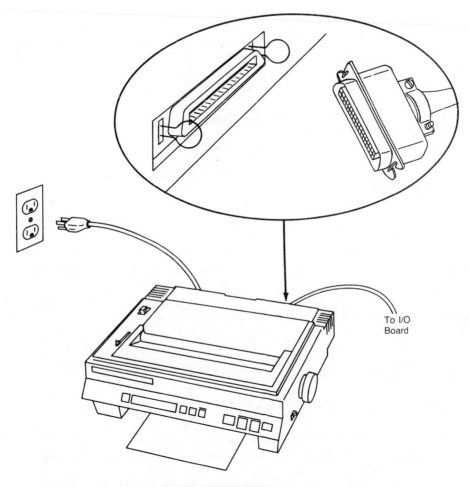

Figure 4–20. Hook up the printer.

80286 to 80386

We assume that the current PC is an IBM PC/AT or clone operating at 6, 8, or 10 MHz with a 30-Mbyte MFM full-height hard-disk drive, two half-height floppy-diskette drives (one 360-byte and one 1.2-Mbyte), a color monitor and extended graphics adapter (EGA), an I/O card containing a serial port and a parallel port, and a 200-watt power supply.

Replacement Parts, 80386

To give you a better real-world feel for the upgrade, we are including part numbers and prices for the suggested components (Table 4–2). We have taken the components and prices from the 1990 Jameco Electronics catalog. Jameco is a mail-order supplier located in Belmont, CA. Their 24-Hour Order Hotline can be reached at (415) 592-8097.

Table 4–2.   80286-to-80386 Upgrade Parts List

Part No.	Description	Cost
JE3520	Jameco 20-MHz 386 Baby Motherboard	$649.95
421000A9A-10	8 ea. 1-Mbyte × 9 SIP Module (8 Mbytes System RAM)	$1279.60
356KU	Toshiba 3.5″ 1.44-Mbyte Internal Floppy-Disk Drive	$109.95
JE2041	ESDI Hard & Floppy Controller	$169.95
M3180E	Miniscribe 150-Mbyte (17-ms) ESDI Half-Height Hard Drive	$1199.95
JE1016	101-Key Enhanced Keyboard	$69.95
TM5156	Casper 14″ VGA Monitor	$399.95
JE1057	Jameco 8/16-Bit VGA Card	$249.95
	TOTAL PRICE	$4129.25

Note that we have selected an ESDI drive for this upgrade, which means the existing 30-MByte drive can't be used. Older style controllers are not compatible with the ESDI format, and you can't use two controllers in the system at once. You could, of course, choose to install a higher-capacity ST-506 drive and keep the 30-MByte unit in service. However, overall performance would be degraded. You can probably get a few dollars for the old 30-MByte drive, or you could use it to upgrade an older machine. We recommend the ESDI approach for maximum performance and to bring the overall upgrade up to state of the art.

Out With the Old, AT

We'll guide you through your 80286-to-80386 upgrade process. We will discuss the selection process in other chapters. There is a preferred sequence to both assembly and disassembly. We'll take you through a sequence that will require a minimum amount of reworking. It's certainly possible to perform either the removal or installation of components in a different order, but other event sequences may require more effort or even give you skinned knuckles. (The solder side of a printed circuit board has many sharp points.)

Remove All Electrical Power, AT

Flip the switch to turn off the system. Unplug the system power cord from the 120-volt receptacle. Disconnect the system power cord from the back of the system unit. Store the power cord for future use.

Unplug the Keyboard, AT

Trace the keyboard cord to the back of the unit. Unplug the keyboard by pulling on the plug, not on the cord. Place the keyboard unit with your surplus parts.

Disconnect the Monitor, AT

The monitor has two cords that must be disconnected, a power cord and a signal cord. First, turn off the monitor. Second, remove the monitor power cord from the 120-volt receptacle (possibly the switched receptacle on the back of the system case if you're using an adapter). Finally, unplug the signal cord; you may have to use a screwdriver to loosen two screws holding the connector in place. Put the monitor and cords with your salvage parts.

Pull the Printer, AT

The printer has two cords that must be unplugged, a power cord and a signal cord. First, turn off the printer. Second, unplug the power from the 120-volt receptacle. Third, unplug the signal cord from the back of the system unit; you may have to loosen two screws holding the connector in place. Finally, flip back the latches and unplug the signal cable from the printer. These spring-like latches can be troublesome, mainly because they are a little delicate and a little sharp. To release them, grip each one, one at a time, firmly between your thumb and forefinger, and squeeze to release the tension; then swing the latch away from the plug. Put the printer, the printer power cord, and the printer signal cable in storage until the upgrade is completed.

Open the Box, AT

Unscrew, remove, and save the five screws holding the top of the system case (box) in place. (See Figure 4–21.) Pull the top forward until it stops, and then lift the top up and off. Store the top for future reassembly.

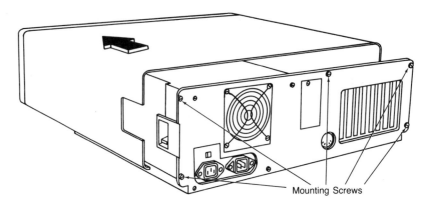

Figure 4–21.   Remove the case cover.

Lift the Cards, AT

Remove each of the expansion cards (printed circuit boards) from the sockets (bus) on the motherboard. (See Figure 4–22.) First, carefully remove any connectors from the expansion cards. Second, remove the screws holding the metal tabs in place. Retain the screws for attaching other cards. Finally, remove each card with a rocking motion. Store the serial and parallel I/O card for future use.

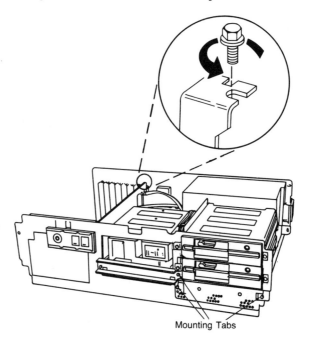

Figure 4–22.   Remove the expansion cards.

(This card has a 25-pin female connector for parallel data transfer and a 9-pin male connector for series data transfer.) Store the rest of the cards in your salvage pile.

Floppy-Diskette Drives, AT

Refer to Figure 4–23. First, remove the small metal tabs holding the drives in place. Keep the tabs and screws for future use. Second, slide the drives forward (out of the chassis) slightly, and disconnect the power and signal cables. Finally, remove the 360-kbyte drive. Leave the 1.2-Mbyte drive in the chassis. Store the 360-kbyte floppy-diskette drive in your salvage pile.

Hard Drive, AT

Refer to Figure 4–24. First, remove the bar holding the hard drive in place. Keep the bar and screws for future use. Second, slide the drive out of the bay slightly, and disconnect the data, control, and power cables from the back (inside) of the hard drive. Finally, remove the drive. Store the 30-Mbyte hard-disk drive in your salvage pile.

Disconnect the Power Supply, AT

You will not be removing the power supply. It is adequate to support the components installed during the upgrade. Unplug the power connection to the motherboard. (See Figure 4–25.) Note that on most power supplies this is a two-piece connector. Grab the connectors; don't pull on the cables.

Move Out the Motherboard, AT

Refer to Figure 4–26. First, remove any remaining electrical connectors from the motherboard. Second, remove all screws holding it. Third, slide the motherboard slightly away from the power supply. You are trying to disengage plastic standoffs from their slots. Finally, remove the motherboard. Very carefully put the motherboard in your salvage pile.

Halfway, AT

That's it. You should now have an empty case staring at you—except for the power supply. Reversing the process with your new components will complete the hand-tools portion of your upgrade.

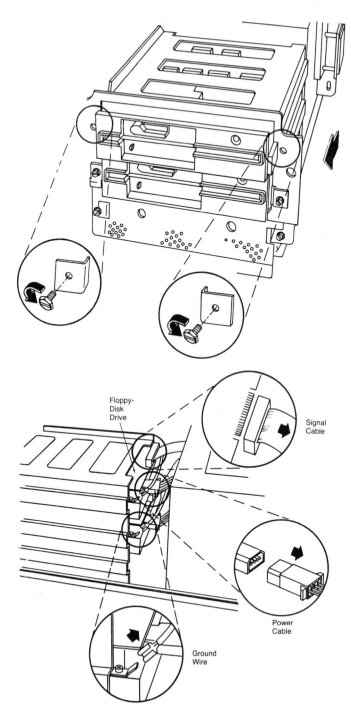

Figure 4–23.   Remove the floppy drives.

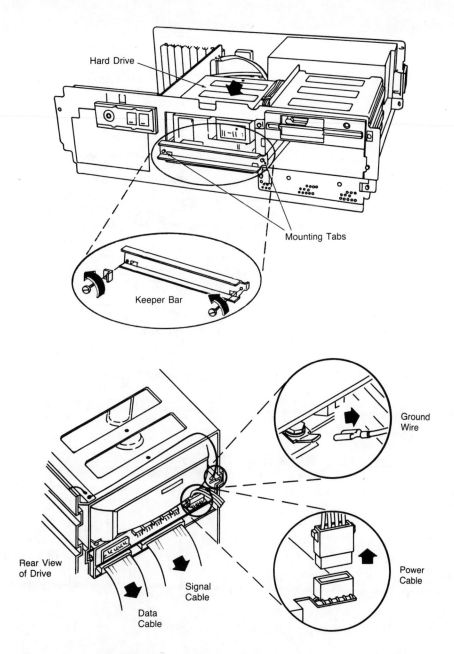

Figure 4–24. Remove the hard drive.

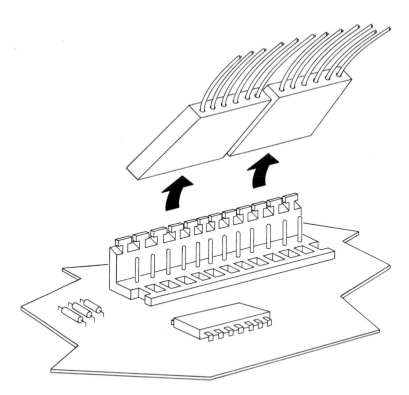

Figure 4–25.   Unplug the power supply.

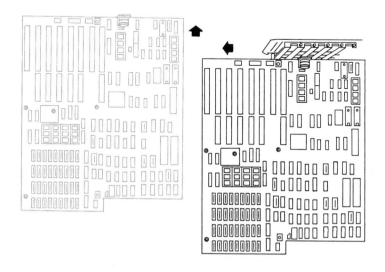

Figure 4–26.   Remove the motherboard.

In With the New

You can begin the rebuilding process by inserting new components that you have selected for your upgrade.

Add Memory, AT

Now is a good time to add the 8 megabytes of RAM to your motherboard. Make a stack of a couple of pieces of cardboard and place the motherboard on top (Figure 4–27). This will help to keep you from cracking the motherboard during the module insertion process (Figure 4–28).

Just like chips, modules can be damaged by the discharge of static electricity from you to them. While you're inserting the modules, keep grounding yourself. One way to avoid damaging static discharge is to touch the computer chassis first and, while keeping your hand on the chassis, pick up the memory module. Avoid touching the leads of the modules.

Modules can also be damaged by bending or breaking leads. As a general rule, you can bend and straighten a lead one time. Bend it more than that, and it will probably break. Once a lead is broken, the module must be replaced. To help avoid bending leads, insert the modules with extreme care using a gentle rocking motion.

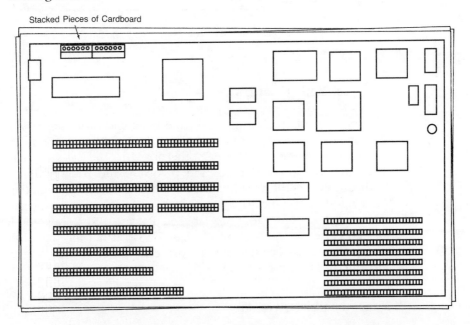

Figure 4–27.   Place motherboard on cardboard or foam.

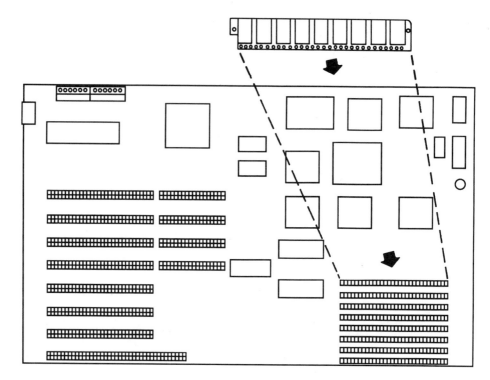

Figure 4–28.   Insert memory modules.

Mount the Motherboard, AT

Position each plastic standoff over the large end of its slot (Figure 4–29), and slide the motherboard into place. Using the screws you removed from the old motherboard, attach the new motherboard to the case. Remember that the multipin slots should be positioned toward the back of the case and the keyboard connector must line up with the hole in the back of the case.

Plug in the connectors that provide power for the motherboard. In most instances, the connectors are labelled P4 and P5. Connector P4 should be located closer to the back of the case. Most, if not all, manufacturers supply connectors with locating pins to prevent you from hooking up the power incorrectly. Don't force them.

Mount the Disk Drives, AT

Install the 1.44-Mbyte floppy-disk drive on the rails in the open bay (Figure 4–30). Mount the hard drive on the lower rails immediately to the left of the

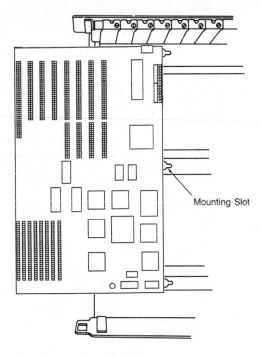

Mounting Slot

Figure 4–29. Mount the motherboard.

floppy drives. Secure the drives with the screws, tabs, and bars you removed earlier.

Connect the power, control, and data cables and the ground wire to the hard-disk drive. Connect the power and signal cables and ground wire to the floppy-diskette drives. Consult your documentation for the location of the terminating resistor. It must be removed from the floppy drive that will be the B: drive in your system. The A: drive must retain its terminating resistor.

Most hard drives also have a terminating resistor. If you are using only one drive, you can probably use the hard drive as it was supplied from the vendor or distributor. If you are using two drives, the second drive, the one that will be the D: drive, likely will not need the terminator. You should remove it according to the instructions supplied with the drive and store it in a safe place.

Install the Disk Controller Card, AT

Refer to Figure 4–31. Insert the controller card into the 16-bit slot closest to the disk drives. (A 16-bit slot has a 62-pin connector and a 36-pin connector.) Be certain to insert the card with a rocking motion until it is well seated. Fasten the metal tab with the screw that you retained. Plug the connectors into the correct locations as shown in the documentation for the controller card.

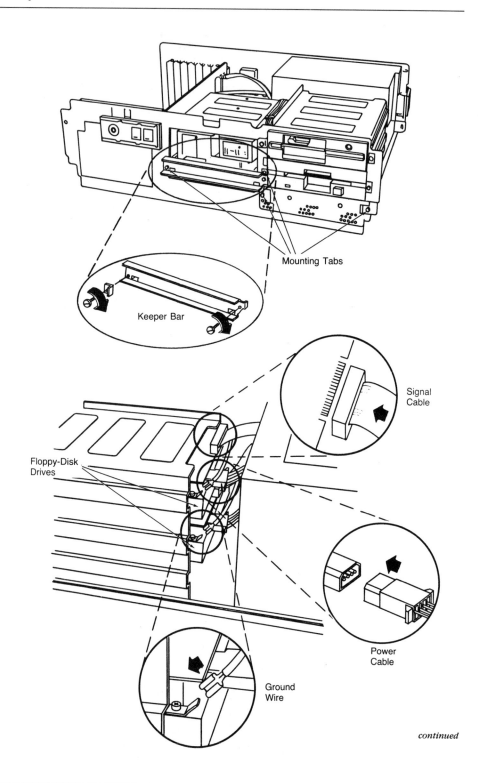

Mounting Tabs

Keeper Bar

Signal Cable

Floppy-Disk Drives

Power Cable

Ground Wire

continued

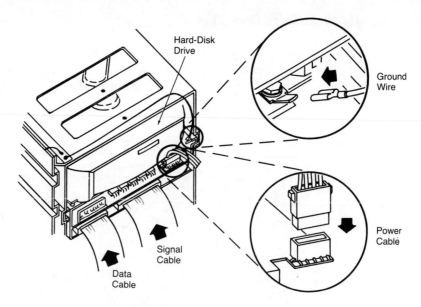

Figure 4–30. Mount the disk drives.

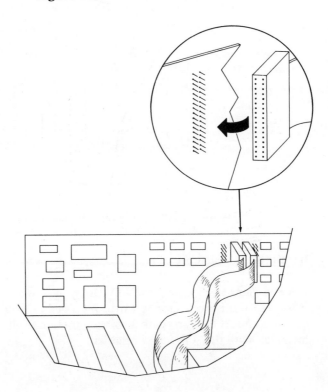

Figure 4–31. Install the disk controller card.

Install the Video Card, AT

Plug the video card into the 16-bit slot that is one over from the slot containing the disk controller card. See Figure 4–32. Be certain to insert the card with a rocking motion until it is well seated. Fasten the metal tab with the screw you retained.

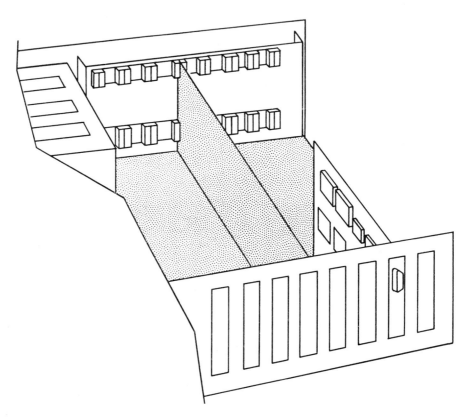

Figure 4–32.   Install the display adapter card.

Install the I/O Card, AT

Refer to Figure 4–33. Plug the I/O card you removed earlier into the 8-bit slot closest to the power supply. (An 8-bit slot has only a 62-pin connector.) Be certain to insert the card with a rocking motion until it is well seated. Fasten the metal tab with the screw you retained.

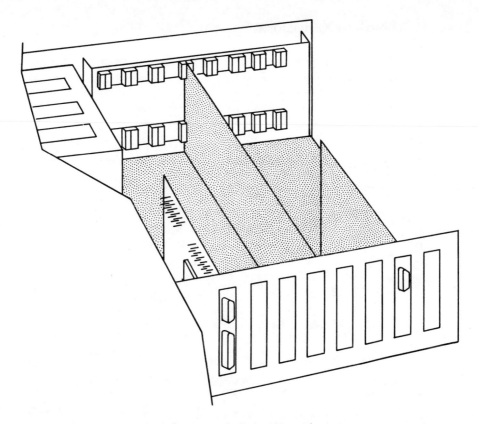

Figure 4–33.   Install the I/O card.

Block the Holes, AT

Be certain that there are no open slots at the back of case. There must be a metal plate covering each unused expansion-slot position. Your PC won't cool properly if a plate is left off. In addition, without the case properly sealed there is more opportunity for radio-frequency (RF) emissions.

Close the Box, AT

Replace the cover. Place it in the track, and slide it back as far as it will go. Secure it with the screws you retained.

Install the Keyboard, AT

Plug the keyboard into the outlet provided at the back of the system unit. (See Figure 4–34.)

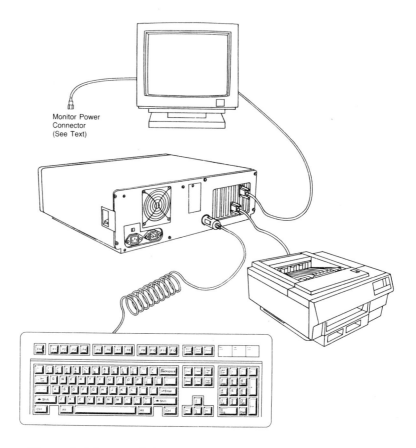

Monitor Power
Connector
(See Text)

Figure 4–34.   Install the keyboard, printer, and monitor.

Install the Video Monitor, AT

Plug the monitor video connector into the receptacle provided on the back of the video card (Figure 4–34). Plug in the power cord for the monitor. Note that most high-end monitors are not equipped with power plugs that can attach to the switched outlet on the rear of your computer chassis. This is for a very good reason: VGA and some EGA monitors draw more power than these switched sockets can provide. If you have been using a short ac adapter to convert your monitor to match the switched outlet, first check the power requirement of your new monitor, and compare it with the available power output on the switched outlet. If the monitor draws more current than the socket provides, don't plug the monitor into the computer socket. Use a wall outlet instead.

Hook Up the Printer, AT

Connect the printer cable to the parallel receptacle provided on the I/O board (Figure 4–34) and to the receptacle with spring clips on the back of the printer. Plug the printer power cord into a source of 120 volts ac.

Check It All One More Time, AT

Review all your connections. Make sure that all the boards are seated well. Using gentle pressure, check to see that the memory modules are securely in their sockets. Check the memory modules to be certain that all have the correct orientation.

Try It Out

Set up your disk drives according to the information that came with the controller and the drives. Your controller and CPU will support 1:1 interleave. Partition your hard drive using DOS FDISK or a similar third-party product. Perform a high-level DOS format, eg., FORMAT C: /S /V. This will put the system files on C: and prompt you for a volume label.

Go through the testing procedures detailed in Chapter 6.

Run some benchmarks of your own. Test your new system by running software that you normally use. Time how long it takes to perform some time-consuming operations on the old and new systems. Is the new system faster than PCs you've been using? Probably so, by a large margin.

You now have enough information to strip your old PC and assemble an upgraded PC in its place. Like the phoenix, the new machine will rise from the ashes of the old one.

Chapter 5

Upgrading Your Printer

Of all the peripherals that you can hang on your PC, it's likely that your printer has the greatest influence on others. Virtually everyone sends and receives letters and memos. The way your letters look can prejudice the way others deal with you. Just as in person, it's only possible to make a first impression once.

Today's technology offers a wide variety of printer options, from low-priced, but relatively high-quality, dot-matrix impact printers to top-of-the-line, high-resolution lasers.

In this chapter, we discuss options for upgrading your printer. Available printer options include adding memory to your printer, adding printer controllers, installing fonts, PostScript, cartridge fonts, fancy printing programs, and printer peripherals.

Improving the Quality of Your Communications

Desktop publishing has been receiving lots of attention lately. Many companies have bought software packages and hardware systems that let their staffs produce extremely good-looking materials. Unfortunately, the printer and software upgrades are not always accompanied by information on how to write more effectively.

Under these conditions, it isn't surprising that extremely good looking but poorly written communications are produced. Fancy letters with pictures and graphs don't "get it" when your message is unclear. We recommend that you take advantage of any opportunities to upgrade your writing skills. The best PC and printer combination in the world can't make up for missing or under-developed communications skills.

Understanding Your Printer Choices

In this chapter, we will consider four basic types of printers. These are the inkjet printer, the laser printer, the dot-matrix printer, and the daisy-wheel printer.

Inkjet Printer

Inkjet printers have received bad press for several years. Early inkjet printers tended to clog easily, required regular—almost daily—cleaning and maintenance, and were messy to work with. Those that didn't clog sometimes put blobs of ink on the paper.

Today's inkjets are a far cry from the early machines. There have been large gains in quality and reliability. Only laser printers have a better reputation for combined quality, speed, and ease of maintenance.

Inkjet printers such as the one in Figure 5–1 work by shooting small droplets of ink onto the paper. The exact droplet specifications vary from printer to printer. However, in general it can be said that the droplets are considerably smaller than the dots produced by dot-matrix printers. (We'll discuss dot-matrix printers later in this chapter.)

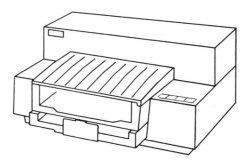

Figure 5–1.   Example of an inkjet printer.

There are several methods for moving the droplets. The primary technique is to accelerate the droplet with electrostatic fields after the drop has been formed. Another is to squeeze the droplet through small orifices in piezoelectric crystals. Piezoelectric crystals change shape when an electric field is applied to them. The shape changes are responsible for accelerating and steering the ink droplets to the appropriate locations.

Reliability

The worst thing that can happen to an inkjet printer is a clog. As with most PC-related equipment, there are very few user serviceable parts. The clogs usually can be removed by soaking the print head or some removable part of it in a solvent. The small size of the orifices makes physical cleaning as opposed to chemical cleaning a very impractical approach. In fact, you will probably mess up your printer if you try to clean the orifice with a wire or anything else.

Good quality control during ink formulation has brought the number of ink-related clogs to nearly zero. To avoid ink problems, you must buy the inks especially made for inkjet printers. It is interesting to note that you have to mix your own inks for the ultrafast, ultraexpensive ($15,000 and up) special-purpose printers.

Quality

Inkjet printers can achieve 300 dots per inch (dpi) resolution. This has become the defacto standard for good quality dot-matrix printers. While inkjet printers don't operate with little wires hitting the ribbon and the paper, small dots are used to form characters and graphics. So inkjet printers satisfy the basic requirements to be called dot-matrix devices.

Full-page 300-dpi graphics are possible with inkjet printers. There is a big difference between 300-dpi text and 300-dpi graphics. Any of the inkjet printers presently being manufactured can produce 300-dpi text. The rub comes when you want to go to full-page graphics at 300-dpi resolution.

Graphics images are generated in the computer memory at a resolution determined by your software. Converting the memory images to images on paper is called *bit mapping*. You can't do full-page bit mapping with the amount of memory that comes standard on most inkjet printers. You need to buy and install a memory-upgrade board. It takes at least 1 megabyte of RAM above and beyond the standard printer configuration to do 300-dpi graphics.

Speed

Speed for inkjet and laser printers is specified in terms of the number of pages per minute that they can print. Run-of-the mill inkjet printers can produce from four to ten pages per minute once the initial page has been prepared. There is a lot of variation in the amount of time it takes to produce the first page. This is a function of both the printer (intrinsic slowness) and the complexity of the material you're asking it to produce (graphics take longer than text).

Operating Materials

As with any printer, the primary operating material is paper. Fortunately, you can use just about any paper in an inkjet printer; you don't need special paper. However, usually you can't use pin feed (continuous) paper; you have to use sheets.

Inkjet printers do, however, require special inks. You won't just load a reservoir with a water-based ink like the ink fountain pens use. The inks have a special solvent to promote very rapid drying.

Cost

Inkjet printers are available with price tags up near $20,000. The more utilitarian, slower models are generally available for under $3000. A list of manufacturers of ink-jet printers is given in Appendix B.

Laser Printers

The basic laser printer (Figure 5–2) uses a laser diode (a semiconductor device) to write information onto a drum coated with photosensitive material. The laser light is pulsed to make very tiny dots. A multisided mirror scans the laser beam from one edge of the drum to the other. The printed image is built up one scan line at a time. A single line of text takes many scans of the laser beam.

To make a fairly long story short, not everything called a laser printer is actually a laser printer. There are alternative light sources and methods for getting the image onto the photosensitive materials.

A line of light-emitting diodes (LEDs) can make the image. With an LED array, you don't have to have a mirror to scan the light across the drum. The array is as wide as the drum, and there is an LED for each dot in the 300-dpi line. (What you have is a 300 LED-per-inch array.) The LED design has some advantages in that it requires fewer moving parts and the overall design requires less maintenance.

A second alternative to laser diodes and rotating mirrors is a liquid-crystal shutter (LCS) with a single light source (frequently a halogen light). The LCS has an element for each dot on the 300-dpi line just as the LED array does. For either the LED or LCS array, any single element can fail and thereby degrade the image. However, the rest of the array will continue to form images on the drum.

The paper wraps around the drum, and the image transfers to it. At this point, the ink (a relatively low-melting-point plastic) is not bonded to the paper. If you ever have a paper jam in a laser printer (a common occurrence), you will probably come away with some of the ink on you. The ink smudges and smears on the paper easily. Rollers and heaters are used to get the temperature high enough with the right pressure to make the ink bond tightly to the paper.

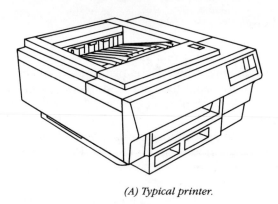

(A) Typical printer.

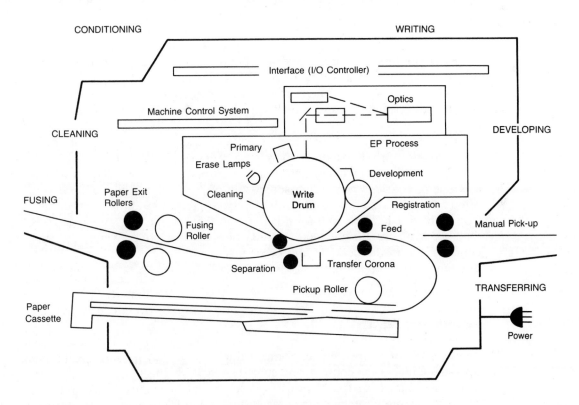

(B) Principle of operation. Courtesy Hewlett-Packard.

Figure 5–2. Laser printer.

Reliability

Laser printers are reasonably reliable. One popular series feeds pages through at about eight per minute without complaint. Most of the failures encountered with laser printers are paper feed problems. Very thin and very thick paper will not feed properly. With thin paper, you may get several sheets emerging at the same time (only one of them with ink on it). When the paper is too thick, it won't feed at all, or maybe an occasional sheet will feed or an occasional sheet will stick. Most page printers (laser, LED, and LCS printers all are classified as *page printers*) come with instructions about the type of paper that should be used with them.

High humidity is a real problem for paper. If you expose a ream of paper to high humidity for too long, the edges of the pages will curl. If you have ever spent much time around a large copy machine, you're already aware of this problem. Near most big copiers, there is a message about rewrapping unused paper.

Laser printers don't feed paper with curled edges any better than copiers do. You have to keep straight, flat paper in the paper tray. During times of the year when the humidity is high, it is best to keep a relatively small amount of paper in the paper tray and refill the tray often from a well wrapped paper supply.

Don't assume that air conditioning will necessarily prevent humidity problems with laser-printer paper. We have seen laser printers brought to their knees by high humidity, even in constantly air-conditioned environments. If you have a problem, consider purchasing some type of sealed container to store your printer paper during times of high humidity. We have found that storage cases from RubberMaid work well for this purpose. They come in a variety of sizes, they are virtually airtight, and the lids pop on and off conveniently. Such containers from RubberMaid and other manufacturers are readily available at discount stores, office-supply stores, building-supply outlets, and even grocery stores.

Laser-Printer Paper

All paper is not created equal. Some is thicker than others, some is heavier, some has a higher rag content, and some has a glossy finish.

As a group, laser (page) printers have special paper needs. Many of the computer-supplies catalogs advertise different kinds of page-printer (usually called "laser-printer") paper. It's important to understand the requirements that laser printers put on paper.

There are two primary requirements: one is imposed by the physical processes involved in getting the image on the paper, and the second is imposed by the paper-handling mechanisms. Laser printers utilize electrical fields (charges) to hold the toner to the paper. The toner is then fused to the paper with a combination of heat and pressure. This requires special electrical and thermal properties for the paper used in page printers.

The intrinsic electrical resistance of paper is determined at the time of manufacture. The two methods of getting the right resistance for this application are either to mix in chemicals to change the bulk properties of the paper or to add chemicals that will affect the surface properties.

Moisture content can change the electrical resistance of the paper. Most paper is manufactured in a room where the relative humidity is 50%. When the relative humidity of the room where the paper is used stays above 50% for an extended period of time, the paper absorbs moisture. The extra water reduces the electrical resistance of the paper, making it more difficult to get the toner to adhere to the paper. This is a source of the variation of print quality with relative humidity. Too much moisture also can cause the paper to wrinkle or to develop "bumps" in the surface. If such irregularities are too severe, the paper will not lie flat on the drum, and the printed image may be unclear.

Paper handling also can be affected by moisture in the paper. In addition to changing the electrical resistance, moisture changes the structure of the paper. Paper exposed to too much moisture for too long begins to curl at the edges. This curling affects the way it passes through the laser printer. A page with too much edge curl is likely to jam.

The packaging that reams of paper are shipped in contains special coatings to prevent the contents from absorbing excess moisture. You should take advantage of the packaging. Take care to close the packaging around partial reams of paper. Also, don't put more paper in your paper tray than you are likely to use in a day when the relative humidity in your room exceeds 60 to 65%.

Another item that affects paper handling is generated during paper manufacturing. When paper is produced, the two sides are not the same. Unfortunately, the distinction is not always readily apparent to your eyes or your fingers. The two sides are the *felt* (top) and the *wire* (bottom). Considering that the paper is supported on a screen during manufacture, it is not surprising that the side in contact with the screen is called the wire side.

The rule of thumb for printers (it's a rule you should apply, too) is to print on the wire side. If you are going to do two-sided printing (there are new printers that can do two-sided, or *duplex,* printing), you should print on the wire side first. The label on many paper packages has an arrow that points to the wire side. Be certain to arrange the paper in your paper tray so that the wire side receives the toner. You must consider whether your paper is fed face up or face down.

If the paper you are using is not marked on the package, there is no easy way to tell which is the wire side. On high-quality bond—the papers with a watermark—you can hold the paper up to the light to read the mark. You should print on the side on which the watermark reads correctly.

Some papers designed especially for laser printers have one side that is noticeably slicker or shinier than the other. You should use this side first. In addition, there are special offset papers that have some clay content to one side of the paper, making it appear very white and almost fuzzy. This type of paper will produce very high-quality results, but generally you can use only one side of the paper.

If yours is an ink-jet printer, there are special papers designed to minimize the amount of paper dust they produce. The surface is very slick and has a relatively hard finish to reduce any ink bleeding. Although you can use standard papers in an ink jet printer, you will get better quality output, and increase the life of your print head, by using stock especially designed for the ink-jet machine.

In the final analysis, our printer friends tell us that except for special cases—clay-coated paper, watermarked paper—you can print on either side. If your printer has extremely close tolerances, you may find that some papers feed better on one side than on the other, but you probably won't be able to tell the difference in print quality just by looking at the finished product, regardless of which side of the paper you use for printing.

Paper weight also affects the likelihood of paper jams. If your paper is too light or too heavy, your chances of a paper jam are increased. The basis weight of paper is determined by weighing 500 sheets (the page size of the paper is also a consideration). Five hundred sheets of the most commonly used paper weighs 20 pounds, so it is called 20-pound paper. There is better quality paper, 24-pound paper, that is used for some applications in which the improved quality offsets the increased price. Some applications can use 15- or 18-pound papers, but the lighter papers—especially anything under 18 pounds—are likely to cause jams.

Once the weight of the paper has been decided, it's time to consider the appearance. Bond paper contains cotton fibers mixed with the wood pulp. Bond feels good and frequently has a watermark stamped on it. Paper can also be made with linen fibers mixed with the wood pulp. These fibers make the paper very durable. Linen paper is used infrequently for laser-printer applications because of its high cost.

Other paper considerations involve special forms, labels, and envelopes. Special forms are available in either fan-fold or individual-sheet format from numerous suppliers. Getting the right labels presents modest difficulties. The rollers used to fuse the toner to the paper can reach 200 degrees Fahrenheit. That is too hot for some label adhesives. You have to check, either by carefully reading the specs or by buying a small sample and trying them. However, if you use the wrong type of label in your laser printer, you run the risk of the labels or the adhesive that holds them coming off inside the printer, causing some real maintenance headaches.

Hewlett-Packard has assembled tips for using envelopes in laser printers. Among their recommendations are:

- Buy only envelopes with diagonal seams and gummed flaps.
- Make a sharp crease on the leading edge of your envelopes (the edge that's first through the paper path).

The bottom line is that you have to spend a little extra money to get paper that is OK to use in a laser printer. Of course, many of the paper products made for office copiers will work in a laser printer, but for a little more money you can purchase paper designed specifically for the needs of laser printers. The better performance and print quality usually are worth the extra cost.

Buy small quantities (a ream or two) of several different papers. Test as many as you can afford until you find one or more that will stand up to your own set of demanding requirements.

Quality

Laser printers produce high-quality output. The standard resolution is 300 dpi. If you are willing to pay for it (over $4000), 600 dpi is available. At 600 dpi, you're getting very close to phototypesetter print quality, at least as far as the human eye can determine. (To ensure maximum quality through the printing process, typesetters use 1200- to 2400-dpi devices, but when you look at the original printed page it is all but impossible to see the difference between 600-dpi and 1200-dpi output.)

The way the manufacturer assembles the components determines printer quality. This is particularly true because most laser printer manufacturers don't necessarily make all the components that go into their machines. A relatively small number of suppliers of printer innards (laser engines) supply printer manufacturers. Canon and Ricoh are but two companies that produce laser engines capable of fine-quality output.

The laser (or its substitute technology), drum, and fixer assemblies are called the *laser engine*. Most printer makers choose to use one of the two engines mentioned above. The printer manufacturers provide the paper-handling functions, logic, memory, and case.

In general, there are two basic designs available today. One, such as the Canon engine, packages toner, drum, and other printing components into a single, removable package. When you run out of toner, you replace the entire printing mechanism. This approach has the advantage that you don't have to track separately how many images have been produced by a given drum. When you replace the toner, you also replace the drum. The disadvantage is that each toner replacement costs more, and, as a general rule, the drum can produce more high-quality images than one loading of toner.

In other engines, the engine components are kept separate. When you run out of toner, you dump a new supply into a reservoir, but you don't replace any of the mechanical components. The drum and other printing components are replaced separately as required. This approach produces a lower overall per-copy cost and, according to some manufacturers, makes possible higher quality output. But it also means that you have to pay more attention to printer maintenance during the life of the machine.

Given this inherent equality because numerous printers start off equal (they use the same laser engine), it shouldn't come as a big surprise to you that print quality does not vary greatly. There is some print variability because of design decisions.

You will see real differences among laser printers in how the final manufacturer designs the paper handling for the machine. For example, the top-end machines use very short, straight paper paths, reducing complexity and improving paper-feed reliability.

The paper path takes on special importance when you are going to use the printer as a shared resource. There will be times when the printer is operating and no one is watching. So, you need a printer that can feed lots of sheets without a paper jam and can stack the sheets in the correct order.

Speed

Speed for laser and inkjet printers is specified in terms of how many pages per minute they can print. Run-of-the-mill laser printers can produce from four to ten pages per minute once the initial page has been prepared. There is a lot of variation in the amount of time it takes to produce the first page. This is a function of both the printer (intrinsic processing speed) and the complexity of the material you're asking it to produce (graphics take longer than text). As a general rule, a printer with more memory will get the first page ready quicker than one with minimal memory. PostScript printers provide a large variety of fonts, but it usually takes longer to compose a page in PostScript or other page-definition language than if the printer uses its own font-generation facilities.

Most single-user applications can easily get along with six or eight pages per minute with 300-dpi resolution.

Materials for Operation

As with any printer, the primary operating material is paper. For guidelines on selecting laser-printer paper, see the section headed "Laser-Printer Paper" earlier in this chapter.

Laser printers don't use ink, they use toner. Toners usually are supplied in a special replaceable cartridge, or you fill a printer reservoir from a packaged container. You have to replace the toner after a specified number of hours of operation or a specified number of pages printed. By the way, there is a secondary market in used toner cartridges for some laser engines. If you buy a refurbished toner/drum assembly from the Canon engine, for example, you will pay about half of what a new assembly costs. Just make sure you purchase the reconditioned parts from a reputable dealer. A laser printer that produces poor-quality output is worse than having a quality impact printer at your service.

Cost

Laser printers are available with price tags from just over $1000 to as high as you want to go. Very high end, publishing quality, shared devices can cost well over $100,000, but that's not the type of printer we are talking about here.

Toner replacement by itself isn't particularly expensive. Toner replacement for an NEC LC890 printer, for example, is priced around $21 to $25, and it gives you enough toner for 2000 to 3000 pages. A "toner" cartridge for a Canon engine, which really includes a lot of hardware besides just toner, is usually around $100 for the same 2000 to 3000 pages. With toner-only replacement types, you still have to replace the printing drum regularly, say every 7000 to 10,000 pages. The drum may cost $130 to $200. The overall cost per page with this type of printer is lower, but you have to stock more replacement parts, and you have to pay attention to maintenance.

Dot-Matrix Printers

The basic principle of dot-matrix printers is much like that of regular type-writers. Ink is transferred from a ribbon to paper. The difference is that in the dot-matrix printer many small wires are used to form the letter or number, whereas the typewriter uses a single preformed letter or number. The dot-matrix printer forms characters on the fly. (As we mentioned earlier, other types of printers also construct images from a pattern of small dots. However, in common usage the term "dot-matrix printer" is used to refer to the type of device we are discussing here.)

The *matrix* portion of the name comes from the arrangement of dots used to form characters. Early models had a total of nine wires in the print head. The wires were arranged in a single column. Characters were made up of dots laid out in a matrix that was nine dots high and six dots wide. Most characters used just the top seven pins (dots), while the descenders (such as on p and q) were formed with the bottom two pins. The matrix was only six dots wide, but eleven positions were available (intermediate columns could be used as long as the dots didn't overlap). The nine-pin (wire) matrix made rather low-quality characters. Much higher quality is achieved currently with 24-pin print heads. Figure 5–3 shows representative units.

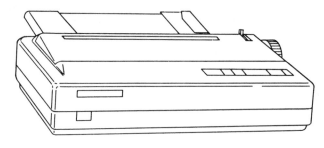

(A) 9-pin printer.

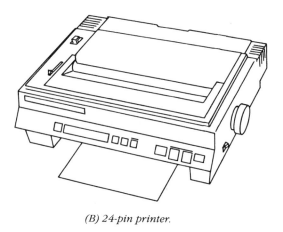

(B) 24-pin printer.

Figure 5–3.   Examples of dot-matrix printers.

The lowest-quality characters for a dot-matrix printer are produced at the highest speed. The high-speed operation is called the *draft mode*. The printer manufacturers are assuming that you already know what you have written, so you can tolerate lower quality to get your printed copy quickly.

A big step up in quality from draft mode is *near letter quality (NLQ)*. The term NLQ is frequently encountered in advertisements for dot-matrix printers. In principle, NLQ refers to making characters that are almost as good as the ones a good quality typewriter can make. But in practice, the quality often leaves something to be desired, especially for nine-pin printers. Especially with older printers, the NLQ settings can be painfully slow, requiring two, three, or more passes of the print head.

Even the inexpensive nine-pin printers have an NLQ mode. They improve character quality by going over each character twice. Simply hitting the same location two times would only make the dots darker. The quality improvement is achieved by making a slight displacement (offset) from the original location both vertically and horizontally. The new character thus produced fills in empty spots of the earlier character.

Although the NLQ mode produces a dramatic improvement in character quality for nine-pin printers, it's still rather far from typewriter quality. In addition, it takes a long time to print a document.

Twenty-four-pin printers in the draft mode make characters that are just barely lower in quality than the NLQ-mode characters of nine-pin printers. The transition from nine to 24 pins in the print head has made a tremendous improvement in the quality achievable with dot-matrix printers.

There are also 18-pin printers that have very high quality output compared with nine-pin models. Since virtually all comments made about 24-pin printers also apply to the 18-pin models, we will refer only to the 24-pin models to avoid complications.

Reliability

Paper handling is a sore point with most people who have to live with a printer for any length of time. It really doesn't matter whether it is a dot-matrix printer or some other type. Getting paper to travel through the printer without tearing or jamming should be a primary goal for printer manufacturers. Having said that, we would hasten to add that most dot-matrix printers work very well on single sheets of paper. Friction feed (pressure) is used to move single sheets. As with any typewriter, there are alignment problems that you must address.

However, pin feed is the dominant paper-moving mechanism in dot matrix printers (Figure 5–4). The actual pin-feed mechanism rarely fails. Problems arise because of misalignment of the paper with the pins. The paper must arrive almost exactly parallel to the pins. If this condition isn't met, the holes in the paper will be mangled or torn. The poorer the alignment, the more likely it is that the paper will become cocked in the printer and cause a catastrophic failure.

With some printers, the pin-feed mechanism is not of high quality. Leaving one of these printers unattended during a long print job is a mistake. You are likely to return to find a mass of unusable paper.

In quite a few dot-matrix printers, incoming and outgoing paper can interfere. Massive paper jams occur when the outgoing pages get dragged back into the print path. Several third-party companies manufacture paper-handling stands designed to prevent or at least reduce the possibility of interference. Even with the help of such equipment, it's still up to you to prevent paper jams.

Quality and Speed

As noted earlier, the best that dot-matrix printers can do is NLQ. For the 24-pin printers, this may be quite good. The tradeoff here is between print quality and printing speed.

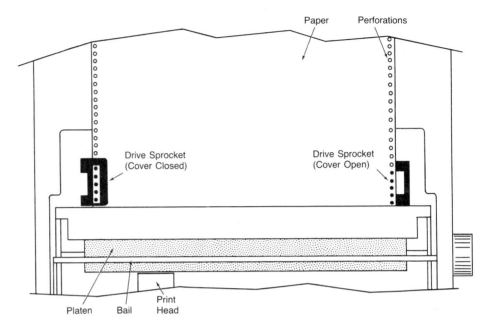

Figure 5–4.   Tractor/pin-feed paper handling.

Some of the better dot-matrix printers can produce more than 250 characters per second in the draft mode. For the same printers, NLQ can be printed at better than 150 characters per second.

Materials for Operation

As with all printers, paper is the most important element required for operation. Most dot-matrix printers can use fan fold paper. This can be handled with either the traction (friction) feed or the pin (tractor) feed. It works much better when used with the pin feed, but it can work either way. Laser cut paper—sometimes called Micro-Perf or some other trade name—looks almost as good as standard sheets once you've removed the pin-feed holes.

The next most important item is the ribbon. Ribbons come in two varieties and can be obtained from any of a large number of local and mail-order supply houses. The ribbons producing the best looking output are the carbon-film ribbons. They can only be used once. The text is very dark and looks consistently good. The older, more conventional ribbons are of the reusable type. The ribbon cycles back and forth until you decide that the inevitable degradation in printing performance demands that you replace it.

Cost

Dot-matrix printers go from very cheap (around $300) to very expensive (around $3500). Most of the nine-pin printers cost less than $800. The 24-pin printers range in price from around $500 to around $3500.

Daisy-Wheel Printers

Daisy-wheel printers are the upscale big brothers of the standard typewriter. The characters are all preformed and located on replaceable circular assemblies that look a great deal like multispoke wagon wheels or like daisies. To change from one type font to another, you simply replace the wheel assembly. Although widely used in some existing applications, daisy-wheel printers are generally a thing of the past. Unless you want very high quality print at a relatively low cost, it is doubtful whether upgrading to a daisy-wheel device is a good choice. And to get a low cost you should look for a used machine, which, of course, can present maintenance headaches.

In operation, an electromagnet actuates a plunger that strikes the desired character. The character has been rotated into position in front of the ribbon. The character strikes the ribbon and makes an impression on the paper. This is a combination of characteristics found in several makes of conventional typewriters.

There is nothing spectacular about the paper-feed mechanism. Daisy-wheel printers have been around for a long time, and they continue to be popular with people who need high-quality printing at a modest cost. Of course, there is none of the flexibility that is to be had with the high quality available with a laser printer. (But, there's none of the high price, either.)

Reliability

There are no other printers quite as reliable as the daisy wheel printers. With very well developed (mature) technology, there is little that can go wrong that has not already been addressed. Daisy wheels can stick or break, ribbons can fail to advance, and paper can jam; all in all these failure modes don't happen very often. When the inevitable failures occur, recovery from them usually requires a short time. Most people who have daisy wheel printers have a small inventory of spare parts. The failures usually involve parts that can be replaced with a small amount of effort by the person using the printer, or at most a local technician.

On the other hand, daisy-wheel printers are mechanically complex. There are a lot of moving parts, and each one must function properly for the whole printer to work right. Select the type of printer according to your application. For mass mailings where the printer will be in operation most of every business day, you obviously need a very high-quality, rugged mechanism. Some companies also offer a light-duty design that you can use for an occasional letter or report, offloading the majority of your printing to a dot-matrix printer. In printers, as everywhere else, you get what you pay for.

Quality

The print quality is tops. It is the standard by which all the others are judged. For example, NLQ means that the printing is nearly as good as that produced by a daisy-wheel printer.

Speed

The speed of even the fastest of the daisy-wheel printers is nothing to write home about. With a speed limit between 40 and 60 characters per second, only the slowest of the dot-matrix printers are in the same ball park. However, what you don't get in speed is more than made up for in quality.

Materials for Operation

Standard fan-fold paper is the fare of choice for daisy-wheel printers. They can accept single sheets when needed. These printers are extremely forgiving of choices of low-weight and heavy-weight papers. They are not finicky like laser printers and others of that ilk.

The same two ribbon choices available for dot-matrix printers are also available for daisy-wheel printers. You can use either the carbon-film ribbon or the multipass inked ribbon. With the latter, it's up to you to figure out when it's time to change ribbons.

You need to maintain an inventory of daisy wheels to accommodate font changes that will inevitably be required. You can't change them on the fly with software, but with most applications you can insert a code that will pause output while you change the wheel, which in itself is not a complicated process.

Adding Memory to a Laser Printer

You've bought a laser printer (or you're planning to buy a laser printer), and someone just told you that your printer needs more memory. What's wrong with the amount of memory the factory puts in the printer? Most laser printers come with at least 512 kbytes of RAM. Why would you want to add more memory? Those are very reasonable questions. And they're ones that can have several answers.

A concept that ties in directly with the RAM issue is *resolution*. The better resolution you demand, the more RAM you need. There are two kinds of resolution that pertain to our topic: text resolution and graphics resolution. Standard laser printers are specified as having 300 dots per inch (dpi) resolution. The difference between lower resolutions, say 150 dpi, and the 300 dpi of the laser printer probably is not readily apparent in normal (10- or 12-point) text. When you use bigger characters, the ragged appearance produced by 150 dpi becomes obvious. For 300-dpi text resolution with average-sized fonts, there is enough RAM on a standard laser printer.

Graphics and larger fonts write a story all their own. You can specify the resolution either for part of the page or for the whole page. At 300 dpi, there is enough standard memory to allow you to print at least ¼ page of graphics (and nothing more). With this minimal RAM configuration, an entire page of graphics will be printed at 75 dpi. That's really rather poor.

Most people using business-graphics software packages want to have their display material look a lot better than their CRT screen. If you fit into this rather large group, then you need to go for 300-dpi, full-page graphics. And that can't be done with the standard memory allocation.

New Fonts

The way you use your laser printer is a big driver in this hardware-upgrade decision. If you want to produce very high quality text and you're happy with the Courier and F and J fonts available with Hewlett-Packard and compatible printers, then you really don't need to upgrade to more RAM than came with your printer.

Okay, you've decided that there's no reason for you to hold back your laser printer. You're not going to tie it down to the assortment of fonts available to an old-fashioned daisy-wheel printer. You're going to let it produce the very best quality text it can. And unlike the case with daisy-wheel printers, you can change fonts in software.

This seems like a software decision, but it is actually a hardware decision, too. You need more memory if you are going to utilize the numerous, readily available downloadable fonts. It takes lots of RAM to set up your page in anything other than very conventionally sized, monospaced text.

If you are to step into the world of documents that look typeset, you have to have both the hardware and the software to support proportional fonts. An excellent choice for downloadable fonts is the Bitstream fonts. They allow you to go from very small (6 point) to very large (24 point) characters in different fonts including Courier (standard typewriter monospaced font), Times Roman (most popular proportionally spaced font), and others.

High-Resolution Full-Page Graphics

To do full-page graphics with 300-dpi resolution, you'll need at least two megabytes of RAM. Why would you want to go to full page graphics? After all, you can print ¼ page at 300 dpi with the standard LaserJet. Surely that's enough when you are busily integrating text with graphics with the newest word-processing or desktop-publishing package.

Yes that's true. But what about those really nifty presentations you'd like to make if only your pie charts didn't look like they have a bad case of measles. Low-resolution graphics (150 dpi and lower) look a great deal like the halftone images you see in newspapers. They aren't too bad when you see them on a sheet of paper. But when they are projected on a screen for the whole world to see, it becomes all too obvious that there is a lot of empty space between the dots.

Once you've decided to buy the extra memory, where do you get it, who installs it, or even better, how do you install it yourself?

The first question is the easiest to answer. Get your additional memory from the same place that sold you the printer. If they are out of business or for some other reason you don't want to deal with them, try the mail-order firms that advertise your printer. A listing of many of the more prominent mail-order firms can be found in Appendix D. You could also check the back of any of the large monthly computer magazines for a list of advertisers.

The second and third questions are almost as easy to answer as the first. Anyone with the ability to read, follow instructions, and exercise due caution around electrical equipment can install the extra memory. You could hire a technician to do it at your site. You could take it back to the dealer who sold it to you to have his technicians install it. Or you could do it yourself.

Doing it yourself gives you the chance to get satisfaction from doing a job well and immediately benefitting from your labors. All you have to do is follow the directions. The instructions supplied by the manufacturer should be followed EXACTLY. If you follow them to the letter, there is no reason for you to expect that you can't do the job yourself. Before you start the job, read and familiarize yourself with Appendix C.

Printing Speed

Printing speed is a big concern for people who have to share printers. You don't want to have to wait forever while Harry's spreadsheets and Mildred's monthly reports get printed. After all, you're important and expensive. While you are sitting around twiddling your thumbs waiting for your turn on the printer, you're costing the company money.

Laser printers are by their nature page printers. When we specify their speed, we do it differently than for character oriented printers such as dot-matrix and daisy-wheel units. Laser printers are rated in pages per minute, while character printers are rated in characters per second. There is a rough comparison between the two measuring systems. If you assume a full printed page contains about 2500 characters, then an eight page-per-minute page printer is roughly equivalent to 333 characters per second.

The fastest of the current dot-matrix printers is capable of roughly 350 characters per second and costs over $3000. The slowest of the current laser printers is rated at four pages per minute (about half the speed of the fastest dot-matrix printer). This printer sells for under $1000. And laser printers offer the benefit of higher resolution, more fonts, graphics, and compatibility with a broad range of applications software. So unless nearly all of your printer output is draft-mode text and speed is extremely important, for initial cost and raw printing speed, the bottom-of-the-line laser printer wins over a high speed dot-matrix impact printer hands down.

It's still pretty clear that the bottom-of-the-line laser printer is not the answer in a busy office. It's just not fast enough to handle big loads. When the initial cost is not as big a constraint as people's time, you can get laser printers rated at over 15 pages per minute. Of course, these printers have very large price tags. But they do keep large queues from developing even in busy offices.

So it's decision time. If you want to upgrade to a page printer and you'll have sole possession or only share it with one other person, then one of the slower (4 to 6 pages per minute), less expensive laser printers or an inkjet printer would be most cost effective. If you're going to have to share it with six or eight other people, you should opt for a considerably faster (8 to 10 pages per minute) model. If some of your coworkers are real printer hogs, then it would be a good idea to go for the fastest page printer you can locate (over 15 pages per minute).

Page Formatting

One time-consuming activity that we haven't mentioned is page formatting. It takes time to produce the page image in memory (format the page). And then it takes time (not very much time) to move the image from memory to the transfer drum. Simple, monospaced fonts take the smallest amount of time to produce the page format. Formatting time goes up with font changes and proportional spacing. The longest formatting times go with high resolution graphics.

Unhappily, there is no absolute number associated with page formatting as there is with page printing. The first page takes 30 seconds or more to format, and then the rest of the document comes rolling out at or near the advertised page-printing rate. Sometimes it seems as if that first page will never be born.

Most of the laser printers on the market use Motorola microprocessors for control and page preparation. Early models used the 68000. Now most of the higher-priced printers use the 68020. Either of these chips is well adapted to handling large amounts of data at high speed. It's quite likely that the 68030 and the new 68040 will begin to show up as more and more pressure is put on the manufacturers to reduce the first-page formatting time.

Fonts

Most of the medium- to high-priced printers allow you to change fonts. So with the decision to upgrade to a new printer comes the decision of what font to use. New fonts are a lot like new suits. The more conservative the font, the more appropriate it is for most business use. Garish, unusual fonts convey the message that you and your business are mavericks and out of step. This may be the message that you are trying to send, but it's not the right message for most businesses. For instance, that is certainly not the message you want to get from your banker, lawyer, or doctor.

Courier is the font that looks a lot like the standard print from the IBM Selectric typewriter. It's a *monospaced* font. That means that each letter or character occupies exactly the same space. A "w" and an "i" are allocated the same space.

Fonts like Courier are usually the default font for printers and word-processing software. Such fonts are easy to handle with software because it's easy to predict how much space will be used up on a line. You just multiply the standard space by the number of characters in the line. (Don't forget! The space between words has to be counted as a character.)

You may remember that there are two common sizes of type: pica and elite. Pica is the larger of the two and is generally assumed to be a 10-pitch type. That means each pica character plus its white space occupies 1/10 of an inch. Another way to say this is that pica type has 10 characters per inch. Elite is 12-pitch type; that is, there are 12 elite characters in one inch.

The standard fonts like Courier that appear in printers come in both 10 and 12 pitch, or in a range of pitches if your printer supports PostScript or other page-description languages. There is also a compressed size that varies between 16 and 17 pitch. In the Hewlett-Packard LaserJet printer, the compressed size is 16.66 pitch.

There is a great deal of confusion generated by the difference between the way font sizes are designated for typewriters and for printers. For printers and the printing industry in general, fonts are specified in point size. A point is approximately 1/72 of an inch. So the larger the font, the bigger is its point size. This is exactly the inverse of pitch. The bigger the pitch, the smaller is the type.

You can get terribly confused if you insist on using both pitch and point size to specify font sizes. For the lower-priced printers, you are offered the equivalent of pica, elite, and compressed type. They can be selected either by hardware (internal DIP switches or control-panel push buttons) or by software. You just try them out to see which is the right one for your application. With the more expensive printers, you can change the size of the built-in fonts by specifying the pitch in a software setup command (frequently called a *setup string*). With the Hewlett-Packard LaserJet, for example, you get to select the font from a setup menu accessed by means of the front-panel switches.

From what we've just said, it looks as though there's no particular reason for getting confused about pitch and point. Your printer (hardware) appears to be ready to operate using pitch alone. The rub occurs because software is not consistent. Most word-processing packages specify font size by using points. Popular spreadsheet and data-base software makes you specify your font by using setup strings that contain pitch information.

"Why can't they just do it one way and leave me alone?" is not a bad question. The answer is that it's part past practice and part interaction with other industries. Character printers had their beginnings with typewriters, so that heritage shows. There is the desire on the part of the manufacturers to maintain part of their history as a sort of backward compatibility. The interaction with the printing industry provides the impetus for consistency with another heritage.

There's more to this than just the desire of the software industry to keep computer consultants and trainers in business. When you leave behind the built-in fonts, there needs to be a consistent method for specifying the large number of font sizes that are available. The sizes range from very small to outrageously large. The point-size method is more intuitive since it has large numbers associated with large print. Primarily because of the intuitive appeal of point size, this method was chosen by word-processing package writers. In addition, it is consistent, as we mentioned earlier, with past and present practice in the printing industry.

Some word-processing packages have become sufficiently sophisticated so that they make material that's ready to go to a phototypesetter. Clearly, there should be a consistent method for specifying sizes for the two printing devices (the printer beside your desk and the phototypesetter). There is such a method, and it is point size.

Swapping Fonts—Economy-Model Printers

Swapping fonts is not possible with most of the older, low priced ($200 to $400) dot-matrix printers. They have different sizes of a single font. The font they use (as noted earlier) is similar to characters on a typewriter. With most of the

Epson dot-matrix printers and clones, you can define your own character set and store it in RAM. Rolling your own is most useful for special characters from another alphabet, engineering or scientific symbols, or perhaps a stylized logo.

There are a few low-priced printers, including the Epson LX 810, that do support more than one font in the NLQ mode. The Epson features Roman (a variation on Times Roman) and a sans serif font. The list price is $299, but it is frequently available for under $200 from discounters and in package deals.

Table 5–1 is provided to give you a feel for the character sizes available from Epson and clone printers. An obvious overlap is standard pica and compressed expanded elite. They both print 10 characters per inch. You can also print each of these sizes in italic print and as emphasized print (each character is struck twice).

Table 5–1.   Character Widths, Epson and Compatible Printers

Character Description	Pitch (Characters per Inch)	Maximum Characters per Line
Pica, standard	10	80
Pica, expanded	5	40
Pica, compressed	17	136
Pica, compressed expanded	8.5	68
Elite, standard	12	96
Elite, expanded	6	48
Elite, compressed	20	160
Elite, compressed expanded	10	80

Some of the low-priced clones include proportional spacing in their repertoire. Printer-generated proportional printing is not compatible with some software-based proportional printing. Both hardware and software could be trying to adjust the spacing between characters based on the shape of the character. The adjustment could be made twice, and you'd get a string of overlapping, unreadable characters.

Most of the recent commercially available word-processing packages have the complete details on which printer does what. Printer-generated proportional spacing is a convenient way to start using proportional spacing. It can have problems, however. To use it with dumb software, you have to tell your software that you are using a monospaced font. This means that you could wind up with very ragged right margins. The software would be trying to generate 50 or 60 uniformly spaced characters per line. With nonuniform character spacing, some lines could be about two-thirds the length of others. It's very unlikely that any would run all the way to whatever margin you set.

If you don't have a recent version of your word-processing package, you probably shouldn't try proportionally spaced printing. This is certainly a case where you need to upgrade your software when you upgrade your printer. Don't base a printer purchase decision solely on proportional printing ability. It's just one element of the entire printer picture.

Font swapping for the under-$400 printer is usually limited to two built-in NLQ fonts. If you want more fonts, you have to design your own or purchase downloadable fonts. The general quality of downloadable fonts for 9-pin dot-matrix printers is not good, in large part because available printer memory is too small to accommodate the print buffer and the data necessary for complicated fonts.

Swapping Fonts—Medium- to High-Priced Printers

As the price of dot-matrix printers edges over $400, the number of built-in fonts and ways to import fonts goes up. With the Epson LQ-510 ($529 list and discounted by up to a third), you only get built-in Roman and sans serif, but there are font cartridges available. The cartridges plug into a socket in the printer and provide alternative fonts. With the Epson, there are five single-font cartridges ($59 each) and one multifont cartridge ($99). The multifont cartridge has Courier, Prestige, Script, OCR-B, OCR-A, Orator, and Orator-S. The OCR-A and B fonts are especially designed to be scanned successfully by optical character-recognition scanning devices. This particular printer is a 24-pin model that is well adapted for light office work.

This printer or one like it would be a good choice if you are upgrading from an older 9-pin printer. In addition to multiple fonts, it has some useful paper-handling features. In particular, it will allow you to make microadjustments in vertical paper movement. The movement can be as small 1/180 inch. This is very handy when you are filling out forms where the answer has to be inside a box or sandwiched between two lines.

Serif vs Sans Serif

The terms "serif" and "sans serif" refer to fonts. In the relatively sedate, standard world of font composition, these are the two basic font categories. There are, of course, italics and the large number of specialty fonts, but we aren't discussing them here because they are not used widely.

The *serif* is the finishing stroke that is placed at the end of a main stroke of a letter or number. It follows that fonts which have these finishing touches are called serif fonts. Times Roman is a serif font with which you are probably very familiar even if you don't know it. This is because many of our nation's newspapers are printed with Times Roman type.

Fonts that lack the finishing serif strokes are called *sans serif* fonts. One of the more popular sans-serif fonts is Helvetica. It is used fairly often in logos and captions. The standard computer output is a very crude example of a sans-serif font.

As you can see from the examples in Figure 5–5, serif and sans serif fonts don't look alike. In fact, you can also see, if you examine the examples closely, that there are differences within each font classification.

This is a line of Helvetica normal

This is a line of Times Roman normal

This is a line of Helvetica bold

This is a line of Times roman bold

This is a line of Helvetica bold oblique

Figure 5–5.   Samples of serif and sans-serif type.

Using Serif and Sans-Serif Fonts

Quite a bit of research has been conducted on the relative merits of serif and sans-serif fonts. The results favor serif fonts as being more readable for extended reading such as books and newspapers. The sans-serif font is generally acknowledged to have a more crisp, clean appearance. It is more appropriate for short communications where the crisp appearance can contribute to getting the message across.

In your personal and business communications, pick a font that you like. To prevent the reader's attention from being diverted from your message, the font should not be too garish. Since most of us don't put out multipage missives on a daily basis, the choice between serif and sans-serif fonts can be made solely on the basis of personal taste. If you do have a reason to produce a long document, you should use a serif font. Times Roman is a perennial favorite. Another appealing serif font is Bookman.

PostScript

Now that we've discussed font sizes and the relative merits of serif and sans-serif fonts, it's time to check out the way fonts are made. There are two major ways to make fonts, *bitmapped* and *scalable*. Bitmapped fonts are just what the name implies. Each character has been designed bit by bit (or dot by dot) to fool your eyes into seeing a nice, smooth curve. If you try to make one of these characters bigger, the edges become ragged. To change font sizes, you have to have a complete new font.

Scalable fonts are made up from outlines that are stored as mathematical formulas. Fonts of any size can be made simply by feeding the size information into the formulas. There are other formulas (algorithms) that fill in the outlines and smooth the curves. You are likely to see the terms scalable fonts and outline fonts used interchangeably. They refer to the same process.

Here comes the hardware connection: The two font-composition methods make very different demands on your hardware. Bitmapped fonts need lots of storage space. Whether you buy them on cartridges or on diskettes, they take up lots of bytes. The space they occupy on your hard disk is room that can't be used by other software. The problem with cartridges is that you typically get only one font per cartridge. It comes in several sizes, but just one style.

Scalable fonts don't take up very much storage space. After all, they are stored as mathematical formulas. What they do require is lots of RAM in your printer. It takes lots of computations to generate the finished fonts. Page printers typically need more than the standard 512 kilobytes to produce scalable fonts. The usual configuration for scalable fonts is 2 megabytes of printer RAM.

With the extra memory, you get the ability to produce fonts of an unbelievably large number of sizes. You aren't limited to integer point sizes. You can make 11.9-point fonts or 7.77-point fonts if you want. You are no longer held captive by the sizes stored in your system. If your presentation could use slightly larger characters, make them. It's simple. Or if you can't quite get everything you want to say on a single page (research has shown that most people stop reading memos and sales pitches after the first page), drop down in increments of a tenth of a point size, and try again until you get what you want. Your readers probably won't notice the size difference, and they are more likely to read your entire message.

How to Get Scalable Fonts The most widely used implementation of scalable fonts is PostScript from Adobe Systems, Inc. The original PostScript printer was the Apple LaserWriter. The typical PostScript page printer clone comes with 35 built-in typefaces and sells for $4500 and up. The basic font types include Courier, Dutch, ITC Avant Garde Gothic, ITC Bookman, New Century Schoolbook, Swiss, Symbol, Zapf Calligraphic, Zapf Chancery, and Zapf Dingbats (a collection of symbols and graphics characters). In addition to PostScript compatibility, the typical PostScript clone is also compatible with the HP LaserJet series.

There are other scalable-font implementations available or to be released soon. For example, printer manufacturers Brother and Canon have released HP compatible printers with scalable fonts. The new scalable-font printers are not likely to occupy a very large share of the market for a couple of years. In addition, they are likely to suffer from the same problem encountered by most new products, bugs. For the immediate future, your best choice for compatibility and quality is a PostScript printer.

There are some lower-cost avenues for getting PostScript on your existing HP compatible printer. There are plug-in cartridges available with Adobe PostScript. Canon has introduced one, and more should be appearing soon. There are also scalable fonts available on floppy diskettes. These can be transferred to your printer if you have an appropriate driver program. Since they aren't built-in, you'll have to reload them every time you turn on your printer.

With any of the scalable-font options, you must have lots of RAM in your printer. This is just a fact of life. Your printer has to have enough room to perform the computations and store the results.

PostScript Appearance   The same advice applies for PostScript fonts as for fonts in general. Try out the available fonts. Pick a font that you like. Figure 5–6 shows some samples.

Be careful to use a font that says what you want to say about your business. Particularly garish and unusual fonts carry the message that you are different and probably don't play by the same rules as others. The more standard fonts intimate that you and your business are conventionally oriented and likely to be dependable. You won't branch off quickly in unexpected directions.

Scalable Fonts and Speed

It takes longer to do the calculations to produce scalable fonts than it does to simply load predefined (bitmapped) fonts into memory. The time penalty is not severe. You probably wouldn't notice it unless someone brought it to your attention.

With any page printer, there is a delay before printing begins while the first page is formatted. If you are accustomed to a character printer of the dot-matrix or daisy-wheel variety, the delay can be disconcerting. Your first reaction will probably be to wonder what's wrong with the printer. The delay is obvious, but when the pages start rolling out, you can accommodate this little peccadillo.

This is Courier

This is Courier Bold

This is Courier Bold Oblique

This is Courier Oblique

This is Helvetica

This is Helvetica Bold

This is Helvetica Bold Oblique

This is Helvetica Narrow

This is Helvetica Narrow Bold

This is Helvetica Narrow Bold Oblique

This is Helvetica Narrow Oblique

This is Helvetica Oblique

This is Avant Garde Gothic Book

This is Avant Garde Gothic Book Oblique

This is Avant Garde Gothic Demi

This is Avant Garde Gothic Demi Oblique

This is Bookman Demi

This is Bookman Demi Italic

This is Bookman Light in

This is Bookman Light Italic

This is Zapf Chancery Medium Italic

This is New Century Schoolbook

This is New Century Schoolbook Bold

This is New Century Schoolbook Bold Italic

This is New Century Schoolbook Italic

This is Palatino

This is Palatino Bold

This is Palatino Bold Italic

This is Palatino Italic

This is Times Roman

This is Times Roman Bold

This is Times Roman Bold Italic

This is Times Roman Italic

Figure 5–6. PostScript font samples.

Printer Languages and Control Codes

Each major printer category has a sequence of characters (frequently called *control codes*) for giving the printer instructions about how to carry out its tasks. For Epson printers and clones, this is a sequence of characters most of which begin with the Escape character (ASCII 27). For fairly obvious reasons, these commands are called *escape sequences*. The commands perform all kinds of unseen tasks, including setting the font size, vertical spacing, tab spacing, page length, and NLQ or draft mode. Fortunately, all this information is handled for us by the printer drivers built into our software packages.

The HP LaserJet series has an official language, PCL. Many of the PCL commands are escape sequences. The escape sequences are not the same ones used by Epson, so it's necessary for different printer drivers to be written to support HP and Epson.

The PostScript language is made up of ASCII strings that more closely resemble standard computer languages than the escape sequences of HP and Epson. (See Figure 5–7.)

PostScript Code Fragment

```
/#copies 1 def wpdict begin
_bd letter _bp 0 13200 10200 _ornt /CourierR 600 _ff
0 13200 10200 _ornt /Helvetica-BoldR 1200 _ff
1200 11693 _m
_SH (This)_S 133 _t (is)_S 133 _t (24)_S 133 _t (pt.)_S 133 _t (Helvetica)_S 133 _t
(Bold)_S 133 _t (Shadow)_S _sh _ep
_ed end
```

This is the final seven lines of PostScript code required to print the line:

This is 24 pt. Helvetica Bold Shadow

In all, the PostScript code to print this single line of formatted text required more than 5 pages of program code.

Figure 5–7.   Plain text and the PostScript code to produce it.

PostScript, the language, can be used to format your document. This level of printer interaction may not be desirable to you, but it's there if you need it.

Chapter 6

How to Test Your Upgraded System

Well, you've upgraded your system. All the hardware has been installed according to the manufacturers' specifications. So what should you do now? Check, double-check, and triple-check everything you were supposed to do.

You've finished all the checking? Super! Now it's time for the smoke test (that's where you turn everything on and watch for smoke). Assuming you've followed all the installation instructions exactly, your PC should pass this test with flying colors.

Following the power-on sequence, you should put your entire system through a series of diagnostic tests. These will help to determine if all the components are working together as they should. If DIP switches are set incorrectly or cables are connected to the wrong ports, you can find these at this stage.

Any elements of your system that didn't pass the system-wide testing need to be examined individually. In addition, you can perform several tests to determine the optimal settings for specific elements such as your hard disk. Do you need to change the interleave? How many bad spots does your disk have?

You can also run element performance tests that will tell you if you actually got the improvements the vendors promised. Did you really get a 200% improvement in throughput by installing the I/O-controller board from Flying Widget Computers?

Burn-in testing in a time-honored method for finding components that are going to quit long before their nominal life expectancy. This technique is used most frequently for testing system memory and hard disks. Certainly it can be applied to any component in your system. Of course, there must be a testing procedure for the suspect component.

In this chapter, we'll take you through smoke, diagnostic, system-specific, and burn-in testing. By following the principles and practices laid out here, you will develop confidence in the quality of your upgrade and understand the characteristics of the upgrades you performed.

Smoke Test

Only after rechecking everything you were supposed to do are you ready for the smoke test. "Smoke" is not an acronym for something. It's what can happen when you apply power to a system that hasn't been assembled correctly.

You've checked everything? OK. You've done all you can by yourself. Let the computer check itself out. There's no point in delaying the inevitable. This is no time for weak knees and faint hearts. Go ahead. Make sure the main power switch is turned off. Then plug in the system. Assuming nothing went "poof!," "snap!," or "bang!," and no smoke came rolling out, you're ready for the next milestone.

Turn on the power to each of the system units. You should do this in a logical sequence. First, apply power to the pieces that weren't changed. Since they are very unlikely to have problems, this should help your confidence level.

If the entire system is new, then apply power first to the peripherals. There is no magic order. One quite reasonable sequence would be the printer first and then the monitor. Both should have their power-on lights lighted. And since both are "packaged" components that you probably didn't do anything to, the likelihood of finding anything wrong at this stage of the testing is remote.

There is a "gotcha!" here. If you've plugged your monitor (or printer) into the switched plug on the back of your PC, then the monitor (or printer) won't come on. If the monitor doesn't power up, plug it into a receptacle that you know has power. (Test it with a lamp that you are certain is working.)

Once you've established that both these peripherals can turn on, flip the power switch on your PC. Be ready to pull the plug if you should hear anything unusual.

Truly, all these cautions are a bit overstated. In 99 out of 100 cases where something does go wrong, the protective circuitry built into your PC and its peripherals simply shuts everything off without further ado.

If you apply power to your PC and nothing happens, refer to Appendix E. It contains information about troubleshooting your hardware. Before digging into the inside of your system, be certain to reread the safety material in Appendix C.

If you still can't figure out what is wrong after going through the steps outlined in Appendix E, get expert help. If you bought an on-site service contract with your PC, get them to come fix your system. Without an on-site contract, you will probably have to take your system to a local technician or mail it back to your supplier. The mail-back route doesn't work well when you bought components from several vendors.

There are usually local technicians available who will service your system. You can find them in your telephone book. They will probably charge you quite a bit for a nonstandard system, since they are unlikely to have immediate access to all the technical manuals they might need. Be certain to supply them with all the information you can about how the system is supposed to be configured. The less time they spend fixing your system, the smaller the charge will be.

Diagnostic Tests

After the smoke-test hurdle, the next logical move is to conduct diagnostic testing to find out if all the components are working together the way they should. This testing is conducted by a fairly complex piece of software. Since neither you nor many other end users are likely to run the software more than once or twice, the cost per iteration is rather high. We will demonstrate the testing using DiagMenu from PC Consultants.

We'll work with you to go through the tests being conducted by DiagMenu. You can use the software from your A: drive, or you can INSTALL it on your hard disk. It's up to you. The only penalty for not INSTALLing it is a slightly longer access time. On the other hand, if this is your first run-through with a new upgrade, you probably should run everything from the floppy drive in the beginning.

Follow the instructions in the documentation for installing DiagMenu and configuring it for your system. This is really a minimal effort because DiagMenu searches to get the answers for itself.

Ready to start the tests? OK, let's go. When you issue the command DIAG-MENU, the program quickly determines certain high level information about your system. Figure 6–1 shows an example screen from running DiagMenu on a 10-MHz AT clone (80286 CPU) without a math coprocessor. In addition to information about the ROM BIOS (Read-Only Memory Basic Input/Output System), there is information about memory configuration, video adapter type, keyboard, game port, the number of parallel and serial ports, floppy drives (with size and capacity information), and hard drives.

There is information here that you may need later, so be certain to keep a copy. After you get to the Execute Diagnostics? (y/n) prompt, do a screen dump to your printer (use the PRINT SCREEN key) so that you will have a permanent record. You should be keeping all your testing information in a notebook for future reference. You never know when something may happen and you'll need to refer to this data. In particular, the addresses of the parallel and serial ports should be recorded.

In Figure 6–1, the parallel ports are located at addresses 3BCH and 378H. That's pretty cryptic. What kind of numbering system uses an H? This is base-16, or *hexadecimal*, notation. (See Appendix A for hexadecimal-to-decimal translations.) The H is to tell you that this is hex and not base-10 (decimal). You're not likely to think that 3BC is a decimal number, but 378 could be.

Don't expect to draw any particular information from either the parallel or serial addresses. Record them; when you add another serial board, for example,

```
PC Consultants' Diagnostics                        12/26/89
Version  2.02  September 01, 1989                    12:27
(c) Copyright, 1987, 1988, 1989, PC Consultants. All Rights Reserved.
-----------------------------------------------------------------------
    AT ROMs    =>     Award    10/01/86
         Processor    =>     80286    10.00 Mhz
         Co-processor =>     Not Installed
         Memory       =>     Sys   640 kb, Ext   512 kb, Exp   0 kb
         Video    =>     Monographics
         Keyboard     =>     Installed
         Game Port    =>     Not Installed
         Parallel Port(s)   2>     3BCH 378H
         Serial Port(s) 2>    3F8H 2F8H
         Floppy Disk(s)     1>     1.2 Mb
         Fixed Disk(s) 1>     Western_Digital   WD93044_A
-----------------------------------------------------   DOS  4.00 reports :
Available Drives  A: - I:  ( 9)
            : 640 kb of RAM
          : 567 kb of RAM available for application programs
      Execute Diagnostics ? (y/n) y
```

Figure 6–1. DiagMenu high-level reporting.

you'll need to put it at the next available address. The printed documentation
will help you remember what already is in the system. The serial addresses
shown in Figure 6–1 are 3F8H and 2F8H. As with the parallel addresses, the H
tells you that these are hexadecimal (base-16) numbers.

   You get information about keyboard and game-port status, number and
format of floppy-diskette drives, and number of and controllers for fixed-disk
drives. In addition, this high-level test reports the *DOS (Disk Operating System)*
being used (4.00 in this case).

   The number of available drives is reported as nine. Does this mean you can
have as many as nine drives on this particular AT clone? No, there are only two
physical drives connected to the PC—one floppy-diskette drive and one fixed-
disk drive. But the hard disk is configured for a number of *logical drives*. The
DOS-level SUBST command was used in the AUTOEXEC.BAT file to set up
several logical (artificial, not physical) drives. This is an artifice frequently used to
make it easier to address a path to a file. For instance, the full path could be

C: \ WP \ UPGRADE \ PIXS \ CHAPTER.7

This is a lot to have to type whenever you want to get to file CHAPTER.7, so
you could use

SUBST I: C: \ WP \ UPGRADE \ PIX

and from then on until you redefine I:, you could get to CHAPTER.7 by accessing I: \ CHAPTER.7.

Now we turn to Figure 6–2. It tells us about SYSBRD, DMA Controller, I/O Port Chip, NMI Logic, Interrupt Controller—the figure seems like alphabet soup. You just wanted to know if it was working, right? What can you do with all this information?

```
PC Consultants' Diagnostics                  12/26/89
Version  2.02  September 01, 1989             12:27
(c) Copyright, 1987, 1988, 1989, PC Consultants. All Rights Reserved.


-----------------------------------Diagnostic Completion Status Screen

      Loading Diagnostic File = sysbrd.dia
SYSBRD : Execution begins.
SYSBRD : Interrupt Controller Test begins.
SYSBRD : I/O Port Chip Test begins.
SYSBRD : Timer Chip Test begins.
SYSBRD : NMI Logic Test begins.
SYSBRD : DMA Controller Test begins.
SYSBRD : Loops = 0001, Errors = 0000
SYSBRD : Interrupt Controller Test begins.
SYSBRD : I/O Port Chip Test begins.
SYSBRD : Timer Chip Test begins.
SYSBRD : NMI Logic Test begins.
SYSBRD : DMA Controller Test begins.
SYSBRD : Loops = 0002, Errors = 0000
SYSBRD : Interrupt Controller Test begins.
SYSBRD : I/O Port Chip Test begins.
SYSBRD : Timer Chip Test begins.
SYSBRD : NMI Logic Test begins.
SYSBRD : DMA Controller Test begins.
SYSBRD : Loops = 0003, Errors = 0000
SYSBRD : Execution complete.
      Sysbrd     =>     Passed
```

Figure 6–2. DiagMenu diagnostic completion status screen, system-board testing.

Fortunately, in the case shown it all worked. What if an error occurs? Step back a minute. Cool down. Take care of first things first. This is a test of chips on the motherboard, so you don't have to worry about any of the peripherals or the plug-in boards. In fact you don't have to worry about the system RAM. We're not testing that now.

Before giving way to panic, try a simple fix. Follow the steps outlined in Figure 6–3. Now run DiagMenu again.

You say it works now? Fantastic!! Move on to the next series of tests.

Oops, it still doesn't work? Unfortunately, you've just gone beyond the scope of this book. You need to call in the hired guns, the computer techni-

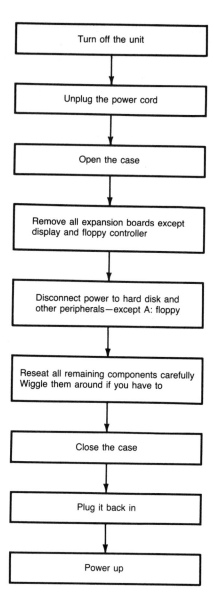

Figure 6–3. Fixing simple problems.

cians. Since the motherboard is a fairly expensive piece of hardware, you should get help. Assuming you've done this upgrade yourself, you need to locate a competent local guru.

To some extent, the cost to repair your system depends on how unique the boards and chips are. Standard components are easy to locate, and the information needed to repair them is quickly available.

If your motherboard is still under warranty, quickly get in contact with your supplier. DON'T ship your motherboard back to them without first contacting them. They will probably want to assign a special number to your problem so that their receiving department can route it to the right place. Without an assigned number, it's likely that your board won't get any service, period. In fact, some companies even refuse to accept shipments that arrive without return authorization (RA) numbers.

Well, we're making progress. You've managed to make it through the basic system-board tests. Figure 6–4 shows a typical system RAM test sequence. Notice that it is tested in blocks that are not sequential. This is not an error. It is an artifact of the way memory addressing is performed.

```
    PC Consultants' Diagnostics                    12/26/89
    Version  2.02  September 01, 1989               12:27
      (c) Copyright, 1987, 1988, 1989, PC Consultants. All Rights Reserved.


    -------------------------------------Diagnostic Completion Status Screen


      Loading Diagnostic File = ramtst.dia
RAMTST : Execution begins
RAMTST : testing block    2
RAMTST : testing block    3
RAMTST : testing block    4
RAMTST : testing block    5
RAMTST : testing block    6
RAMTST : testing block    7
RAMTST : testing block    8
RAMTST : testing block    9
RAMTST : testing block   16
RAMTST : testing block   17
RAMTST : testing block   18
RAMTST : testing block   19
RAMTST : testing block   20
RAMTST : testing block   21
RAMTST : testing block   22
RAMTST : testing block   23
RAMTST : Addressing test begins
RAMTST : testing lower memory, no interrupts are allowed
RAMTST : Loops = 0001, Errors = 0000
RAMTST : Execution complete
    Ramtst     =>     Passed
```

Figure 6–4.   DiagMenu diagnostic completion status screen, system memory (RAM) testing.

Be very careful while performing this test. When it says "testing lower memory, no interrupts are allowed," don't try it to find out what can go wrong if you interrupt the testing sequence. Stay away from the keyboard until the testing is completed. It won't take long.

Assuming that you've come through this test with flying colors, you can move on to video-adapter testing.

"Whoa!" you say. "Not so fast! My test didn't go so well." Don't trash your PC just yet. Problems with RAM are among the most common of PC difficulties. Follow the steps outlined in Figure 6–3, and rerun DiagMenu.

All right! That did it! Success; proceed to testing the video system.

Whoops, it's still not fixed! Follow the information given in the DiagMenu documentation to determine the bank of chips where the error occurred. Follow the sequence shown in Figure 6–3 with one exception: Rather than merely reseating components, replace all the chips in the bank where the error occurred. Then rerun DiagMenu.

If you don't have an extra set of chips, try swapping the chips in two blocks of memory. Rerun DiagMenu to see if the memory error followed the chips from the block that first reported an error. If so, the quickest way to correct the problem is to replace all of the chips in that block.

Want to save money instead of time? OK. Swap one chip at a time from one block to another until the error moves to another block. Now you know precisely which chip is causing the problem. Replace it.

Finally, success! You did it! Go on to testing the video adapter.

It doesn't take a detective to realize that the video tests shown in Figure 6–5 are much more involved than any others we've run. Specifically these are tests of a monochrome video graphics adapter. Some of the tests for a color system are different. DiagMenu recognizes CGA, EGA, and VGA systems and conducts customized tests.

```
PC Consultants' Diagnostics                    12/26/89
Version  2.02  September 01, 1989                 12:27
(c) Copyright, 1987, 1988, 1989, PC Consultants. All Rights Reserved.

-------------------------------------------------------------------

              Diagnostic Completion Status Screen

          Loading Diagnostic File = mdamga.dia
MDAMGA : Execution begins.
MDAMGA : CRT Controller Read/Write Test begins.
MDAMGA : Text Cursor Position Test begins.

              Text Cursor Position Test Screen.

The cursor should move from the Upper Left Corner
                to the Lower Right Corner
                to the Lower Left Corner
                to the Upper Right Corner
                and finally to the Center.
                Did the Cursor move correctly (y/n) ? y
```

continued

```
MDAMGA : Text RAM Test begins.

                The MONO screen will blank for 7 seconds.

MDAMGA : Text Attribute Test begins.

                    Text Attribute Test Screen.

        (A series of lines of characters appear on the screen)

                Is this screen correct (y/n) ? y

        (A series of lines of characters appear on the screen)

            The screen above should STOP blinking.

                Is this screen correct (y/n) ? y

MDAMGA : Character Set Test begins.

                    Character Set Test Screen.

                Is this screen correct (y/n) ? y

MDAMGA : Graphics RAM Test begins. The MONO screen will blank for 7 seconds.
MDAMGA : Graphics Pattern Test begins.

                    Graphics Pattern Test Screen.

    (Graphics Patterns of Increasing and Decreasing Complexity Appear)
    Did a series of Graphic Patterns appear on the screen (y/n) ? y
    (Graphics Patterns of Increasing and Decreasing Complexity Appear)
    Did a series of Graphic Patterns appear on the screen (y/n) ? y

MDAMGA : Text Paging Test begins.

                    Text Paging Test Screen.

        Did a screen full of "0"s appear (y/n) ? y

        Did a screen full of "1"s appear (y/n) ? y

MDAMGA : Loops = 0001, Errors = 0000
MDAMGA : Execution complete.
    Mdamga      =>      Passed
```

Figure 6–5. DiagMenu diagnostic completion status screen, video-adapter testing.

If you had been seeing appropriate material on the screen before you performed this test, about the only thing the test can show is a minor defect in the video board or video memory. Follow the steps in Figure 6–3 to attempt to correct any minor problems; then rerun DiagMenu.

If you're successful, move on to parallel- and serial-port testing.

No luck? The problem just won't clear up? Make a quick call to your video-board vendor. Make arrangements to send the board back. Ask to have a replacement sent to you while your board is going back to them. You shouldn't have to wait for a round trip of your video board just to be able to use your PC.

Follow the steps in Figure 6–6 for installing or moving your video board. Once you've installed the new (rebuilt) video board, then test it. All should go well unless you didn't get the board plugged in correctly. If by some chance this board doesn't test as functional, follow the steps in Figure 6–3, and then rerun the test.

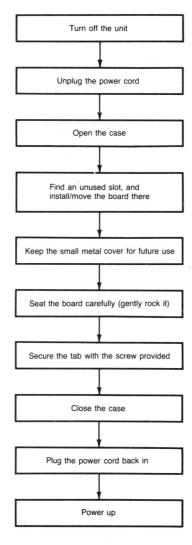

Figure 6–6.   Installing or moving a board.

Oops, the new replacement video board doesn't work! Uh-oh, there's trouble in paradise! You may have found a bad slot on your motherboard. Now you have to work to get a new motherboard from your supplier. Write down what happened and what you did. Step-by-step documentation is a lot more convincing than a statement like "I know its broken because I fixed it and it still doesn't work." It may take a letter or two to get what you want, but keep at it. Motherboards aren't cheap, and you deserve one that works the way it should.

Assuming you met with success, we'll proceed to testing the parallel ports (Figure 6–7). A word of caution — if you have a parallel port that doesn't have a printer or other parallel device connected to it, don't try to output a test pattern to the empty port. If you do, the system will hang, and you'll have to reboot it.

```
PC Consultants' Diagnostics                     12/26/89
Version  2.02  September 01, 1989                12:27
(c) Copyright, 1987, 1988, 1989, PC Consultants. All Rights Reserved.


-----------------------------------------------------------------

              Diagnostic Completion Status Screen

     Loading Diagnostic File = parall.dia
PARALL : Execution begins
PARALL : Output a test pattern to the printer at LPT1 ? y
PARALL : Output a test pattern to the printer at LPT2 ? y
PARALL : Execution complete
     Parall  =>    Passed
```

Figure 6–7.   DiagMenu diagnostic completion status screen, parallel-port testing.

Next comes the serial-port test (Figure 6–8). If you have one or more serial ports not in use, try to find a very cheap printer with a serial-interface card. It is necessary to have a device connected to each serial port. When a serial device is not there, the testing will be phased out after a time interval determined by the program, and the serial ports will be declared to have failed the testing.

What should you do if the board actually tests bad? That is, you've put a serial device at each port and one or more of the ports still test bad. If you have gone through the steps in Figures 6–3 and 6–6 and you haven't corrected the problem, it is indeed time to call in the local experts (the computer technicians), or to replace the bad board.

But before you assume the board is really bad, try one more test. Hook up a serial printer, a modem, or something else and try to operate it. Software that tests computer hardware is a wonderful aid to computer maintenance and testing, but it is not infallible. If you try a real serial device on a real port with a couple of applications and you can't get it to work, then assume there really is a hardware problem with the board.

```
PC Consultants' Diagnostics                          12/26/89
Version  2.02  September 01, 1989                     12:27
(c) Copyright, 1987, 1988, 1989, PC Consultants. All Rights Reserved.


----------------------------------------------------------------------

                 Diagnostic Completion Status Screen

      Loading Diagnostic File = serial.dia
SERIAL : Execution begins
SERIAL : {03F8} Register integrity test begins.
SERIAL : {03F8} Register integrity test passed.
SERIAL : {03F8} Internal register loopback test begins.
SERIAL : {03F8} Internal register loopback test complete.
SERIAL : {03F8} Internal data loopback test begins.
SERIAL : {03F8} Internal data loopback test complete.
SERIAL : {02F8} Register integrity test begins.
SERIAL : {02F8} Register integrity test passed.
SERIAL : {02F8} Internal register loopback test begins.
SERIAL : {02F8} Internal register loopback test complete.
SERIAL : {02F8} Internal data loopback test begins.
SERIAL : {02F8} Internal data loopback test complete.
Serial  =>   Passed
```

Figure 6-8. DiagMenu diagnostic completion status screen, serial-port testing.

Before you get technicians into the act, you should recognize that boards costing under $100 and in some cases $200 are considered throwaways. It'll cost more to repair them than it will to replace them. If you're having problems with a $70 I/O board, replace it yourself. Get your supplier to send you a replacement if you have any sort of guarantee. If you don't, it doesn't hurt to ask, especially if you spent quite a bit of money with them.

Ask your supplier for help. It's a good negotiating tactic, and that's what you're doing now—negotiating. Remind them of your purchase total. Suggest that you might be a future customer if they prove they can be depended on when the chips are down. Above all, don't be abusive; it might make you feel better, but it doesn't accomplish your goal.

We've managed to move by the port tests, and now it's time to do the diskette tests (Figure 6–9). If your system has two diskette drives and you are running the program from your hard disk, put formatted diskettes into drives A: and B:. If you are running the program from drive A:, put a formatted diskette in drive B:. In the latter case, DiagMenu will use the program diskette for testing purposes.

This is a test that your system is unlikely to fail unless you have recently installed a new diskette drive and haven't taken the opportunity to test it. If that happens to be the case and the software identified the presence of two drives back at the high-level reporting we saw first, then all is likely to be well.

```
     PC Consultants' Diagnostics                        12/26/89
     Version  2.02  September 01, 1989                    12:27
      (c) Copyright, 1987, 1988, 1989, PC Consultants. All Rights Reserved.


-----------------------------------------------------------------------
                    Diagnostic Completion Status Screen
      Loading Diagnostic File = floppy.dia
 FLOPPY : Execution begins.
 FLOPPY : Read Test begins
 FLOPPY : test drive = 0 head = 1 cylinder =  0
 FLOPPY : Loops = 0001, Errors = 0000
 FLOPPY : Execution complete.
     Floppy    =>    Passed
```

Figure 6–9. DiagMenu diagnostic completion status screen, floppy-diskette-drive testing.

The most frequent cause for problems associated with the installation of a new floppy-diskette drive in a dual-drive system is failure to remove the terminating resistor from the first drive in the chain. If you don't remove it, the system can't work. It thinks that there are two A: drives, and it doesn't know what to do.

The terminating resistor usually looks like a memory chip that isn't black, or it may obviously be a bank of small resistors that plugs in sideways parallel to the drive controller board. You should have removed it and stored it for future use. Occasionally, the terminating resistor is not removable, and you have to reposition a jumper to take it out of the circuit. Follow your drive instructions at this point.

If the terminating resistor was correctly removed and you put a formatted diskette into each drive, the test should have been completed successfully. If drive B: failed the test, follow the sequence of steps given in Figures 6–3 and 6–6 for safely removing electrical power from the PC, and then check to be certain that the diskette drive is connected to the floppy diskette controller and the power supply. Close up the case, and restore electrical power. Rerun the test.

Now it works. Hey, that's great! It must have been a loose connection. Let's move on to testing the hard-disk interface and drive(s).

"Not so fast!" you say. "My floppy-diskette drive didn't make the cut. It's still failing the tests." Well, you have three possible places where the trouble lies: the controller, the power supply, and the diskette drive.

Eliminate the controller and power supply as sources of trouble by one at a time exchanging cabling with the other diskette drive and retesting. This is a fairly tedious task and one where a single mistake can result in neither drive working. (The problem isn't permanent. Once the cables are back where they belong, all will be well again.)

Attach labels to all cables. Record the original label/cable orientation. Record the changes as you progress. Don't forget to move the terminating resistor when you make the A: drive into the B: drive and vice versa (it all happens at once).

If, after all this, the drive still doesn't work, replace it. Most diskette drives cost only about $100. Negotiate with your supplier for a new drive or the return of your money. Be certain to have documented what you did to determine that the drive is defective. A well documented case usually receives the supplier's prompt attention.

Figure 6–10 is an abbreviated version of the fixed-disk test performed by DiagMenu. During each of the loops shown, a number of steps are taken as the hard disk is exercised vigorously.

```
PC Consultants' Diagnostics                          12/26/89
Version  2.02  September 01, 1989                      12:27
(c) Copyright, 1987, 1988, 1989, PC Consultants. All Rights Reserved.


------------------------------------------------------------------

              Diagnostic Completion Status Screen

        Loading Diagnostic File = fixdsk.dia
FIXDSK : Execution begins.
FIXDSK : Controller Test begins
FIXDSK : testing drive = 0 head = 1 cylinder = 0
FIXDSK : Loops = 0001, Errors = 0000
FIXDSK : Crescendo Seek Test begins
FIXDSK : testing drive = 0 head = 3 cylinder = 525
FIXDSK : Loops = 0001, Errors = 0000
FIXDSK : Read/Write/Read Test begins
FIXDSK : testing drive = 0 head = 0 cylinder = 0
FIXDSK : Loops = 0001, Errors = 0000
FIXDSK : Execution completed
     Fixdsk      =>      Passed
```

Figure 6–10. DiagMenu diagnostic completion status screen, fixed-disk-drive testing.

The crescendo test is especially unnerving. Your entire PC will shake during the lower-speed portion of the test. During the higher-speed portion, you may think the hard drive will develop wings and fly out of the case. All this apparently does no permanent damage. We've conducted the test several times on our PCs with no signs of deterioration.

The read/write/read test is a very effective method for determining hard-disk recording-surface quality. The disk is read, written to, and then read again. If errors occur in the first read or the write, the error is detected by the second read. This technique is used by most software that tests for errors in the hard-disk recording surface.

This is one instance in which a failing mark does not necessarily mean the device is not serviceable. We have had at least one hard-disk drive that is in daily service fail the fixed-disk test. (This book is being written using it.) There apparently is some incompatibility between the testing program and the hard-disk controller. This particular hard disk has passed surface testing by other software without problems.

So, if you encounter a failing grade at this point, be a bit chary about ripping out your hard drive. First see if it will read and write successfully. Copy material back and forth to floppy diskettes. Use the DOS COMP command to see if the transfer occurred without problems. If you can't copy files at all or not reliably, then you do indeed have a big problem. You have either a controller, hard-disk, or power-supply problem.

The problem could be bad locations on the drive, and if this is the case a low-level reformat or the use of a program that will mark bad spots so DOS won't use them may be all that you need to do. Obviously, you should try all of these things before deciding to replace the hard drive. And, be sure you make a second full backup of the disk before you start to work with it. A second backup is important because you may have uncovered something that will cause some data loss beyond what occurred before the last backup. Therefore, don't write the backup over existing backup disks or tape. Start a new backup to preserve the current state of the drive as well as the existing backup that probably was done at some earlier time.

If the hard disk comes up to a constant speed (you can tell by listening), you probably don't have a power-supply problem. However, if it can't get to a constant speed and you didn't upgrade to a 200-watt power supply when you added a hard drive, you need to do it now. It's also possible that your 200-watt power supply is not quite as good as it should be.

You can make some preliminary power-supply tests by removing from the computer everything not actually needed to run the hard drive. Take out serial and parallel boards, remove any extended or expanded memory-expansion boards, disconnect the power from floppy-disk drives, and remove their controller if it is separate from the hard-drive controller. These steps reduce drain on the power supply. If the drive now functions normally, either the power supply is at fault, or one of the components you removed has a power-drain problem.

Bring each of the components you removed back on line one at a time, noting when you begin to have problems. If the problem recurs before all of the components are replaced, again remove everything not necessary, and replace only the one component that caused the problem to show up again.

This type of step-by-step approach to isolating problems is one of the best ways to troubleshoot electronic equipment, and it doesn't require special testing equipment or deep technical knowledge of the components being tested.

If you have only one hard drive, you can't change the cabling to test for wiring problems coming from the controller. With two hard drives, you could interchange them to test for wiring and controller problems. (All of the labelling caveats made about performing this task for floppy-diskette drives apply here.

Don't forget to follow the power-down and power-up sequences given in Figures 6–3 and 6–6.) Beyond simply swapping cables, making sure that the connections are in the right places, seeing that any terminating resistors that should have been removed were removed, etc., you need a technician.

Basically, the only thing you can do to check your hard disk is a simple test for loose connectors. Be certain to follow the power-down and power-up sequences given in Figures 6–3 and 6–6. Unplug and plug in again the power supply and controller connectors. Close up your case and try to copy files. If the copy works, rerun the diagnostics. If you still can't copy files, call in the experts.

If file copy works but you can't get a clean bill of health from the diagnostics, you can proceed as though all were well. We haven't had problems (yet) even though the drive doesn't check out all the way in the diagnostics. We do make backup copies of everything we care about keeping.

System-Specific Tests

If the diagnostic testing has detected one or more systems that are performing at lower levels than you expect or not working at all, you need to test those individual systems. Repeating global diagnostic testing is not the way to get to know more about what's going wrong with specific systems and components. We have to find software that is appropriate for the task at hand.

Benchmarks

Benchmarks can help you compare your system with others (external comparisons). Another testing method that is potentially as useful or even more useful for you is comparison of the performance of your PC before and after the upgrade (internal comparisons).

There are benchmarks to test computational speed (both with and without math coprocessors), disk I/O, and printer speed to name a few. One problem with benchmark routines is that there are no standards. Benchmarks from different companies get answers that aren't the same even though they claim to be measuring the same performance characteristics.

Let's examine a few benchmarks in detail. We have several different ones, including two versions of one. We'll show you what to expect when you crank up the software, and we'll run a few on the same machine to show the differences in answers.

For any of these benchmarks, it is better if you can run them both before and after your upgrade. A comparison of the particular performance of your PC is the best measure of how successful you've been.

PC Magazine Labs Benchmark Series 5.0

One widely accepted and diverse set of benchmarks is published by *PC Magazine* through their testing arm, PC Labs. One of the very nicest features of this software is the price—it's free. You can write to them at

PC Magazine Labs
One Park Avenue, 4th Floor
New York, New York 10016

to request that they send you a copy of their most recent PC Labs Benchmark Series. Let's stroll through their software.

This software will address performance, compatibility, and quality. The caveat accompanying the software cautions you not to make comparisons between this version (5.0) and earlier versions produced by the same organization. Clearly, if one organization doesn't maintain testing compatibility, compatibility is very unlikely to be found between organizations.

In the areas of performance measurement, we note that the program will measure the performance of the processor, coprocessor, disks, video, memory, and printer. This is one of a very small number of software packages that attempts to establish printer performance. The program also will measure the quality of EGA and VGA adapters.

Under the performance-measurement umbrella, we find processor speed tests. There is a real assortment of tests from basic processor instructions, to integer arithmetic, to string manipulations, and on to floating point arithmetic. Other software packages perform some of the same tests, but most don't allow you to choose which ones will be conducted. Notice that the menu item can be chosen by striking the space bar after you have reached the item by using the up and down cursor keys.

You probably will be interested in determining your hard-disk performance. The PC Labs program will perform both BIOS- and DOS-level disk access to determine access speed. An important aspect of disk performance that is tested is the speed at which small and large files can be read and written. Here are two tests that will come very close to telling you just how well you've done with your disk upgrade. Of course, the ultimate test is how well the system performs on your data rather than the artificial sets established by the program writers.

The program will test conventional, expanded, and extended memory for you. This will help you determine if you have managed to effect a system improvement when you upgraded memory. You should expect to see a dramatic improvement if you went from an 80286 to an 80386 system. The chips involved with the 80386 system are generally faster than the ones in the 80286 system.

There is also the printer test. During this test, a stored letter is printed, and the number of characters printed per second is determined. You have to interact with the program by hitting a key to let it know that the printer has finished its job. There is a request early on for a special character sequence for your printer that is to be terminated with END. Feel free simply to strike the END key. You won't hurt anything.

The PC Labs Benchmark displays are a bit more sophisticated than for most similar routines. You don't normally have a mixture of text and graphics. The specific numbers it gives are nice, but the relative ones it shows at the bottom of its display tell the story almost as well as the graphics.

The PC Labs Benchmark program is the only multipurpose benchmarking routine we'll examine. We'll take a look now at two versions of the same CPU-performance benchmark program.

Landmark CPU Speed Test

As we discussed earlier, different versions of the same program may not get the same results on performance. This is shown quite clearly in Figures 6-11 and 6–12. We are looking at the tests produced by the 0.99 and 1.05 versions of the Landmark CPU Speed Test from Landmark Software of Sunnyvale, CA. You can see that the tested PC was 6.1 times faster than a PC/XT according to version 0.99 and only 5.2 times faster according to version 1.05. Certainly the PC didn't slow down between the times the two versions were run. You have to view any results you get from benchmark software with a grain of salt. Keep in mind that this genre is most useful for internal comparisons.

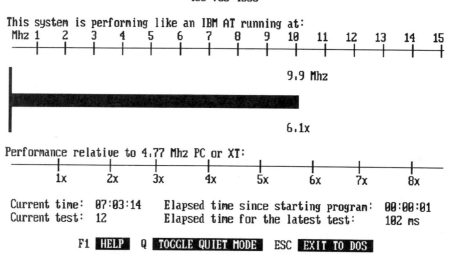

Figure 6–11.   Landmark CPU test with SPEED99.

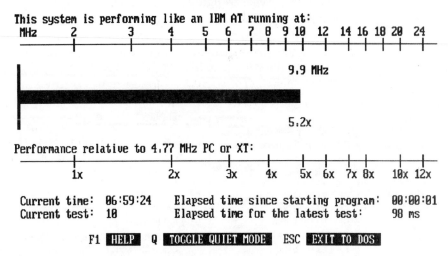

Figure 6–12. Landmark CPU test with SPEED105.

Utilities

There's more benchmark-only software available, but we've explored a representative sample with you. Next, we will look at some examples of utilities available for use with your system.

Norton Utilities Verson 4.5

Most of the PC vendors will quote benchmark values from Norton. They are giving you results from tests run on their hardware using the Norton Utilities from Peter Norton Computing of Santa Monica, CA. The Norton Utilities cost about $75 from the larger mail-order software suppliers. The Advanced Version can be obtained for about $110. The list prices are $100 and $150, respectively.

We'll examine three programs available from the Norton Utilities—Disk Test (DT.EXE), System Information (SI.EXE), and Speed Disk (SD.EXE). These files can be executed individually or through the Norton Integrator (NI.EXE). We'll show you the method through the integrator since it contains helpful documentation.

Disk Test   The disk test is not a performance test like the PC Labs Benchmark disk test. This program tests the integrity of the hard-disk recording surface. It attempts to read and then write back to the disk. There is no internal measure of how long any of this operation takes. For the 30-Mbyte hard disk on the tested PC, it takes roughly four minutes for Disk Test to do its job.

Figure 6–13 shows the first page of the Norton Integrator with Disk Test chosen as the software to be run. The right-hand side of the screen image contains helpful documentation about Disk Test. At the bottom of the screen page, there is the command line with optional switches just as it will be given to the operating system as soon as a carriage return is struck.

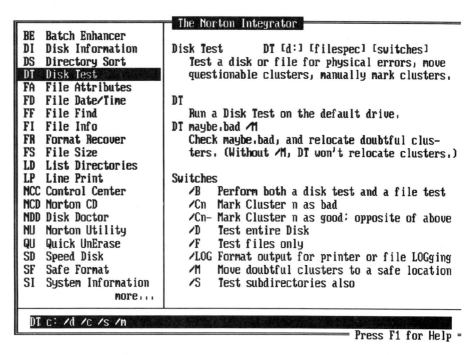

Figure 6–13.   Norton Utilities Disk Test selection.

The results of this test are shown in Figure 6–14. You should note that Disk Test found a bad cluster (number 3686). The cluster was already marked as bad, so no action was necessary. If it had not been marked as bad, it would have been marked, and any information residing in that cluster would have been moved if possible. This would have been done because the /M (move doubtful data) and /C (mark cluster) options were chosen.

System Information   The material supplied by System Information is similar to that made available during the initial stages of DiagMenu. In addition, there are three benchmark numbers—computing index, disk index, and per-

```
DT-Disk Test, Advanced Edition 4.50, (C) Copr 1987-88, Peter Norton

During the scan of the disk, you may press
BREAK (Control-C) to interrupt Disk Test

Test reading the entire disk C:, system area and data area
   The system area consists of boot, FAT, and directory
      No errors reading system area


   The data area consists of clusters numbered 2 - 15,513
      3,686th cluster read error: already marked as bad; no danger



Press any key to continue...
```

Figure 6–14.   Norton Utilities Disk Test results.

formance index. The computing index is the number frequently quoted by computer-hardware vendors. Figure 6–15 shows the second page of the Norton Integrator with System Information as the software to be run. On the right is the short form documentation. At the bottom of the screen page is the command line. The hard-disk drive (C:) is specified there. Without a designated drive, the disk index and performance index will not be computed.

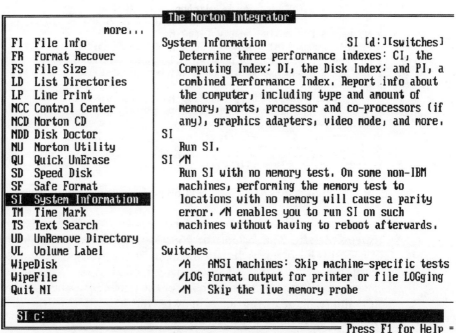

Figure 6–15.   Norton Utilities System Information test selection.

As you can see from Figure 6–16, the performance measurements are made with respect to an IBM XT. For the tested PC (10-MHz 80286 AT clone), the computing index is 9.8. That is, this PC is 9.8 times faster than an IBM XT at doing the tasks the program samples. This is in marked contrast with the 2.4 times faster than an XT that was the result of the 8088 instruction set execution conducted by the PC Labs Benchmark program. A result of 9.8 on one hand and 2.4 on the other—which are you supposed to believe? Once again, we have to go back to our earlier statement: Benchmarks are best used as internal measures. Run both programs on your hardware both before and after you upgrade your PC. The change in values, not the absolute numbers, is important.

```
SI-System Information, Advanced Edition 4.50, (C) Copr 1987-88, Peter Norton

          Computer Name: IBM AT
       Operating System: DOS 3.20
      Built-in BIOS dated: Wednesday, October 1, 1986
         Main Processor: Intel 80286                Serial Ports: 2
           Co-Processor: None                       Parallel Ports: 2
  Video Display Adapter: Monochrome (MDA)
     Current Video Mode: Text, 80 x 25 Monochrome
   Available Disk Drives: 10, A: - C:, E: - K:

DOS reports 640 K-bytes of memory:
    259 K-bytes used by DOS and resident programs
    381 K-bytes available for application programs
A search for active memory finds:
    640 K-bytes main memory      (at hex 00000-0A000)
     64 K-bytes display memory   (at hex 0B000-0C000)
    512 K-bytes extended memory  (at hex 10000-18000)

  Computing Index (CI), relative to IBM/XT: 9.8
      Disk Index (DI), relative to IBM/XT: 2.5

Performance Index (PI), relative to IBM/XT: 7.3

Press any key to continue...
```

Figure 6–16. Norton Utilities performance measurements.

Speed Disk   The last of the Norton Utilities we'll examine is Speed Disk. Again, this is not a benchmark program. It is a utility designed to improve your hard-disk performance. It does that by making your files contiguous. Under DOS, your files are spread out all over the hard disk. Where a file goes is solely a function of available space when the file is written to the disk. When DOS places your files on the disk, it makes no extra effort to keep them in contiguous sectors. Speed Disk rewrites your hard disk to make as many files contiguous as possible. CAUTION: Never run this or any other routine that alters your hard disk without having a recent backup of all your hard-disk files.

Figure 6–17 is a display of the Speed Disk menu complete with switches on the command line shown at the bottom of the figure.

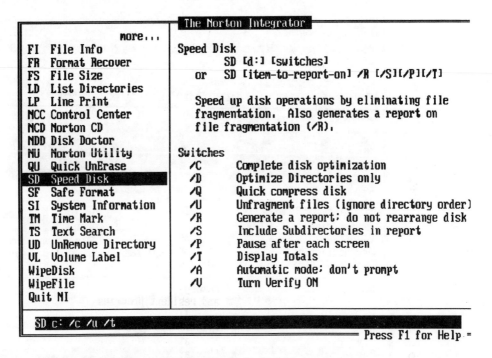

```
┌─────────────────────────────────┤ The Norton Integrator ├──────────────────────┐
│                     more...     Speed Disk                                       │
│  FI  File Info                       SD [d:] [switches]                          │
│  FR  Format Recover              or  SD [item-to-report-on] /R [/S][/P][/T]      │
│  FS  File Size                                                                   │
│  LD  List Directories                                                           │
│  LP  Line Print                  Speed up disk operations by eliminating file    │
│  NCC Control Center              fragmentation.  Also generates a report on      │
│  NCD Norton CD                   file fragmentation (/R).                        │
│  NDD Disk Doctor                                                                 │
│  NU  Norton Utility              Switches                                        │
│  QU  Quick UnErase                 /C       Complete disk optimization           │
│  SD  Speed Disk                    /D       Optimize Directories only            │
│  SF  Safe Format                   /Q       Quick compress disk                  │
│  SI  System Information            /U       Unfragment files (ignore directory order) │
│  TM  Time Mark                     /R       Generate a report; do not rearrange disk  │
│  TS  Text Search                   /S       Include Subdirectories in report     │
│  UD  UnRemove Directory            /P       Pause after each screen              │
│  VL  Volume Label                  /T       Display Totals                       │
│  WipeDisk                          /A       Automatic mode; don't prompt         │
│  WipeFile                          /V       Turn Verify ON                       │
│  Quit NI                                                                         │
│                                                                                  │
├──────────────────────────────────────────────────────────────────────────────  │
│  SD c: /c /u /t                                                                  │
└═══════════════════════════════════════════════════════════ Press F1 for Help ═══┘
```

Figure 6–17. Norton Utilities Speed Disk screen.

Figure 6–18 contains a map of the 30-Mbyte hard disk used in the tested PC. If you'll quickly scan the legend at the lower right, you'll see that most of the disk is occupied. Only a small number of clusters are seen to be empty in between clusters that are occupied. You can also locate the bad cluster (number 3686) reported by Disk Test. It shows up as a block with a "B" in it.

Figure 6–19 shows disk statistics superimposed over the hard disk map. You may notice that 98% of the files on the hard disk are not fragmented (they are contiguous). That's because we make it a regular practice to run a hard-disk cleanup routine such as Speed Disk.

As a point on disk use, you should note that the statistics report shows there are 58 directories on this disk—the root directory and 57 others. And there are 1419 files. If all 1419 files were in only one or two directories, it would be almost impossible to find the file you want. It is extremely important to arrange your hard-disk file system so that you can retrieve files quickly—after all, time wasted is money wasted.

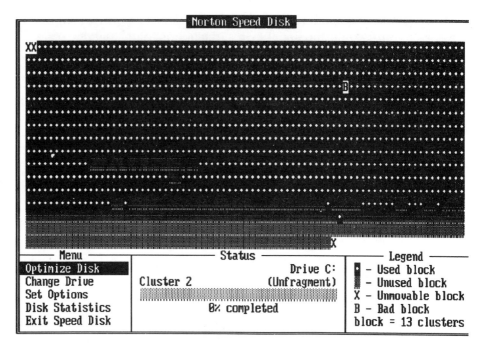

Figure 6–18. Norton Utilities disk map.

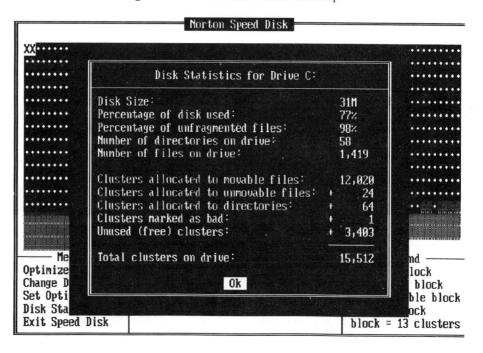

Figure 6–19. Norton Utilities Disk Statistics.

Optune, The Gazelle Optimizer Version 1.1

Optune is a hard-disk management tool from Gazelle Systems of Provo, UT. It can restructure your hard disk in a way similar to that accomplished by Norton's Speed Disk; it can check for correct low-level format; it can test and alter the interleave if necessary to maximize performance; and it can test the disk surface for bad places. Many people use it without qualms or problems.

However, here is a word of caution: Optune may not work if you have a Western Digital disk controller. The Optune warning file contained a caution for Western Digital RLL controllers only. However, when we used it with a much older MFM Western Digital controller, the entire disk contents were wiped out. Remember: DON'T LET ANY SOFTWARE MESS AROUND WITH YOUR HARD DISK UNLESS YOU HAVE A RECENT BACKUP OF ALL FILES YOU WANT TO KEEP.

The menu structure of Optune consists of Optimize, Tune-Disk, Check-Disk, and Verify/Fix-Disk. There are options for using the Verify/Fix-Disk feature that you should examine carefully. Be especially wary about using the Bit Test options for Verify Type. The safest option is Read-Only. Of course, it also won't let any adjustments occur. So you can have safety without action. If you want the program to act for you, first back up all the files you want to be able to recover, and then proceed with Fix-Disk.

Again, there seem to be incompatibilities between the way Optune reads and writes information to the hard disk during the interleave test and the way Western Digital stores information on the hard disk for future use. Whatever the source of the problem, following the interleave test (which was conducted without asking the program to change anything), our hard disk was unusable.

Burn-In Tests

Burn-in tests are best conducted at night or over weekends. They occupy the system for extended periods of time. During the tests, it is important that no one disturbs the system.

Despite the name, nothing will actually get burned. This is simply a second trial by fire for the upgraded hardware. The first trial was the smoke test.

One simple burn-in test for your hard disk is to set up a batch file that executes Disk Test until you interrupt it. An example DISKTEST.BAT file is shown below.

```
DISKTEST.BAT
:START
C:
CD\NORTON
DT C: /D /S
GOTO START
```

This program will execute the disk test until the power fails, the hard disk fails, or you interrupt it with a ⟨CTRL⟩C or ⟨CTRL⟩BREAK. Of course, if you have more than one disk you need to burn in, include one or more additional lines specifying the drive name(s) following the DT portion of the command.

Now that you've tested your new system as much as you can tolerate, you should have confidence in its ability to serve you for many days to come. You would be well advised to keep a log of these tests and conduct them again on a periodic basis, say every six months. You can use the results to tell you if there is any deterioration in the performance of your system. When you first suspect trouble, take steps to have it corrected. Don't wait until your system is dead. Preventive maintenance is the answer.

Chapter 7

How to Build a PC
From Scratch

Building a PC from scratch is not as formidable a task as it was ten or even five years ago. Most of the microcomputers in business and many in home use are IBM or IBM compatibles. Today there is a modest amount of confusion surrounding *microchannel architecture (MCA)* and *enhanced industry standard architecture (EISA)* versus the AT data bus. We'll discuss these design decisions later.

Most of the basic systems available are standard IBM-AT compatibles utilizing Intel 80286 microprocessors. The more advanced systems available maintain the IBM-AT bus structure and use the Intel 80386 microprocessors. Some of the new boards are 80386-based systems with 33-MHz CPUs. You can stay with the AT bus and still go with one of the hottest chips in PC computerdom today.

Basic units typically contain eight expansion slots. In the expansion slots, you put printed circuit boards that will serve as additional memory, serial and parallel communications drivers, fax boards, and modems, to mention a few. This list is certainly not complete.

All this is very good, but you need to know where to go to find the books of dreams, the wish books, the books filled with boxes, boards, and components. Many items will be well beyond your budget (these are the wishes), but there will be some that can be squeezed in if you configure your system just right.

There are numerous decisions for you to make. Will you mix and match— that is, will you get products from just one manufacturer, or will you shop around for the best deals regardless of manufacturer? With what other computers must you maintain compatibility? How much of your existing equipment do you want to retain? Are you going to go with 8- or 16-bit data buses? Are you going to put it all together yourself, subcontract part of it, or buy a whole new system?

We'll discuss these and other issues. Ultimately, you must be satisfied that whatever you decide to do is right for you. If you are planning upgrades for an organization, you must be convinced that what you want is right for them, too.

We will not be discussing how to build computers that aren't compatible with the AT bus. Certainly this leaves out the machines with 32-bit data buses, the current IBM series (PS/2s) and machines that will be compatible with the EISA bus standard, and any other computers that do not use Intel microprocessors.

Sources of Information

Where do you go to get ideas? Obviously, we think you can get some very useful ideas right here. However, we're not presenting a shopping guide to PCs. Those are available elsewhere. We will try to help you find the right sources and then develop a logical basis for constructing your PC.

Magazines

The back pages of most of the major computer magazines contain advertisements from component and complete-system suppliers. Included in the list of magazines are *Computer Shopper*, *PC Magazine*, *PC Resources*, *PC Computing*, *Family Computing*, *PC World*, *Byte*, *Computer Buyers Guide*, and *Personal Computing*. Examining any or all of these sources will provide you with a quick and reasonably comprehensive overview of what's available.

Among the many companies advertising in these magazines, there are a number that specialize in selling system components and assembled computers made from the components they advertise. For instance, Jameco Electronics of Belmont, CA, has available an 80-page catalog of boards, monitors, printers, disk drives, back-up tape drives, keyboards, software, chips, PCs, and supplies.

In addition, the same magazines contain articles about specific applications of older and advanced products. Some of these will be of no practical use to you, but scanning the tables of contents can turn you on to real gems of wisdom.

Clubs

Special-interest groups (SIGs) have grown up in most of the major cities around the country. Many of these groups have restricted themselves to IBM-compatible PCs and activities affecting PCs. These people can be a great source of practical advice. Many of them have built or upgraded their own systems. They can share real-life horror and success stories.

You can usually locate your nearest SIG through local computer retailers. Frequently, retailers have the club meeting schedule posted in their stores. The SIG members buy lots of computers and equipment, so the stores usually try to stay on good terms with them. If you don't see a meeting schedule, ask the clerk or manager about the local SIG. Should you meet with resistance or ignorance, go elsewhere.

Word of Mouth

Your associates and acquaintances are another good source of PC building information. It's quite likely that some of them have computer anecdotes they will be willing to share with you. You'll have to separate the fiction from the facts—the editorializing from the reporting—but you'll find enough information about systems that work well and, equally as important, systems that don't to make the time spent worthwhile.

You probably know at least one person either at work or away from your job who has already assembled a PC. Unfortunately, there are no big letters embossed on this person's chest proclaiming, "I ROLLED MY OWN PC." You will have to ask enough questions to identify your potential information source. It's possible that others will point out the expert to you. Or you may have to stumble around until you locate him yourself. You need to spend as much time as you can collecting information from this person. Keep up the acquaintance. You may want to talk again as your project moves along.

Technical Departments

The technical departments of the major computer stores usually have very competent staffs. These people can advise you about mixing and matching the products they sell. Some of the staff will have worked for other companies as well and therefore have additional knowledge you need. Cultivate them.

The larger mail-order houses also maintain technical advisers. The mail merchants frequently go to a great deal of effort to hire and keep well qualified technical staff to assist you when you call.

Planning

Before you march off to order your components and begin assembling your new PC, you need to do some planning. This is the stage that is most often ignored by individuals and some companies. It is seldom fun, often difficult, and frequently boring. What it has to recommend it is the product. Without planning, you are much more likely to put together a system that either will not work at all or will fail to operate the way you want—it can't quite do the job.

Size

A rather simple issue that is overlooked quite often is size. How big can your PC be? Do you have to be able to move it easily from one place to another? Will you have to be carrying it around in a car, on the subway, or in an airplane? How large is the space where you will be working? Can the PC fit on your desk, or must it be located under the desk?

If your PC must be easily portable, you have design issues. How much can it weigh? What are the maximum height, length, and width that you are willing to tolerate? The smaller the PC has to be, the tougher it is going to be for you to build it yourself. Most of the motherboards and plug-ins for very compact PCs are proprietary. They aren't readily available through mail order or conventional retail outlets.

The manufacturers of portables or laptops want you to buy their PCs and then have them or their dealers perform the upgrades. As an example, a representative of one manufacturer of laptop computers said in a letter to us, "Because of the complexity and space restrictions, most upgrades are contracted out to service organizations. If the upgrade does not require major rework and can be swapped out relatively easily, then the upgrades will more than likely be a dealer upgrade.... The persons who set these upgrade policies are the product managers for each machine."

It would appear that for the immediate future you will be frustrated if you want to roll your own laptop. While the market for complete systems is large, there are very few directly interchangeable parts. Most alterations to existing systems require extensive modifications. There is very little incentive for third-party developers and manufacturers to produce laptop components. The bottom line seems to be: if you want a laptop PC, you are going to have to buy it from an established dealer.

Where you can relax the size restrictions a bit, you stand a chance of putting together a nice, compact system. A little shopping through catalogs reveals that there are a number of what are called *baby* AT and '386 motherboards. These are motherboards that are usually no larger than the motherboards in an old PC/XT. In case you're not familiar with the differences, the XT-size boards are available in both 8.5″ × 12″ and 8.75″ × 13″, while the AT-size boards are roughly 12″ × 13.75″. You can see that the XT-size boards will fit in a smaller box (case) than the AT-size boards.

Home Is Where the Cards Fit

A typical AT-size case is roughly 16.5″ deep, 20.75″ wide, and 6.75″ tall. That's not a small box. It is a reasonably good height for viewing your monitor. Check the location where you will be using your PC. If you can't accommodate a box this large, go for a more compact design.

Do some looking to find the best deal on a box (case) in which to house your PC. Most computer magazines have advertisers that sell cases. Go for a case that has a nice finished look and is made of heavy-gauge sheet metal. Generally, you can tell the sheet-metal gauge (thickness) by looking at the weight of the case. The heavier the case, the thicker the sheet metal. Thin sheet metal will buckle under loads. You'll probably want to put your monitor on top of your machine, and you certainly don't want the case to flex or be permanently deformed because of the weight of the monitor.

You will get the option of choosing a case with a top that slides off after you remove some screws or one that swings up after screws are removed. This is an opportunity to make future work on your PC easier. Sliding the top off a PC while you are trying to keep the entire machine from tumbling into your lap or off onto the floor is no fun. Avoid that problem by getting the swing-up top.

Be aware, however, that some case manufacturers claim the "flip-top" models do not offer adequate RF (radio frequency) shielding. We have seen some excellent flip-up models that appear to be relatively tight, but if interference with broadcast and other radio services is an important consideration, be sure to ask the case vendor about the amount of shielding offered by the models you're considering.

Another source of cases is old PCs. Dealers will sometimes take trade-ins that aren't functional or are in such bad shape that it isn't cost-effective to fix them. Check around; you may be able to get a case from an old PC or PC/XT clone for a very nominal cost. Industries in your area may have used-equipment sales where you can get an older PC for just a few dollars.

Since you are planning to build up your own machine, you are interested only in the case. If there happens to be a functional piece or two inside the case, you're ahead. However, be very cautious about using any components in the case. It's tough to find intermittent problems, and they are a primary reason for disposing of older PCs. Our advice is to scrap everything except the case. It's much more trouble than it's worth to debug a system made up of old and new components. Start with new components; they'll have three or more years of useful life ahead of them.

Compatibility

With what other equipment must you maintain compatibility? Are there other older computers with which you have to be able to communicate? Will your computer be expected to control a piece of equipment? Will it be expected to replace an existing computer in specific applications—software or hardware?

Establishing and maintaining compatibility—developing interfaces—is a job that can occupy a large portion of an engineer's day for an extended period of time if the project is of moderate size. You should expect to spend at least one day (six to eight hours) thinking about and writing down the interface requirements for your new PC.

If yours is to be a stand-alone PC that never communicates with another machine, your job is a lot easier. You can put together any kind of machine you want. Of course, a bit of looking ahead or forward thinking may save you considerable future aggravation.

External Systems

Another compatibility issue involves what external systems your PC has to talk to. If you anticipate that your PC may be used to control a piece of equipment, you must know if the interface is serial or parallel and at what speed data will be transferred. (Here, we're talking about equipment other than a printer or an external disk drive.)

Serial interfaces with a PC are usually done in accord with wiring and signal levels described as *RS-232C*. This is a rather broad standard, and manufacturers implement it in a number of different ways and still maintain that they are RS-232C compatible. The signal levels are usually not the problem. The problem is that there are various ways of configuring the control of data flow (*handshaking*). The data-in, data-out, and ground lines are standard. The other 22 pins (for a PC-type connection) or 6 pins (for an AT-type connection) and how they are interconnected pose the problem.

Certainly, the data-transfer rate can be an issue. The rates are typically 300, 600, 1200, 2400, 4800, 9600, and 19200 baud (bits per second). Virtually all devices will support data transfer at rates below the maximum. Initiate attempts to communicate at 300 baud. Once you have established communications at this speed, then you can hunt for the fastest reliable speed. The easiest way to find the correct transfer rate is to increase the bit rate incrementally until communications fail. Back up one step, and that's your preferred communications speed.

Some older equipment may be configured to communicate over the 8-bit data bus that was standard before the AT was introduced. Parallel 8-bit communications are a problem. The standard AT data bus is 16 bits wide and operates at 8 MHz (eight million cycles per second). The standard PC bus was 8 bits wide and operated at 4.77 MHz.

It is almost impossible to find a PC-style (8088 or 8086) motherboard. Even if you could find one, this would be such an emasculated system that it wouldn't be reasonable to build it.

This is a place where a little research is in order. There are solutions, but they typically involve parallel-to-serial conversion devices that are beyond the scope of this book. Two good places to go for information are the manufacturer of the equipment you want to control and Black Box Corporation, Pittsburgh, PA. Black Box is one of the largest computer communications products companies, and they maintain a technical support organization to help you with problems like this. Their telephone number for technical support is (412) 746-5565.

Your solution probably isn't cheap, but at least you won't be wasting your time building an 8088- or 8086-based machine. If all else fails, there are 8088- and 8086-based PCs available for under $500 from discounters. You would have an awfully tough time building one for less. You can get one for even less if you are willing to buy a discontinued model (like an IBM PC Jr.) or an orphan (defunct manufacturer). Look in the back pages of the magazines mentioned above.

Other Computers

Communicating with other computers can be almost as big a problem as controlling external equipment. If you limit yourself to communicating with PC-compatible computers, your job is somewhat easier.

You can buy a multifunction card that will provide a serial port, a parallel port, and probably a game port where you could connect a joystick. Some cards have installed memory and a clock/calendar. The latter is unnecessary for AT and '386 motherboards (it's built-in). Through the serial port, you could establish a direct connection with another computer if you have the right software, such as Brooklyn Bridge from White Crane Systems or Laplink Plus from Traveling Software.

Serial communication is slow and clumsy at best. The only reason to use it is if you can't exchange data more efficiently. A much more efficient data-transfer method is to take a floppy diskette from your machine and place it in the machine where you want it to be read.

There's a rub. The two machines have to be able to read and write to the same medium. If you build a PC with only a 3.5-inch floppy-diskette drive, you won't be compatible with older systems using 5.25-inch floppy-diskette drives. That's fine if you never have to communicate with an older system. But if you have to communicate through the serial port, you'll quickly start wishing you had the right size floppy drive.

We recommend that you put one floppy-diskette drive of each size with the largest capacity possible in your new PC. These drives cost around $100 apiece. You can put both into your machine for under $250. We strongly encourage you to do this.

Presently, the data-storage limits are 1.2 megabytes for 5.25 inch drives and 1.44 megabytes for 3.5-inch drives. There are smaller drives (2 inches) being used in some laptop PCs, and higher data storage densities (4 megabytes and larger) are under development. There are also some devices that use specialized hardware and software to store up to 43.2 megabytes on a 3.5 inch floppy diskette. Unfortunately, this equipment can't read or write the IBM-formatted diskettes. A lower-capacity (21.4 megabytes) drive from the same manufacturer will read but not write IBM-formatted diskettes. If you are interested in this technology, contact Brier Technology, San Jose, CA, (408) 435-8463.

Telephone Lines

Don't forget the possibility of communicating with other computers and computer users that are too far away for the direct transfer of data via diskette to be timely. (Actually, for massive amounts of data, sending it on floppy diskettes through the mail or with one of the overnight delivery services is certainly cost effective.)

You will need to install a modem (either internal or external) to be a party to these long-distance (off-site) communications. The choice of an internal or external modem depends largely on where your real estate is least crowded. If you can spare the slot, we would recommend an internal modem. It makes for the neatest installation. There are fewer wires running around, since the only connection required is from the wall-mounted phone jack to the modem. The modem gets its power from the PC.

Modems are readily available with data-transfer rates up to 9600 baud. You get the most for your bucks with the 2400-baud modems. These are available from discounters for under $100. The 9600-baud modems cost over $500, and very few people have them. The prices on all the modems are dropping. Be certain that any modem you purchase is Hayes-compatible. Hayes sets the standards for features and functions. Bundled with the modem, you will probably get communications software as well.

Regardless of the physical location of your modem, you will be using a serial port. Serial ports are particularly sought-after. Many other peripherals such as printers, scanners, and fax machines use them. Some motherboards can accommodate only two serial ports. Carefully consider your present and future uses for serial ports. If you think you will need more than two ports, be certain that you buy a motherboard that can support at least four serial ports. Otherwise, you may have to invest in a multiplexing board, and they aren't cheap. Buy a serial A-B-C switch (all the peripherals plug into the black box, but only one at a time is connected to your computer), or simply plug in one peripheral after you have unplugged another.

With your modem, you can connect to dial-up information services (databases, current events, and stock-market happenings are a few examples), local and national bulletin boards, electronic mail services, technical-information services maintained by software and hardware vendors, and on-line conferences. All this is in addition to the more conventional host and terminal relationship you can establish with a mainframe computer at work or across the country. Clearly, a modem is a valuable asset and should be included in your plans for your new PC.

Direct Replacement

An additional constraint on your hardware choices would be having to use your new computer as a replacement for an existing machine. Fortunately, this is a tough problem only when the existing computer is interfaced to another machine through an eight-bit parallel data bus. We discussed this problem and the possible solutions under External Systems.

If the present computer has lots of data stored in it, see if some of the data can be written off to diskettes or simply deleted. After you've reduced the stored materials as much as possible, make plans to get one or more hard disks to handle the existing data plus what you will be putting on it. A good rule of thumb is to increase the storage capacity by a factor of four. If the existing machine needs to store 20 megabytes, then arrange to store at least 80 megabytes (20 megabytes times four).

It is simply amazing how fast hard-disk space can be filled. In practice, it is probably not possible to put too much storage space on a computer system. With very large hard disks, you have to give serious consideration to data-transfer rates and the types of controller interfaces you use. Look up the possibilities in Chapter 2.

For one or two hard disks larger than 100 megabytes, we would suggest going with an ESDI controller. If you are going to install several hard disks, then you should give very serious consideration to a *Small Computer System Interface (SCSI*—pronounced "scuzzy") controller. Of course, the hard disks must be compatible with the controllers. Processing speed can be a problem when you are building a replacement computer. It's unlikely that you will be building a PC that is slower than the one you're replacing, but think about it. In many applications, computers are I/O-bound. Sometimes the speed of the system isn't limited by the CPU clock rate, but rather it's limited by the rate at which it can collect data or send the data to another device. Other times, the system is limited by how fast data can be manipulated internally.

It's possible that an 8088-based computer with a large RAM cache and a slow hard disk can outperform an 80286- or even an 80386-based machine with a moderately fast hard disk. Look carefully at the machine you are replacing. Talk to the people using it. See if they know of any improvements that may have been made to change it from being a real dog into a machine they can live with. Be certain to make your replacement PC at least a little bit better.

Software compatibility is an issue that seldom has any hooks in it for you at the microprocessor level. Intel, the manufacturer of the 80xxx series of CPUs, has exercised care to assure backward compatibility. There may be a few software programs still in existence that take timing information directly from the data bus or CPU clocks. This type of software was a problem during the transition from IBM PCs and PC/XTs to PC/ATs with their faster clock speeds.

The most likely source of conflict is with peripherals. If the old system had a monochrome monitor and you build one with a state-of-the-art color card and monitor, the software might not work. You may have to reconfigure it for the color system. With some older software, especially software that's been written at your site or was written specifically for your application, it may be impossible to configure it for a color monitor. The converse can also be true. It may be impossible to go from a color monitor to a full-page monochrome monitor.

Of course, if you use a color display adapter inside the computer, you will have to upgrade the external display to support it. However, some color cards can drive a monochrome monitor, so you could delay the display upgrade until a later time.

Another peripheral device that can be a problem is the printer. If you bring in a new laser page printer to replace an old dot matrix printer, you may have problems with the software. Older software is not likely to have drivers for laser printers.

When you're building a replacement system, do some investigating to see if there may be a software "gotcha" waiting for you. Locate the software documentation and see how to install it.

From your perspective, the right answer is to replace the software. The users of the software may not see it that way. If you can show them some real, near-term benefits from using new software, you may be able to get them to change their minds. If negotiations fail and they insist upon retaining the existing software, there are two ways you can proceed. You can change your system design, or you can try to find someone to write patches for the existing software. The latter path is likely to be very expensive and therefore is not recommended.

Performance

You've spent quite a while thinking about compatibility. Your system design has been structured to take into account the issues you encountered. Given the constraints you've already imposed, now it's time to consider choices that are a bit more fun. How fast is fast enough? Is there a good reason for going with the fastest CPU possible? Is math-coprocessor support needed? How much memory is enough? Does this system really need the speed and quality available from a laser printer? How about VGA plus? Is 800 × 600 resolution not good enough? Can a 19 inch high-resolution color monitor be used effectively? How fast do the hard disks need to be?

CPU Speed

Any experienced PC user knows that no machine is ever fast enough. There are always applications that could be run in a reasonable length of time if only my machine were 10%, 50%, or 200% faster (pick one). Your design considerations have to include cost.

An 80286-based motherboard is significantly cheaper than an 80386-based system. A quick tour through a recent Jameco catalog shows that a 33-MHz 80386 motherboard costs 6.5 times as much as a 20-MHz 80286 motherboard. But 20-MHz 80386 motherboards are available that are only 1.6 times as much as 20-MHz 80286 motherboards. With time and the advances of technology, the price differentials will be reduced. You should make the best case you can for the fastest CPU you can afford.

If there is any way you can, put together an 80386-based system. The CPU has been designed for easy movement between real and protected modes. This makes the path to multitasking easy for software developers. That means that you will soon have usable multitasking at a reasonable cost. Multitasking alone makes the cost worthwhile in many business environments.

Math Coprocessors

The need for coprocessor support depends largely on the applications you're running. Most business-related work does not require a math coprocessor. Engineering and scientific work frequently requires a math coprocessor. As an example, Lotus 1-2-3 does not show any benefits from having a coprocessor present until the trigonometric and other comparable mathematical functions are used.

Coprocessors are not cheap. The Intel 80287-10, the coprocessor designed for 10-MHz PC/AT clones, lists for $410 but is available during sales for under $250.

A third-party vendor, Integrated Information Technology (IIT), has begun marketing CMOS math coprocessors that are pin-for-pin compatible with the Intel chips. Reviews in several magazines suggest that the IIT chips are considerably faster than comparable Intel chips. The IIT 2C87-10, the coprocessor intended for use with 10-MHz PC/AT clones, lists for slightly over $250. The list price on an Intel 80387-33 is $995. The comparable IIT chip, the 3C87-33, lists for $649. Now is certainly a good time to include a coprocessor in your system if your use justifies the price; even with the price breaks, math coprocessors are still expensive.

Memory Requirements

As with speed, there's never quite enough memory to handle those really big problems that need to be solved. Fortunately for you and your system design, memory prices have been declining recently. For a period of about two years, the costs were so high that many systems were configured with only enough memory to take care of immediate needs.

Application programs are being written that must have more than the 640 kilobytes conventionally available to DOS. Lotus introduced 1-2-3 version 3.0 that required a minimum of 1 megabyte. Articles in the trade press suggest that Lotus 1-2-3/G, likely to be released in 1990, will require a minimum of 6 megabytes. That's more memory than can be installed in many systems that use 256-kilobyte memory modules (SIMMs).

You must use the more expensive 1-megabyte SIMMs to get to the 6-megabyte minimum. If you are a Lotus 1-2-3 aficionado, you will need to put together a system that will satisfy their minimum requirements. There are other application programs that will run happily in 1 to 2 megabytes when it's made available to them.

There is an interaction between hardware and software decisions. Your hardware must be able to support the software you use. If your software requires large amounts of memory, then you must configure your new system to accommodate the increased memory. Conversely, if your system has only a modest amount of memory beyond the 640-kilobyte barrier, some of your software decisions are made for you. If you have chosen to assemble a system using 256-kilobyte SIMMs because of their cost advantage, you can't install 6 megabytes of memory. You are limited to 4 megabytes and to software that will run in that amount of memory.

Printers: To Lase or Not to Lase

Page printers, and especially laser page printers, are wonderful. The available print quality is hard to distinguish from typeset. The speed with which pages emerge makes you wish you never had to wait for output again. But can you realistically design a single-user system with a laser printer? The minimum price for a laser printer is near $1000. That's almost double what a dot-matrix printer of adequate quality costs. Unless you have to do your own correspondence, there's very little you can use to justify including a laser printer in your single-user system.

If the printer is to be attached to more than one computer, then the speed and quality advantages enjoyed by the laser printer versus the dot-matrix printer begin to outweigh the cost disadvantage. If the laser printer serves two users, each of whom would have had a $500 dot-matrix printer without it, then there is no cost disadvantage. The costs are equivalent. For a system with three users for a single bottom-end laser printer, the price advantage belongs to the laser printer. Above three users, the $1000 printer begins to suffer. It isn't fast enough to support more than three users in the fashion to which they want to be accustomed.

Color Monitors and VGA

You have to make display decisions for your system. Will you go with graphics displays? Will you go with color? Our recommendation is go with color and graphics. Text-only cards are for XT compatibles that are used as dumb workstations. We've already recommended against building an XT-compatible system; so it's clear that we won't recommend text-only cards. Graphics cards allow you considerable flexibility including making graphs and presentation graphics, mixing text and graphics, and using text viewing features for proportional fonts, to name a few.

Color monitors are becoming standard equipment. They are moving from a status symbol to the office workhorse. Most users prefer color to monochrome, at least with EGA and VGA. With CGA, the resolution is so low (the characters are big, fat, and grainy) that asking you to look at it for several hours at a time is very close to torture. Both EGA and VGA make acceptable text and graphics.

The higher resolution possible with VGA (800 × 600 standard and 1024 × 768 extended) allows you to go to screens with more than 25 lines (34 or 60) that look good. (The characters are readable from the normal viewing distance.) Graphics are sharper, cleaner, and more interesting with VGA. There's one more immediate choice associated with VGA—16-bit or 8-bit data bus. The better choice is 16-bit. It's twice as wide, so two times the information can be transferred in a given time interval. You really can tell the difference.

Monitor size is also a consideration. The small characters produced in 34 and especially 60 lines per screen are much more easily viewed with a 16-inch or 19-inch monitor. Unfortunately, the prices for these monitors range from near $1000 on up. The best compromise is a 14-inch monitor. The characters are not so small as to be completely unreadable, and the prices for VGA compatible analog monitors start near $500. Be sure to specify a monitor that has a resolution of at least 800 × 600.

Hard-Disk Speed

Most computer operations that occur in offices are I/O-bound. That means you can pick up big performance improvements by putting high-speed I/O devices in your system design. Certainly, hard disks are a dramatic improvement over floppy-disk-only systems, but we've assumed that you are building your system around one or more hard-disk drives. We discussed the plethora of hard-drive types and interfaces in Chapter 2.

An office computer system is not likely to need more than 70 or 80 megabytes on a single hard disk unless you're maintaining some really massive mailing lists or inventories. You know the application where your system must work. Be certain you have a good understanding of the amount of data it will have to be storing for rapid access.

Most systems can get by quite nicely with a 70-megabyte hard disk using a 16-bit MFM interface with a 1:1 interleave. As we noted earlier, the 1:1 interleave is only beneficial for systems operating at or over 16 MHz. That's all the 80386 systems and the 16- and 20-MHz 80286 systems.

Most 70-megabyte hard drives have average access times between 20 and 28 milliseconds. The data-transfer rate is about 5 megabits per second (625 kilobytes per second). Of course, you can go to RLL and ESDI interfaces and compatible hard drives. With them, the average access times may go down to 16 or 17 milliseconds—not a big improvement—and the data-transfer rates can go up by factors between 1.5 and 3.

Most ESDI drives are considerably larger than 70 megabytes and have proportionally larger price tags. There are RLL-interface drives available with about 70 megabytes capacity, but you only gain the 1.5 times faster data transfer. There aren't any really big gains here.

You should seriously consider controllers with built-in RAM caches for systems where performance is or is likely to be really dragged down by the hard drive. With the RAM-cache enhanced controllers, the average access time drops to 0.5 millisecond (500 nanoseconds). That's slower than even the slowest RAM access speeds on the original PC (150 nanoseconds), but it's about 40 times faster than an unassisted controller. That's enough to make a real killer out of what was a wimpy system.

Performance Design Wrap-up

Your job is to design and build the best (highest performance) system for your application. We've made suggestions that we feel will help you assemble that best system. It still falls to you to do the really hard job—maximize performance and minimize costs. That's a tough assignment, but given what you've learned, you're up to it.

In summary, here's our suggested system:

1. One standard AT-size case with a flip-up top
2. One 200-watt power supply
3. One 101-key enhanced keyboard
4. One standard AT-size motherboard with a 25-MHz 80386 CPU
5. Two floppy-disk drives, one 1.2-Mbyte 5.25″ and one 1.44-Mbyte 3.5″
6. One 70-Mbyte hard drive with an MFM controller capable of a 1:1 interleave
7. One serial and parallel I/O board
8. One laser page printer
9. One 2400-baud modem
10. One 80387-25 math coprocessor
11. 4 megabytes of 80-nanosecond RAM chips

Procurement

It's your job to get the best deal on the system you designed. It's decision time again. You've specified exactly the system you want. You've tried to maximize performance and minimize costs. You've produced a set of really great functional requirements. You may even have some specific hardware specifications. Do you want someone else to do the procurement and assembly for you based on your system requirements?

You could turn the job over to someone else now. Virtually any computer store would be happy to take your functional requirements and shoehorn in their equipment. This won't minimize your costs, but it will allow you to go back to doing other things.

Most medium- to large-size towns have small operations where custom computer systems are designed and built. These people are usually hungry for business and anxious to work with you. Be very careful when dealing with them if you have to have your system assembled quickly. These shops typically have very competent staffs, but their resources are limited. Fast turnaround is not a general characteristic. Get a list of customers from the shop. Call them and ask about good and bad interactions. If the shop won't supply a list to you, go elsewhere.

There are also mail-order suppliers and some large custom fabrication shops that advertise in the magazines we listed earlier. Either of these places will put together your system for you. They are both likely to use components they have on hand or can get discounts on so that they can maximize their profit.

If you've decided to do the procurement and assembly yourself, read on.

Sources of Components

Get the best prices! That's your battle cry for this part of system assembly. To do that you need information. You need to know where to go to find products. Once you've found your products, where are the best prices? Can you benefit from problems others have? Look into distressed merchandise. We'll discuss these and related topics.

Quality Components

Certainly, you want the very best components to go into your computer system. Fortunately, you don't have to buy from the large computer merchandisers. You can usually get exactly what you want from a mail-order company. Exercise caution. Check out back issues of the magazines. Any company that has been advertising two years or more is probably stable and a good place to invest your money. After all, if something goes wrong, you want to be able get it fixed or get your money back. That's tough to do when the company doesn't exist any longer.

Discounters

There are a number of discounters that advertise, too. These organizations may not have a technical staff to talk with you. The support they offer is likely to be very elementary or peripheral. If you know exactly what you want, then order from a discounter. Don't expect any help if you encounter difficulties during installation or testing. These companies are in business to move as many components as possible, not to assist you when you have trouble. If you can live without the technical support, the price is right.

Distressed Merchandise

Distressed merchandise comes principally from insurance claims, manufacturer overruns, and discontinued products. The prices look unbelievably good. They are usually well below any you can find elsewhere. It may be that you can live with peripherals that aren't this year's model but are still very functional. In that case, you can save a bundle. Do check out the products before you buy. The ads don't always give you enough information to make a good decision. Use the model numbers to find out exactly what it is you are thinking about buying.

Local Fire and Bankruptcy Sales

While you're assembling your components, keep an eye out for fire and bankruptcy sales at local and not-too-distant computer stores and shops. Often you can pick up components for 10 cents on the dollar. Auctions are also a great place to go to find bargains. Of course, if the component doesn't work or you have trouble installing it, there's no technical support group to turn to.

Mailing Lists

Get on as many mailing lists as you can. That may seem like a cruel trick to play on your postman, but that's how you find out about good deals. Suppliers can't afford to put their entire catalogs in the magazine ads.

Comparison Shopping

Once you've assembled a good supply (you're the judge) of catalogs and fliers, it's time for comparison shopping. When you know exactly what you want, you only have to find the supplier with the best price. Don't overlook quantity or total-cost discounts.

Standard Interfaces

Many peripherals and cards have standard interfaces. It's certainly possible that house-brand components from reputable dealers are a very good deal. We've bought such products, and we haven't been burned. Motherboards are an even better example of standard interfaces. Many suppliers use the same control chips, ROM BIOS, and CPUs. The interfaces are all defined by IBM PC and PC/AT compatibility. Peripherals that use serial interfaces exhibit the worst adherence to established standards. Ask for a pinout (a diagram or table showing what signals or voltages are connected to each pin) for any serial devices you buy.

Single Source or Mix and Match

It would be nice to think that all your trials would be over if you bought all your system components from a single supplier. Unfortunately, there's no guarantee that all the products from a single vendor will work together.

Shop around. You'll be no worse off if you buy standard components from ten different suppliers than if you bought them all from one place. If you decide to get some nonstandard products, you'd better stick with one or at most two suppliers. You're likely to need to talk with someone with fairly intimate knowledge of such products.

Construction (Assembly)

Considering where you are in this chapter, it's pretty likely that you've decided to put the system together yourself. However, it's not too late to change your mind. Getting all the parts and tools together and putting aside blocks of time large enough to do the job are not trivial.

You can still get local computer job shops to assemble the system from your components. Of course, they'll probably charge more for assembly alone than if they were buying the components and assembling them.

Collect the Components

Great! You're ready to put your system together. Before you start assembly, make a checklist. Write down all the pieces that you need for the system. Check off each component as you locate it. Place them together on a large flat work space. If the component arrived in protective foam or a plastic bag, leave it protected until you're ready to install it.

Be certain that you have all the pieces it's going to take for your system. Check the list for completeness, and then look over the components for obvious flaws—broken connectors, missing cables, wrong number of chips. Now is the time to correct any problems before you get heavily involved in assembling the system.

Have the Right Tools

You won't need very many tools to assemble this system. A suggested group is shown in Figure 7–1. You can probably do the entire job with nine tools: two flat-blade screwdrivers, one medium and one small; two Phillips-head screwdrivers, one medium and one small; two nut drivers, one ¼" and one ³/₁₆"; one pair of needle-nose pliers; one IC (integrated circuit) installation tool; and one IC removal tool (in case you do it wrong the first time). It wouldn't hurt to have an inexpensive multimeter for continuity checks.

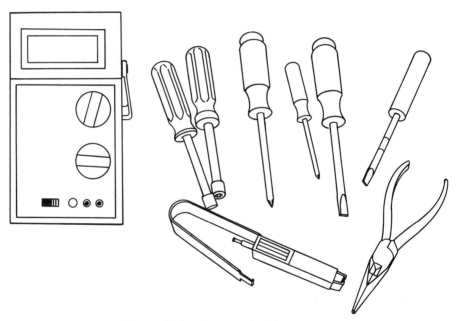

Figure 7–1. Suggested tools.

Be Safe

Safety is paramount during any operations that may involve electricity. You need to practice personal safety, and you need to employ practices that will keep your components safe. Don't expose them to static discharges. Appendix C discusses safe operations with and around electrical equipment.

Put It Together

Good construction practices are simply an extension of common sense to the task at hand. You should keep the work area clear of everything not involved in the system assembly. Have the tools on hand that you need to do the job. Locate the parts that will be used, and position them near the work area. Always let someone know that you will be working around electrical equipment, and arrange to have them check on you periodically.

Install the Power Supply

Place the power supply in the case as shown in the drawings provided with both the case and the power supply.

Mount the Motherboard

Using the screws provided, attach the motherboard (Figure 7–2) to the case. Remember that the multipin slots should be positioned toward the back of the case.

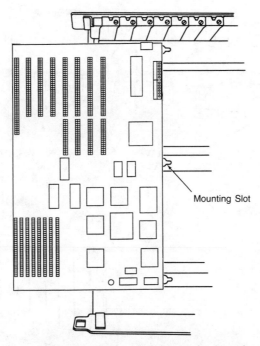

Mounting Slot

Figure 7–2. Install the motherboard.

Mount the Disk Drives and Controller Card

Install the floppy-disk drives on their rails in the open bay. Mount the hard drive on its rails immediately to the left of the floppy drives.

Remove the metal cover behind the slot closest to the disk drives. Save the cover for future use, and retain the screw. Insert the controller card into the slot closest to the disk drives. Be certain to insert the card with a rocking motion until it is well seated. Fasten the metal tab with the screw that you retained.

Install the Video Card and Monitor

Remove the metal cover behind the slot adjacent to the controller card. Save the cover for future use, and retain the screw. Plug the video card into the slot adjacent to the one containing the controller card (Figure 7–3). Be certain to insert the card with a rocking motion until it is well seated. Fasten the metal tab with the screw you retained. Plug the monitor video connector into the receptacle provided on the back of the video card. Plug the power cord for the monitor into the receptacle provided on the back of the power supply. Be certain to check to see that the receptacle can handle the power requirement of your monitor.

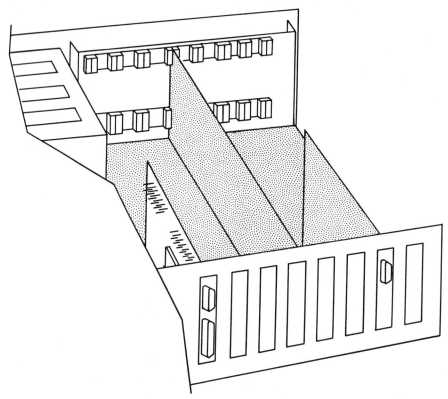

Figure 7–3.   Install the display-adapter card.

Install the Multifunction I/O Card

Remove the metal cover behind the slot adjacent to the video card. Save the cover for future use, and retain the screw. Plug the I/O card into the slot adjacent to the video card. Be certain to insert the card with a rocking motion until it is well seated. Fasten the metal tab with the screw you retained.

Install Additional Memory

Do not touch the pins of the memory modules. Using great care, insert the 1-megabyte SIMMs (Figure 7–4) into the locations shown in the drawing accompanying the motherboard. Notice that the SIMMs are installed in groups called *banks*.

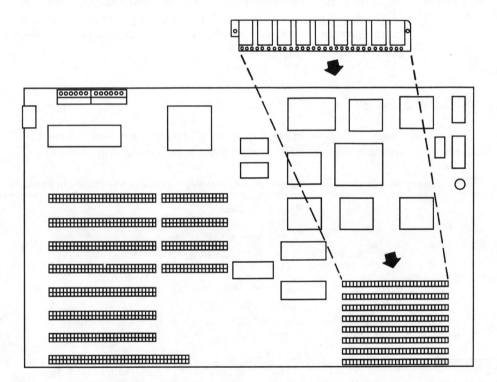

Figure 7–4.   Install the memory modules.

Hook Up the Printer

Connect the printer cable to the parallel receptacle provided on the I/O board and to the receptacle with spring clips on the back of the printer. Plug the printer power cord into a source of 120 volts AC (alternating current).

Install the Keyboard

Plug the keyboard into the outlet provided at the back of the system unit.

Check It All One More Time

Review all your connections. Make sure that all the boards are seated well. Using gentle pressure, check to see that the SIMMs are securely in their sockets.

Try It Out

Go through the testing procedures detailed in Chapter 6.

Run some benchmarks of your own. Test your new system by running software that you normally use. Time how long it takes to perform some time-consuming operations on the old and new systems. Is the new system faster than PCs you've been using?

Example Systems

Table 7–1 shows the cheapest 80286-based system with a hard-disk drive that we can assemble from the Jameco Electronics catalog for 1990.

Table 7–1.   Component List, Inexpensive 80286 Upgrade

Part No.	Description	Cost
JE3005	8/12-MHz 80286 Motherboard	$199.95
41256-100	18 ea., 100-ns 256K × 1 RAM chips (512K RAM)	$71.10
JE2019	Flip-Top Baby AT Case	$69.95
JE1032	200-Watt Power Supply	$89.95
JE1016	84-Key Keyboard	$59.95
JE1022	5.25″ 1.2-Mbyte Floppy-Disk Drive	$99.95
JE1065	I/O Card for AT	$59.95
M8425A	Miniscribe 20-Mbyte 3.5″ Half-Height Hard-Disk Drive, 68-ms avg. access time with 5.25″ mounting hardware	$339.95
AMBER	Casper 12″ Amber Monochrome Monitor	$99.95
JE1050	Monochrome Text/Graphics Card	$59.95
SP2000	9-Pin IBM Compatible Printer	$199.95
	TOTAL SYSTEM PRICE	$1350.60

Table 7–2 shows a high-performance 80386-based system we assembled from the Jameco Electronics catalog for 1990 and the Jade Computer Winter 1989/90 sale flier. We chose to use the Jade sale flier because the Jameco catalog didn't have any laser printers. We elected to go with a bottom-of-the-line laser printer (4 pages per minute) to hold down the total system price.

Table 7–2.   Component List, High-Performance 80386 Upgrade

Part No.	Description	Cost
JE3028	AMI 33-MHz 386 Full Size Motherboard	$2599.95
421000A9A-70	1 ea. 1-MByte SIP Module (1 Mbyte RAM)	$189.95
421000A9B-70	7 ea. 1-MByte SIMM Module (7 Mbyte RAM)	$1329.65
80387-33	Intel 33-MHz Math Coprocessor	$649.95
JE2011	Vertical Case With 300-Watt Power Supply	$279.95
JE1016	101-Key Enhanced Keyboard	$69.95
JE1022	5.25″ 1.2-Mbyte Floppy-Disk Drive	$99.95
MF355B	Mitsubishi 1.44-Mbyte 3.5″ Floppy-Disk Drive	$119.95
JE1077	Multi I/O With Floppy Controller	$69.95
M9380E	Miniscribe 330-Mbyte Full-Height Hard-Disk Drive	$1699.95
JE2041	ESDI Hard- & Floppy-Disk Controller Card	$169.95
M9070S	Nanao 16″ Multiscan Color Monitor	$1099.95
GC1501	Orchid Technology 8/16-Bit VGA Card	$299.95
9600E	Prometheus 9600/4800/2400/1200-Baud Modem	$749.95
FAX96	Niche Tek 9600-Baud Fax Board	$349.95
The following items are from the Jade Computer sale flier.		
Page 12	Hewlett-Packard LaserJet IIP	$1098.00
Page 12	Extra Toner, 1 ea.	$88.00
Page 12	250-Sheet Bottom Cassette	$178.00
Page 12	Legal Tray	$78.00
Page 12	Envelope Tray	$88.00
Page 12	2 ea. 1-Mbyte RAM Card	$796.00
	TOTAL SYSTEM PRICE	$12104.95

Chapter 8

Upgrade Strategies

Every upgrade has a strategy. That is quite an assertion, and it probably comes as a surprise to you. You thought you just wanted to make your PC work better, faster, smarter—whatever. Why are we talking about strategies?

Well, it works a bit like this. Let's consider an analogy to travelling. When you travel, you have to know where you want to go. Knowing where you want to go is important, but you also have to decide how you're going to get there. Are you going to drive a car, ride the bus, take a plane, or maybe just walk? It all depends, right?

It depends on how far you have to go, how quickly you have to get there, and how much money you have to spend. When you make the decisions about how long, how much, and what travel mode, you're plotting strategy to reach your destination.

Upgrading your PC probably doesn't feel that straightforward. You've been making travel decisions for years. They're easy. Mapping out a PC-upgrade strategy takes the same kinds of steps you do almost intuitively for travelling. Obviously, the first step is to state where you want to go. It can be technical: I want the fastest central processing unit (CPU) I can get with a math coprocessor and an enhanced-small-device-interface (ESDI), 90-megabyte hard drive. Or it could be functional: I want a computer that'll sort my mailing lists faster.

Goals set? Great! Next you have to decide how much you're willing to spend. Set a maximum and a minimum. You understand the max, right? Don't spend more than you can afford. Why the minimum? That's your opinion about what it'll take to put your system together. If you come in below the min, give yourself a treat. Buy an extra piece for your system—hardware, software, you name it. It doesn't matter. You've done a super shopping job, and you deserve a treat.

Now let's move on to how you'll make it. There are lots of ways to get there. A couple of very broad-stroke options are mix-and-match versus single-source and all-at-once versus incremental.

The first option is a compatibility issue. How can you be assured that all the components you buy will work together in your system? The second option concerns urgency. Must the upgrade be done immediately? Can the expenditure occur now? Do potential technology improvements and price decreases argue for incremental improvements?

We'll go over these topics with you as well as suggestions for what to do with old but working components.

Goal Setting

Goal setting is an extremely important part of your upgrade strategy. Unless you know what you want to accomplish, you are likely to have problems. You can end up spending much more than necessary because you are buying components you don't need. Or you can find that your PC won't do what you need because you haven't upgraded to the right level.

Your best bet is to set a functional goal. This should be in the form of one or more statements about how you want your PC to operate. Since your PC can't work without software, your functional goals will affect both hardware and software decisions. Here are some example functional goals:

1. Calculate spreadsheets at least ten times faster.
2. Display graphics.
3. Print high-quality letters lots faster.
4. Communicate with the home-office computer at 9600 baud.
5. Send and receive fax messages.
6. Spend less time waiting for XYZ program to execute.
7. Stop video-monitor (CRT) blinking.
8. Make disk I/O at least 100 times faster.
9. Store more data for immediate access.
10. Get rid of squishy-feeling keyboard.
11. Read and write to 5.25- and 3.5-inch floppy diskettes.

Some of these functional goals can lead to specific system decisions much more easily than others. Let's look at the stated goals in more detail.

1. Calculate spreadsheets at least ten times faster. This functional goal looks clearly stated, but the technical details are fuzzy. If the intention is to make the entire spreadsheet process ten times faster, then the objective may be achievable. A good deal depends on the current hardware and software configuration. Certainly, if your current PC is a 4.77-MHz IBM PC, XT, or clone, you could upgrade to a 20-MHz 80286 CPU for the raw processing

power to achieve your goal. If your PC spends a good deal of time doing disk accesses (reading data) during your spreadsheet work, then you will have to consider improving data-transfer speeds to reach your objective.

2. Display graphics. This is a clear statement that can be implemented. This requires a video-display board capable of displaying graphics (mono-chrome or color), a monitor compatible with the video-display board, and software capable of generating graphics.

3. Print high-quality letters lots faster. This goal is difficult to reach because it isn't clear. How much faster is fast enough? As noted earlier, much depends on where you are now. If you have a dot-matrix printer that produces near-letter quality (NLQ) documents at less than 50 characters per second (cps), an upgrade to a printer able to generate NLQ in excess of 150 cps will seem faster. Will it seem lots faster? That's hard to say. It is a subjective call. Maybe you need to move up to a laser printer. The slowest of these prints at about four pages per minute (roughly 166 cps). When you state your goals, try to be as quantitative as possible.

4. Communicate with the home-office computer at 9600 baud. Here's an objective that is clearly stated and probably achievable. Certainly, 9600-baud modems can be purchased. Of course, you do have to have modems able to operate at 9600 baud at both ends of the line.

5. Send and receive fax messages. This objective is well stated but not perfect. There are fax boards that operate at either 4800 or 9600 baud. Your objective should specify the data transmission and reception speed.

6. Spend less time waiting for XYZ program to execute. This is definitely a desirable goal, but it doesn't give you very much information. This could be broken into two or more objectives. For example:

   A. Increase CPU computational speed by a factor of two.

   B. Install math coprocessor compatible with new CPU.

   C. Increase disk data-transfer rate by a factor of two.

   Now the objectives—A, B, and C—are clearly stated. It may be that you can't reach them. If you already are using a 33-MHz 80386 CPU, you may have to wait awhile before there is a CPU that can double your computa-tional speed. Objective B is clearly stated and can be implemented without significant problems other than cost. If you are using a hard disk with an MFM controller, you can accomplish objective C by installing an ESDI controller and compatible hard-disk drive.

7. Stop video-monitor (CRT) blinking. Blinking CRTs are characteristic of IBM PCs and 100% compatible clones. The transition to ATs eliminated the video-board speed problems. The objective is clearly stated, but here is a case where a software change can eliminate a hardware problem. Installing an ANSI.SYS file with appropriate driver software could solve your problem.

8. Make disk I/O at least 100 times faster. This is a clearly stated functional objective, but it looks like a wild dream. It's always possible to state objectives that can't be achieved today. This one is not in that category. Reviewers in several recent computer magazines have tested ESDI drives with RAM cache controllers. The disk I/O was found to be at least 2000 percent faster than MFM drives with 1:1 interleave.

9. Store more data for immediate access. This is a well stated functional specification. It could be implemented by installing high-density floppy-diskette drives if you have double- or single-density drives. You could also install an additional hard-disk drive if you have only one. Or you could install a larger hard-disk drive to replace the current one.

10. Get rid of squishy-feeling keyboard. This functional objective may mean something to you, but it is very difficult to communicate to another person. It's difficult to get others to agree on keyboard feel. Still, you can achieve this objective. You will have to test keyboards in person. You can't farm this acquisition out to someone else.

11. Read and write to 5.25- and 3.5-inch floppy diskettes. Here's an understandable functional objective. In fact, you could say that it's a technical objective. Or is it? Do you need high-density drives (1.2 megabytes and 1.44 megabytes, respectively), or will double density (360 kilobytes and 720 kilobytes, respectively) suffice? Be as specific as possible. It will make it easier for you to find and install the right components.

The message should be clear to you: State your functional objectives with as much detail as possible. If you have trouble translating a very broad-stroke functional requirement into specific system changes, look around for help.

Where to Find Help

Where do you go to get help? Clearly, you can get help from the examples we present. We cannot address all the possible PC configurations and modifications that can be made to them. We will try to help you find the right sources to assist you in converting your functional requirements into technical specifications.

Magazines

The major computer magazines contain product reviews. In the reviews, there are often tables of performance data that can assist you. To be able to get a great deal of benefit from such sources, you must have a fairly good idea about what components you need to replace or add. Included in the list of magazines are *Computer Shopper, PC Magazine, PC Resources, PC Computing, Family Computing, PC World, Byte, Computer Buyers Guide,* and *Personal Computing.*

Examining the tables of contents of back issues of any or all of these sources will provide you with a quick and reasonably comprehensive overview of the kinds of technical data available.

SIGs

Special interest groups (SIGs) have grown up in most of the major cities around the country. The purpose of such groups is sharing information. Many of these groups have restricted themselves to IBM-compatible PCs and activities affecting PCs. These people can be a great source of practical advice. Many of them have upgraded their own systems. They can share real-life horror and success stories.

You can usually locate your nearest SIG through local computer retailers. Retailers often have the club meeting schedule posted in their stores. The SIG members buy lots of computers and equipment, so the stores usually try to stay on good terms with them. If you can't find a meeting schedule, ask the clerk or manager about the local SIG. If they don't know, try at another store.

People You Know

People you know at work or elsewhere are another good source of information. It's quite likely that you could arrange to be the recipient of some computer anecdotes. You'll have to separate the fiction from the facts—the editorializing from the reporting—but you'll find enough information about systems that work well and, equally as important, systems that don't work to make the time spent worthwhile.

You probably know at least one person either at work or away from your job who has bumped into a problem similar to if not the same as the one puzzling you. Unfortunately, no one goes around wearing a T-shirt proclaiming, "I CAN HELP SOLVE YOUR PROBLEMS." You will have to ask enough questions to identify your expert. It's possible that others will point out the expert to you. Or you may have to stumble around until you locate one yourself. Once you've cornered an expert, spend as much time as you can collecting information. Keep up the acquaintance. You may want to talk again as your project moves along.

Technical Departments

The technical departments of the major computer stores usually have very competent staffs. These people can advise you about ways to accomplish your goals by using the products their company sells. Some of the staff may have worked for other companies as well and therefore may have a broad knowledge base. Talk to them. Extract as much specific and generic information as possible. Do not make decisions based on recommendations from a single source. When assembling a PC system, second and even third opinions are necessary.

The larger mail-order houses also maintain technical advisers. Mail-order houses where you can expect to find excellent advice and advisors include CompuAdd Corporation, Austin, TX; Northgate Computer Systems, Plymouth, MN; Dell Computer Corporation, Austin, TX; Tussey Computer Products, State College, PA; and Zeos International, St. Paul, MN. This expertise is just a telephone call away. Use it.

Technical Requirements

You must be careful to consider the ramifications your proposed changes can have on other components. For example, if you're planning to install a hard disk in a floppy-only system, you probably need a new power supply. If your power supply isn't up to the task, your PC won't work properly. For instance, it might not be able to get your hard drives up to normal operating speed.

Check the papers that came with your PC to determine the wattage rating of the power supply. If you can't find the information, you'll need to get it from the plate that's attached to the power supply itself. To do that, you will have to open the system case.

Be certain to open the case only after having read Appendix C. Shut off and disconnect all peripherals, switch off the power, and unplug the power cord. Open the case, and find the wattage rating on the power-supply information plate (Figure 8–1). Close the system box, plug in the power cord, connect all peripherals, switch on the peripherals, and switch on the main power.

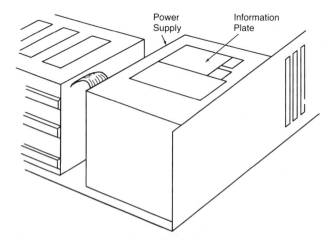

Figure 8–1.   Power-supply information plate.

If the original power supply is rated for less than 150 watts, you need a new supply. A 200-watt power supply is sufficient under normal circumstances for at least two floppy-diskette drives, two hard-disk drives, the normal complement of plug-in boards, and the motherboard.

If you are upgrading to a system with lots of memory and data storage, you may need a 250- or 300-watt supply. Check the power requirements for each of the devices you intend to have in your system, not just the new components. For instance, large hard disk drives have more mass (several platters) to move and therefore require more power to start and keep them rotating than does a small hard-disk drive of 20 to 40 megabytes capacity. The power-supply rating must exceed the sum of the ratings of the components in your system. A good safe operating margin is 40%; i.e., keep the power-supply power rating at least 40% more than the sum of the ratings for all the components in your system.

Now that you've translated your functional objectives into technical requirements, you are ready to move on to the next stage of your PC upgrade.

Spending Limits

You've developed a set of functional requirements for your system, and now it's time to figure out how to pay for it all. The first thing you should do is grab one or two catalogs and write down the prices of all the components you'll need to build the system you've specified. Get as many prices as you can from both catalogs. When you can't match components exactly, use a reasonable substitute.

Once you've gotten total prices from two sources for your upgraded system, you need to consider very carefully any questions the prices may raise. For example, one very good question is, "Can I afford this upgrade now?" If you can answer this "Yes," then go for it. Otherwise, you are faced with some tough decisions:

1. Delay until all the money is available.
2. Upgrade incrementally.
   A. Components to add now.
   B. Components to add later.
3. Adjust the upgrade to stay within available funds.

One possible alternative, if the total estimated cost is within 20% of your budgeted amount, is to do an extensive search to find the components at lower prices elsewhere. Numerous suppliers advertise in the magazines we mentioned above. With judicious shopping, you can probably shave up to 20% from your original price estimate.

As with all budget shopping decisions, you must worry about the integrity and longevity of your supplier. Will they replace components that fail during the warranty period? Will they stay in business long enough to honor the warranty?

We'll discuss these and other budget-related issues in Chapter 9. For now, you should consider the upgrade costs to be justifiable and appropriate if the parts you need to meet your functional objectives can be purchased with the funds you have available.

Pick Your Parts

Aside from concerns about price, availability, and supplier integrity, compatibility is a major concern for you as the one responsible for the system upgrade. How can you ensure that parts you buy will be compatible, i.e., work together? Two obvious strategies are:

1. Buy your components from a single supplier.
2. Buy only compatible components from as many suppliers as you need to perform the upgrade.

Getting your upgrade components from one supplier sounds like a good way to assure compatibility. Sometimes it works, but it doesn't address compatibility with components already in your PC. You have to be certain that you won't be making a serious blunder like expecting boards designed for the 4.77-MHz 8-bit PC data bus to operate properly on the 8-MHz 16-bit AT data bus.

Fortunately, there are industry standards. All manufacturers don't necessarily adhere to the standards, but most do. The major departures involve serial communications devices and the RS-232C standard. Unfortunately, this standard leaves a good deal of the implementation to the discretion of the manufacturer. This produces a situation where you, the buyer, have to assure yourself that your serial devices are using the same lines for each function. Never buy a serial device without getting a list or drawing of the *pinout*. The pinout details the signals present on each of the pins in the connector.

Aside from the stated problems with serial communications devices, there is no great impetus for you to get your components from a single supplier. This is especially true if the supplier carries several product lines.

Get the components from whomever has them at a price you can afford. This strategy is followed by most PC manufacturers for the products that go into their systems. You can use it to your advantage as well.

Present Needs

You know the urgency of the upgrades better than anyone else. If you can't get your inventory run because it's too big to fit on a single 360-kilobyte diskette, you have an immediate need for an upgrade. Or maybe you are trying to set up a real-time data base application and your PC is too slow—I/O-bound. In situations such as these, cost should not be a major concern. Timing is the issue. You need to get the upgrades done as quickly as possible so that the PC can be used for its intended purpose.

Benefit-to-Size Ratio

The size (cost) of an upgrade doesn't determine the usefulness of the upgrade. For somewhere in the neighborhood of $12,000, you can put together a 33-MHz 80386 system with a 330-megabyte ESDI hard drive. (See the example in Chapter 7.) A system like that is outrageously fast, but for data-base applications where the work is I/O-bound, the blinding speed of the CPU is irrelevant.

You can get better performance by upgrading to a 16-MHz 80286 CPU with 2 megabytes of RAM, a 330-megabyte ESDI drive (if you need one that large), and a disk-caching ESDI controller with 4 megabytes of RAM. The upgrade will cost under $3400 (assuming you already have a slower 80286 system), a whole lot less than the cost of the new system. You get extremely fast I/O from the disk-caching controller.

This controller complete with RAM and an ESDI hard drive can improve the performance of your system by at least 2000%. Certainly an upgrade that cuts the amount of time you have to wait for your hard drive by 2000% is extremely useful. This is clearly a better path for you if you hear your hard drive working very often. In addition, it costs less than the make over to the super hot-dog 80386 system.

Cost Control

Everyone needs to keep costs under control. This includes purchases relating to PCs and PC upgrades. You can help with this rather large task by weighing carefully your options. You can shoot for a top-of-the-line system, or you can get a system that will address your specific problems. Sometimes the top-of the-line system is the only one that can do the job; frequently it is too costly.

Consider getting a system that is one or two steps down from the very top. The very best in technology usually carries a very hefty price tag. Consider the following prices for motherboards taken from the 1990 Jameco Electronics catalog:

AMI 16-MHz '386 Baby Motherboard, $999.95

AMI 20-MHz '386 Baby Motherboard, $1199.95

AMI 25-MHz '386 Full-Size Motherboard, $1899.95

AMI 33-MHz '386 Full-Size Motherboard, $2599.95

For most applications, the 20-MHz '386 is more than adequate. As you can see, it is available for $1400 less than the top-of the-line 33-MHz model. If you insist on having more number crunching ability, the 25-MHz model will save you $700 over the cost of the 33-MHz unit.

Another avenue for savings is provided by the house brands carried by a number of the mail-order suppliers. Some of these items are available for very deep discounts during special promotional events. Keep your eyes open for bargains. Get on as many computer mailing lists as possible. Once you're on a few, the others will find you. Not all low-price components are a good deal, but those that represent very well established technologies such as 2400-baud modems are likely to be good investments. We have purchased components through promotional deals, and we haven't been burned.

Users

When you are busily establishing your current PC needs, it is extremely important that you consider how many people may be using the PC or PCs that you are upgrading. There are two questions that you should consider for each PC that is used by more than one person:

1. Is the percentage use about equal; i.e., is there a dominant user?
2. Do all users have the same level of computer expertise?

Your PC upgrade should be designed with the needs of the dominant user in mind. If that user is an entry-level secretary, there is no reason to make the system be a supercharged speed demon. It's likely that the majority of its tasks will be word processing. Even if an occasional user of that PC has a real need for flat-out speed, don't acquiesce. Let that user find a different system to use.

When you're planning this upgrade, keep the experience of the users in mind. The new user may have no idea how fast the computer is. There is very little difference between the slowest and fastest PCs when you first sit in front of them. They all have a monitor and a case. Without looking inside the case or being knowledgeable about model numbers, you can't easily tell the slow ones from the fast ones.

There is no useful purpose served by giving a rank novice a super-fast PC. There is too much money tied up in such a machine to fritter it away by constraining the machine to do word processing or small-time data-base management. If you are going to upgrade an 8088 (IBM PC, XT, or clone) computer for a novice to use, the best bet would be to set it up as a 12-MHz 80286 machine (use a baby motherboard), include a 40-megabyte hard drive, and upgrade the power supply to 200 watts. That is a very reasonable minimum configuration on which to do word processing and data-base management.

Expectations

Part of the strategy you have to develop relates to future use of any PCs you're upgrading. Try to project what kinds of work may be expected from the PC and its users one or two years from now. You are very likely planning the current upgrade for present and very near-term activities. Stretch your thinking as best you can. Your credibility won't be very high if you have to start talking about another upgrade shortly after you finish this one.

This is probably one of the hardest parts of your upgrade strategy. Ask for help. There's no shame in admitting that you don't know everything about what may happen in the future. Check with current users. Maybe they've heard about big changes in direction. Also be certain to check with management as high up as you can go. In most organizations, the closer you get to the top, the more knowledgeable the individuals are about long-range plans. They may not be willing to divulge any information, but at least you will have tried.

Analyze carefully any information you can glean. When you receive conflicting reports, think about them for awhile to see if there is any common ground that you can use for making decisions. Obviously, if one report says that you're going to close up shop in 12 months and another says that you'll be swamped with new work, there's little common ground. Weigh the relative reliability of your sources, and then be a bit more pessimistic than the most optimistic report you can trust.

If your best projection says that you will need ten new clerk typists within 18 months, you had better plan to have PCs available for them. If you have enough old 8088 machines that you can upgrade to 80286s, go for it. With that much lead time, you can set up a schedule to have four PCs upgraded every six months. Or you may want to do six or seven at once and then wait 10 or 12 months before upgrading the rest.

A much tougher problem would be if your reliable sources tell you that your company is likely to get a major new contract that will require six new engineers for the next 18 months. Engineers typically will want or think they need speed-demon PCs. They are, as a group, computer literate and rather knowledgeable about speed ratings.

Problems arise for you because they will be spending a fairly large portion of their time writing reports about their work. They clearly do not need a 33-MHz 80386- or 80486-based PC to do word processing. You may want to consider having six older PCs upgraded to word-processing status (16-MHz 80286 CPU and a 40 megabyte hard drive) for each of them so you won't have to hear complaints about not enough PCs when reports are due.

Upgrade only two or three PCs to macho status. No one does computations all the time. Set up shared resources. You certainly don't want to put lots of bucks into upgrades for PCs that may not be used two years from now.

Do the best you can to anticipate changes in directions for computer use. You can't be right all the time. However, you'll be much more valuable to your organization if you plan for changes rather than waiting until they are on top of you before you do something. In the parlance of the bureaucrats, be proactive rather than reactive.

While you're doing your strategic planning, don't lose sight of emerging computer-use trends at other organizations. Suppose you are suddenly called upon to set up a PC for desktop publishing, or maybe your boss wants to install expert-adviser software for the order clerks. Are you ready with the right recommendations for hardware and software upgrades?

There is someone we haven't developed an upgrade strategy for in this planning process—you. There are pieces of software that can help you do your job better. You should investigate scheduling and time-management software for your own use. When you have to follow the progress of several upgrades at one time, scheduling software can be a big asset if you'll take the time to use it. It'll show you where difficulties are in a very logical, detailed fashion. Most PC packages will run on 8088 machines, but they'll do better on 80286 or 80386 machines with quick hard-disk drives.

Packages to consider include Agenda from Lotus Development, InstaPlan w/PERT from InstaPlan, Project Scheduler 4 from Scitor, Time$heet Professional from Software Partners, and Timeline from Symantec.

Leftovers

There are always leftovers. Whether it's from the Thanksgiving turkey or a PC upgrade, you have to decide the fate of materials that weren't used. Normally, you can do better than putting the leftovers in the trash. If nothing else, try to find a needy recipient.

Fall-Back

You should never, never get rid of the parts you removed from an upgraded PC until it has been working properly for a few weeks. Most components that are going to have a significantly shortened lifetime will fail during the first six weeks of daily operation (extend the period for intermittent operation). If you've retained the parts you removed, you have a fall-back position. You can replace them and have a functioning PC again. Admittedly, it may not be quite as good as you have come to appreciate, but at least it will work while you are trying to get replacements for the failed parts.

If you are not horribly cramped for space, keeping leftover parts for at least one year is a reasonable practice. It may happen that the parts can be used in a machine that hasn't been upgraded, or you may find that they will work in a different upgraded machine to bring that PC back to life. This fall-back position can work for you because PCs use lots of interchangeable components.

Do be very careful about trading memory chips back and forth. Be certain that you have chips all of one speed and storage capacity. On very old IBM PCs and XTs, the memory chips had odd storage capacities by today's standards. With these machines, it's wise to replace the entire motherboard rather than worrying about individual chips.

Good Riddance

Once you've kept the old parts as long as possible, it's time to determine what you'll do with them. There are some options that you may want to consider before you consign them to the garbage dump. Options available to you include:

1. Exchanging them for parts you may be able to use or selling them through a local PC-SIG.
2. Selling them through a local dealer who is willing to deal with used parts on consignment.
3. Checking through the want ads in computer magazines to find suitable recipients.

Through one or more of these avenues, you may be able to convert your leftovers into cash or components you can use. Remember, one man's garbage is another man's treasure. Don't just scrap your old components. Try to find them a home. You can get more out of it than just a warm, happy feeling.

Examples

Let's consider some upgrade examples targeted for specific applications. This does not mean that other uses of any of the suggested configurations wouldn't be appropriate. These are our suggestions for systems that should adequately address the tasks as we understand them.

With any of these examples, it would certainly be possible to implement the upgrade in an incremental fashion. If a power supply upgrade is recommended, it should be the first item installed in an incremental upgrade. This will prevent inadvertent overloading of the old power supply at some point during the upgrade.

We'll specify the upgrades by the CPU that's being replaced, the new CPU, and the suggested use we think the system will satisfy. We'll take prices and catalog numbers from the Jameco Electronics 1990 catalog, unless otherwise noted; some of the example hard-disk subsystems are from CompuAdd, for example.

Note that we have used dozens of mail-order companies over the years with excellent results. We are not recommending one over another in this book. We have, however, limited our real-life examples to a few companies to make comparisons, price changes, and configurations easier to track. In the back of this book, you'll find a comprehensive list of mail-order firms and an annotated list of products. Use this for research as you work on upgrade configurations.

Upgrade 1: 8088 to 80286 for Word Processing

We assume that the current PC is a floppy-diskette-based IBM PC or clone with a monochrome monitor and graphics adapter, a serial port, and a separate parallel port. Such a machine is likely to have a 150-watt or smaller power supply. We recommend upgrading to a 200-watt power supply to support the hard-disk drive(s). A suggested component list is given in Table 8–1.

Table 8–1.   Component List for Upgrade 1

Part No.	Description	Cost
JE3010	16-MHz Motherboard (XT Footprint)	$299.95
JE1032	200-Watt Power Supply	$89.95
41256-100	36 ea., 100-ns 256K × 1 RAM Chips (1 Mbyte RAM)	$142.20
	As noted in the text, the following I/O card is optional.	
JE1065	I/O Card for AT	$59.95
356KU	Toshiba 3.5″ 1.44-Mbyte Internal Floppy-Disk Drive	$109.95
FD55G	Teac 5.25″ 1.2-Mbyte Internal Floppy-Disk Drive	$119.95
1006VMM2	16-bit MFM 286/386 Hard-Disk Controller (Supports 1:1 Interleave)	$169.95
47207	Seagate 40-Mbyte (28-ms) Half-Height Hard Drive (CompuAdd)	$399.00
JE1016	101-Key Enhanced Keyboard	$69.95
	TOTAL PRICE (including I/O card)	$1460.85

If the serial and parallel port are on a single I/O board, you don't need to replace it. We suggest retaining the monochrome monitor. It can be replaced at a later time. If you decide to replace it, we suggest that you go with VGA because CGA and EGA produce characters that are difficult to look at for extended periods (especially CGA).

We suggest the 16-MHz 80286 rather than the 12-MHz version because this is the lowest CPU speed that benefits appreciably from 1:1 interleave (this allows much faster track-to-track searches). In addition, the 16-MHz version will not have to be replaced if the user moves on to data-base or spreadsheet work.

Upgrade 2: 8088 to 80286 for Spreadsheets and Accounting (Small to Medium)

We assume that the current PC is a hard-disk (10-megabyte) based IBM PC/XT or clone with a monochrome monitor and graphics adapter, a serial port, and a separate parallel port. Suggested components for the upgrade are listed in Table 8–2.

Table 8–2. Component List for Upgrade 2

Part No.	Description	Cost
JE3010	16-MHz Motherboard (XT Footprint)	$299.95
JE1032	200-Watt Power Supply	$89.95
51100P-10	18 ea., 100-ns 1 Mbyte × 1 RAM Chips (2 Mbytes RAM)	$233.10
	As noted in the text, the following I/O card is optional.	
JE1065	I/O Card for AT	$59.95
356KU	Toshiba 3.5″ 1.44-Mbyte Internal Floppy-Disk Drive	$109.95
FD55G	Teac 5.25″ 1.2-Mbyte Internal Floppy-Disk Drive	$119.95
1006VMM2	16-bit MFM 286/386 Hard-Disk Controller (Supports 1:1 Interleave)	$169.95
47207	2 ea., Seagate 40-Mbyte (28-ms) Half-Height Hard Drive (CompuAdd)	$798.00
JE1016		$69.95
	101-Key Enhanced Keyboard	
	TOTAL PRICE (Including I/O Card)	$1950.75

Such a machine is likely to have a 150-watt power supply. We recommend upgrading to a 200-watt power supply to support larger hard-disk drive(s). If the serial and parallel port are on a single I/O board, you don't need to replace it. We suggest retaining the monochrome monitor. It can be replaced at a later time. If you decide to replace it, we suggest that you go with VGA because CGA and EGA produce characters that are difficult to look at for extended periods (especially CGA).

We suggest the 16-MHz 80286 rather than the 12-MHz version because this is the lowest CPU speed that benefits appreciably from 1:1 interleave (this allows much faster track-to-track searches). Applications such as spreadsheets and data-base work that are typically I/O-bound benefit from the faster disk searches. In addition, the 16-MHz CPU will not have to be replaced if the user moves on to data-base or bigger spreadsheet work. You'll only need to upgrade memory, hard drives, and the hard-drive controller.

Upgrade 3: 8088 to 80286 Data-Base Management (Small)

We assume that the current PC is a hard-disk (10-megabyte) based IBM PC/XT or clone with a color monitor with color graphics adapter (CGA), a serial port, and a separate parallel port. Such a machine is likely to have a 150-watt power supply. We recommend upgrading to a 200-watt power supply to support larger hard-disk drive(s). Table 8–3 lists suggested components for this upgrade.

Table 8–3.   Components for Upgrade 3

Part No.	Description	Cost
JE3010	16-MHz Motherboard (XT Footprint)	$299.95
JE1032	200-Watt Power Supply	$89.95
51100P-10	36 ea., 100-ns 1 Mbyte × 1 RAM Chips (4 Mbytes RAM)	$466.20
	As noted in the text, the following I/O card is optional.	
JE1065	I/O Card for AT	$59.95
356KU	Toshiba 3.5" 1.44-Mbyte Internal Floppy-Disk Drive	$109.95
FD55G	Teac 5.25" 1.2-Mbyte Internal Floppy-Disk Drive	$119.95
1006VMM2	16-bit MFM 286/386 Hard-Disk Controller (Supports 1:1 Interleave)	$169.95
M3085	2 ea., Miniscribe 70-Mbyte (20-ms) Half-Height Hard Drive	$1199.90
JE1016	101-Key Enhanced Keyboard	$69.95
TM5156	Casper 14" VGA Monitor	$399.95
JE1057	8/16-Bit VGA Card	$249.95
	TOTAL PRICE (Including I/O Card)	$3235.65

If the serial and parallel port are on a single I/O board, you don't need to replace it. We suggest scrapping the CGA adapter and color monitor because CGA characters are particularly difficult to read for extended periods. We suggest that you replace them with a 14-inch high-resolution color monitor and a VGA card.

We suggest the 16-MHz 80286 rather than the 12-MHz version because this is the lowest CPU speed that benefits appreciably from 1:1 interleave (this allows much faster track-to-track searches). Applications such as spreadsheets and data-base work that are typically I/O-bound benefit from the faster disk searches. In addition, the 16-MHz CPU will not have to be replaced if the user moves on to bigger data-base work. You'll only need to upgrade hard drives and possibly the hard-drive controller.

Upgrade 4: 8088 to 80286 Data-Base Management (Medium)

We assume that the current PC is a hard-disk (10-megabyte) based IBM PC/XT or clone with a color monitor and color graphics adapter (CGA), a serial port, and a separate parallel port. Suggested components for this upgrade are listed in Table 8–4.

Table 8–4. Components for Upgrade 4

Part No.	Description	Cost
JE3010	16-MHz Motherboard (XT Footprint)	$299.95
JE1032	200-Watt Power Supply	$89.95
51100P-10	36 ea., 100-ns 1 Mbyte × 1 RAM chips (4 Mbytes RAM)	$466.20
	As noted in the text, the following I/O card is optional.	
JE1065	I/O Card for AT	$59.95
356KU	Toshiba 3.5" 1.44-Mbyte Internal Floppy-Disk Drive	$109.95
FD55G	Teac 5.25" 1.2-Mbyte Internal Floppy-Disk Drive	$119.95
JE2041	ESDI Hard & Floppy Controller Card	$169.95
M3180E	2 ea., Miniscribe 150-Mbyte (17-ms) Half-Height Hard Drive	$2399.90
JE1016	101-Key Enhanced Keyboard	$69.95
TM5156	Casper 14" VGA Monitor	$399.95
JE1057	Jameco 8/16-Bit VGA Card	$249.95
	TOTAL PRICE (Including I/O Card)	$4435.65

Such a machine is likely to have a 150-watt power supply. We recommend upgrading to a 200-watt power supply to support larger hard-disk drive(s). If the serial and parallel port are on a single I/O board, you don't need to replace it. We suggest scrapping the CGA adapter and color monitor because CGA characters are particularly difficult to read for extended periods. We suggest that you replace them with a 14-inch high resolution color monitor and a VGA card.

We suggest the 16-MHz 80286 rather than the 12-MHz version because it is able to keep up with the very rapid (10 megabits/second) data-transfer rate of the ESDI hard drive. Applications such as spreadsheets and data-base work that are typically I/O-bound benefit substantially from the faster data transfer rate and disk searches. In addition, the 16-MHz CPU will not have to be replaced if the user moves on to bigger data base work. You'll only need to upgrade memory and the hard-drive controller.

Upgrade 5: 8088 to 80286 Data-Base Management (Large)

We assume that the current PC is a hard-disk (40-megabyte) based IBM PC/XT or clone with a color monitor and color graphics adapter (CGA), a serial port, and a separate parallel port. Suggested components for this upgrade are listed in Table 8–5.

Table 8–5.   Components for Upgrade 5

Part No.	Description	Cost
JE3010	16-MHz Motherboard (XT Footprint)	$299.95
JE1032	200-Watt Power Supply	$89.95
51100P-10	36 ea., 100-ns 1 Mbyte × 1 RAM chips (4 Mbytes RAM)	$466.20
421000A9A-10	4 ea., 1 Mbyte × 9 SIP (4 Mbytes RAM) Total memory is 8 Mbytes.	$639.80
	As noted in the text, the following I/O card is optional.	
JE1065	I/O Card for AT	$59.95
356KU	Toshiba 3.5″ 1.44-Mbyte Internal Floppy-Disk Drive	$109.95
FD55G	Teac 5.25″ 1.2-Mbyte Internal Floppy-Disk Drive	$119.95
46510	CompuAdd HardCache/ESDI Controller	$495.00
4210000A9B-10	4 ea., 1 Mbyte × 9 SIMM (4 Mbytes RAM for HardCache)	$639.80
M3180E	2 ea., Miniscribe 150-Mbyte (17-ms) Half-Height Hard Drive	$2399.90
JE1016	101-Key Enhanced Keyboard	$69.95
TM5156	Casper 14″ VGA Monitor	$399.95
JE1057	Jameco 8/16-Bit VGA Card	$249.95
	TOTAL PRICE (Including I/O Card)	$6040.30

Such a machine is likely to have a 150-watt power supply. We recommend upgrading to a 200-watt power supply to support larger hard-disk drive(s). If the serial and parallel port are on a single I/O board, you don't need to replace it. We suggest scrapping the CGA adapter and color monitor because CGA characters are particularly difficult to read for extended periods. We suggest that you replace them with a 14-inch high resolution color monitor and a VGA card. In addition, we suggest that you fully populate memory on the motherboard. This will allow you to work with 6- and 7-megabyte data bases in memory.

We suggest the 16-MHz 80286 rather than the 12-MHz version because it is able to benefit from the very rapid (4 megabytes/second) data-transfer rate of the ESDI hard-drive and cache controller. Applications such as spreadsheets and data base work that are typically I/O-bound benefit to an almost unbelievable extent from the use of the cache controller.

Upgrade 6: 80286 to 80386 for Data-Base Management (Medium)

We assume the present PC is an IBM PC/AT or clone operating at 6, 8, or 10 MHz and equipped with a color monitor and extended graphics adapter (EGA), an I/O board containing both serial and parallel ports, a 5.25-inch 1.2-megabyte floppy-diskette drive, a 30-megabyte MFM hard disk, and a 200-watt power supply.

This machine as configured could handle word processing and light-duty spreadsheet, accounting, and data-base management activities. While not ideal, it can serve in those capacities if you are willing to wait for it. For medium-duty data-base management, the CPU is too slow, and the available high-speed storage is too limited. Our recommendations for an upgrade are shown in Table 8–6.

Table 8–6. Components for Upgrade 6

Part No.	Description	Cost
JE3520	Jameco 20-MHz 386 Baby Motherboard	$649.95
421000A9A-10	4 ea., 1 Mbyte × 9 SIP (1 Mbyte RAM) Total memory is 4 Mbytes.	639.80
356KU	Toshiba 3.5" 1.44-Mbyte Internal Floppy-Disk Drive	$109.95
JE2041	ESDI Hard & Floppy Controller Card	$169.95
M3180E	2 ea., Miniscribe 150-Mbyte (17-ms) Half-Height Hard Drive	$2399.90
JE1016	101-Key Enhanced Keyboard	$69.95
TM5156	Casper 14" VGA Monitor	$399.95
JE1057	8/16-Bit VGA Card	$249.95
	TOTAL PRICE	$4689.40

As configured in the table, this PC can handle most data-base management work with ease. Note that we are not suggesting a mathematics coprocessor. Most spreadsheet and data-base software does not access the coprocessor except for fairly complicated mathematical computations such as trigonometric functions.

Upgrade 7: 80286 to 80386 for Data-Base Management (Large)

We assume the present PC is an IBM PC/AT or clone operating at 6, 8, or 10 MHz and equipped with a color monitor and extended graphics adapter (EGA), an I/O board containing both serial and parallel ports, a 5.25-inch 1.2-megabyte floppy-diskette drive, two 40-megabyte MFM hard disks, and a 200-watt power supply.

This machine as configured could handle word processing and medium-duty spreadsheet, accounting, and data-base management activities. While not ideal, it can serve in those capacities if you are willing to wait for it. For heavy-duty data-base management, the CPU is too slow, and the available high-speed storage is too limited. Our recommendations for an upgrade are shown in Table 8–7.

Table 8–7.   Components for Upgrade 7

Part No.	Description	Cost
JE3525	Jameco 25-MHz 386 Baby Motherboard With 32 kbyte Cache Controller	$1299.95
421000A9A-80	16 ea., 80-ns 1 Mbyte × 9 SIP (1 Mbyte RAM) Total memory is 16 Mbytes.	$2719.20
356KU	Toshiba 3.5″ 1.44-Mbyte Internal Floppy-Disk Drive	$109.95
46510	CompuAdd HardCache/ESDI Controller Card	$495.00
4210000A9B-10	4 ea., 1 Mbyte × 9 SIMM (4 Mbytes RAM for HardCache)	$639.80
M9380E	2 ea., Miniscribe 330-Mbyte (16-ms) Half-Height Hard Drive	$3399.90
JE1016	101-Key Enhanced Keyboard	$69.95
TM5156	Casper 14″ VGA Monitor	$399.95
JE1057	Jameco 8/16-Bit VGA Card	$249.95
	TOTAL PRICE	$9383.65

This upgraded system is almost $3000 less than the very fast system specified in Chapter 7. This system is better prepared to store data because it uses two (rather than one) 330-megabyte hard drives. With 16 megabytes of system RAM, this PC can handle all but the very largest data bases.

Upgrade 8: 80286 to 80386 for Spreadsheets and Accounting (Medium to Large)

We assume the present PC is an IBM PC/AT or clone operating at 6, 8, or 10 MHz and equipped with a color monitor and extended graphics adapter (EGA), an I/O board containing both serial and parallel ports, a 5.25-inch 1.2-megabyte floppy-diskette drive, two 40-megabyte MFM hard disks, and a 200-watt power supply.

This machine as configured could handle word processing and medium-duty spreadsheet, accounting, and data-base management activities. While not ideal, it can serve in those capacities if you are willing to wait for it. For medium- to heavy-duty accounting and spreadsheet manipulations, the CPU is too slow, and the available high-speed storage is too limited. Our recommendations for an upgrade are shown in Table 8–8.

Table 8–8. Components for Upgrade 8

Part No.	Description	Cost
JE3525	Jameco 25-MHz 386 Baby Motherboard With 32 kbyte Cache Controller	$1299.95
421000A9A-80	8 ea., 80-ns 1 Mbyte × 9 SIP (1 Mbyte RAM) Total system RAM is 8 Mbytes.	$1359.60
356KU	Toshiba 3.5″ 1.44-Mbyte Internal Floppy-Disk Drive	$109.95
46510	CompuAdd HardCache/ESDI Controller Card	$495.00
4210000A9B-10	4 ea., 1 Mbyte × 9 SIMM (4 Mbytes RAM for HardCache)	$639.80
M3180E	2 ea., Miniscribe 150-Mbyte (16-ms) Half-Height Hard Drive	$2399.90
JE1016	101-Key Enhanced Keyboard	$69.95
TM5156	Casper 14″ VGA Monitor	$399.95
JE1057	Jameco 8/16-Bit VGA Card	$249.95
	TOTAL PRICE	$7024.05

This upgraded system is moderately less powerful than the one specified for the large-data-base management system. The principal differences are the amount of system RAM and the size of the hard drives. For sheer speed, either the CPU or disk I/O, the two systems are equivalent.

If this system is to be used solely for medium-sized applications, you could save $600 by going to the 20-MHz CPU. You would have to use 100-ns SIPs and an expansion memory board. When the expenditures reach these levels, the 20% improvement in processor speed is probably worth the additional $600.

Upgrade 9: 80286 to 80386 for Number Crunching

We assume the present PC is an IBM PC/AT or clone operating at 6, 8, or 10 MHz and equipped with a color monitor and extended graphics adapter (EGA), an I/O board containing both serial and parallel ports, a 5.25-inch 1.2-megabyte floppy-diskette drive, two 40-megabyte MFM hard disks, a math coprocessor, an add-in memory board with 2 megabytes of RAM, and a 200-watt power supply.

This machine is configured to handle number crunching (intensive mathematical calculations). While not ideal, it can serve in this capacity if you are willing to wait for it. For heavy-duty number crunching, the CPU is too slow, and the available high-speed storage is too limited. Our recommendations for an upgrade are shown in Table 8–9.

Table 8–9.   Components for Upgrade 9

Part No.	Description	Cost
JE3028	AMI 33-MHz 386 Motherboard With 64-kbyte Cache Controller	$2599.95
421000A9A-70	1-MByte SIP Module (1 Mbyte RAM)	$189.95
421000A9B-70	15 ea., 1-MByte SIMM Module (15 Mbytes RAM) Total system RAM is 16 Mbytes.	$2849.25
JE3031	AMI 8-Mbyte 32-Bit Memory Card	$269.95
80387-33	Intel 33-MHz Math Coprocessor	$649.95
356KU	Toshiba 3.5″ 1.44-Mbyte Internal Floppy-Disk Drive	$109.95
46510	CompuAdd HardCache/ESDI Controller Card	$495.00
4210000A9B-10	4 ea., 1 Mbyte × 9 SIMM (4 Mbytes RAM for HardCache)	$639.80
M9380E	2 ea., Miniscribe 330-Mbyte (16-ms) Half-Height Hard Drive	$3399.90
JE1016	101-Key Enhanced Keyboard	$69.95
TM5156	14″ VGA Monitor	$399.95
JE1057	8/16-Bit VGA Card	$249.95
	TOTAL PRICE	$11923.55

This system has the computational abilities that were reserved for minicomputers less than five years ago. Obviously, this is not an inexpensive system. Considering that the original system as specified probably cost in excess of $5000, the total investment is approaching the level of the cheaper minicomputers and workstations. Certainly, the video display could be improved by going to a 19-inch monitor with a Super VGA card or even beyond that.

We have tried to present you with several configurations that satisfy specific requirements. With some thought, you should be able to locate your upgrade within the boundaries we've established.

Chapter 9

Dollars and Sense—How to Analyze an Upgrade Plan

Y ou have to spend money to make money. That sounds like a paraphrase of some famous quote. In our case, it's certainly true. You have to let go of quite a bit of the green stuff to upgrade PCs. But used right, upgraded PCs will more than recoup your investment. There's a catch there, right? You have to use them properly. That's where the ball's in your court. We'll make suggestions about our view of appropriate uses, but ultimately it's all up to you.

In Chapter 8, we talked a good deal about upgrade strategies. One of the strategy issues was money. How much does it cost? Where can I get the best value? Should I spread out the upgrade in order to spread out the costs? We touched on these and other money-related topics. We're going to revisit upgrade strategies, but this time we'll look at money issues in more detail.

Don't look now, but someone's looking over your shoulder. Your upgrade decisions are being second-guessed by lots of other people. Some of them think they know more than you about what kinds of PCs you need. Others are certain you are very knowledgeable about PCs, but they're worried about the way you're planning to throw away money—well, that's the way they see it. The latter group is made up of the people in your organization who count and are accountable for money.

You can make converts of the first group of backseat drivers. Ask for their input. Make them a part of the process. Even if their suggestions are ludicrous, at least appear to give them careful consideration. Be certain to give credit to your team of advisors. It'll make them feel better, and it won't hurt your credibility. It'll make you appear to be a better manager and team player.

Not all the people worrying about the way you spend money are accountants. Your boss is worried that you may make him look bad. If you can't show a return on investment for the upgrade pretty fast, he'll have to explain to his boss why he's invested in unprofitable machinery.

It's not all as bleak as it may appear. You've planned the upgrade to take care of specific problems. This isn't a joyride. You're not dragging a new video game into the office; you have legitimate reasons for these expenditures.

Write down your strategy and the decisions that support it. Be sure to examine all the costs involved with the upgrade. Don't stop with the current costs; do your best to project future costs. Wait a minute; slow down. Take time to think. Be certain you know the costs of doing business without the upgrade.

What's it worth to have a PC that works for you instead of the other way around? That's worth a lot to you, right? Make that clear to others. Be quantitative. Attach a realistic dollar value to working with the upgraded PCs.

Here's a thought: Will you be able to conduct business without interruption if you don't upgrade? Assuming the answer is no or only marginally, say so. This can be a very telling point when the naysayers start their chants.

If you do your homework well, your arguments for upgrading your PCs will be convincing. Unfortunately, you can't depend on someone else to pull together the details for you. You're going to have to go slogging through the swamp of costs and budget projections yourself. You're the only one who can do the job just right. Sure, you can get historical data from your accounting department, but they won't know how to assemble it to tell your story. You know what are telling arguments in your organization. Is it important to show that you can save enough time to replace some part-time help? Is freeing technical and managerial staff to get on with their jobs rather than constraining them to putter around while a computer chugs along an adequate rationale? It's your call.

We'll look at these topics and others, including training costs and benefits. We'll work through some example analyses to give you a flavor for how it can be done.

Budgets

If you don't have it, you can't spend it. And if you can't spend it, you can't do the upgrade you need. That's a nasty situation to be caught in. It's the kind of problem that can nail any of us.

However, we're going to assume that you are not caught in that bind. You can get to some moneys or you wouldn't be reading this chapter. Maybe you can't get it all at once; we'll discuss priorities for incremental upgrades. The really tough job is up to you—getting and hanging onto enough money to pull off the upgrade.

Goals

You know what goals are; they're what soccer players make when the ball goes into the net. No, they're what we talked about in Chapter 8. You've forgotten already? Check it out again (or for the first time).

You've worked through an upgrade strategy, right? You've set your goals; you have a functional requirement. Let's suppose you want to cut in half the time your customers have to wait while clerks get account information. You've converted this functional requirement into technical specifications. You're going to upgrade the clerks' PCs from 4.77-MHz 8088 XT clones with 65-ms hard-disk drives to 12-Mhz 80286 machines with 28-ms 3:1 interleave hard drives. You remember that you need to upgrade the power supply to 200 watts.

Here's a point that we discussed in Chapter 8: set two thresholds for cost— an upper (maximum) and a lower (minimum). The upper limit's clear, right? You can't spend more than you have. The lower limit is probably not quite so obvious. Why set a lower limit? Isn't the lowest cost you can get desirable? Of course it is. The lower limit is your estimate of what the system will cost to assemble. If you come in under this lower limit, then you deserve a reward. You've done a great job of shopping.

Information

Let's take time for a small digression. You can't work with budgets and plans without knowing what costs you're facing. That means you have to have the right information. There are lots of places to get information; we discussed several in Chapter 8.

Magazines and catalogs are good sources of information. You'll get a great deal of very useful information from looking through the ads in the major computer magazines. When you find an interesting ad, be sure to send off for their literature. There's usually more good stuff in the catalogs you send off for. In fact, the more mailing lists you're on, the better. Large quantities of junk mail may clutter up your office, but you need as much material as you can get if you're going to do a good job of comparison shopping.

Included among the magazines you may want to scan are *Computer Shopper*, *PC Magazine*, *PC Resources*, *PC Computing*, *Family Computing*, *PC World*, *Byte*, *Computer Buyers Guide*, and *Personal Computing*. While going through back issues of several of these magazines may not be all encompassing, you'll be getting a good feel for what's available and what it costs.

To be able to get a great deal of benefit from these sources, you must have a fairly good idea about what components you need to replace or add. That leads us back to goals and from there to implementation.

Implementation

So far, so good. Now where do you go from here? You've developed a set of functional requirements for your system, and now it's time to figure out how much it's going to cost. As we said above, the first thing you should do is get magazines and catalogs. Grab one or two catalogs, and write down the prices of all the components you'll need to build the system you've specified.

While you're putting together prices, don't get caught by the shipping and taxes "gotchas." Check out the total weight of the components you need. If you can stand the week or so delay, let them travel by truck. Air delivery is expensive and probably unnecessary for upgrades. See if you're going to have to pay state taxes on your purchases. The absence of state taxes was once a very good reason for buying good quality computer components from mail-order suppliers. You could save anywhere from 3% to 10% of the price of your system. That's not a bad deal.

You've assembled the costs, and now you have to answer a couple of crucial questions:

1. Can I afford this upgrade now?
2. Can I justify this expense?

If you can answer "yes" to the first question, then go for it. If not, you're faced with some tough decisions:

1. Hold off until you get the money.
2. Perform the upgrade incrementally.
   A. Which components get installed now?
   B. Which components get added later?
3. Adjust the upgrade to stay within available funds.

One possible alternative, if the total estimated cost is within 20% of your budgeted amount, is to do an extensive search to find the components at lower prices elsewhere. Numerous suppliers advertise in the magazines we mentioned above. With judicious shopping, you can probably reduce the bottom line by as much as 20%.

Suppliers

As with all purchase decisions, you must worry about the integrity and longevity of your suppliers. Will they replace components that fail during the warranty period? Will they stay in business long enough to honor the warranty?

How are you to find out if the supplier you've located will be around long enough to honor warranties? There's no surefire answer, but there is a technique that works fairly often. Look through back issues of the magazines we mentioned above. You are looking for suppliers that have been advertising for at least a year. A supplier that's been around longer than a year will probably stick around to honor your warranty. Be very wary of startup companies. They may offer bargain prices, but the chances are very good that they'll go out of business before your warranty expires.

How about supplier integrity? Beware of unbelievably low prices. There's a fairly narrow range (about 10%, maybe 25% for loss leaders) from highest to lowest advertised prices for a given component. All reputable suppliers have overhead and suppliers of their own. Talk with the suppliers. If they don't come across as knowledgeable and on the up-and-up, forget them.

There are dealers that specialize in odd-lot and other forms of distressed merchandise. This equipment is OK if you aren't going to want to return it or have someone at the supplier's shop work on it. These same dealers also carry orphan equipment—models no longer produced or models from manufacturers that have gone under. This is still good stuff, but there's no convenient way to get service or replacement. The best bet is for you to stay well away from such dealers.

All at Once or Incremental

Incremental or immediate—those are the choices for doing your PC upgrade. Which way will you go? Most people go for the immediate upgrade. It lets you get started enjoying the benefits from the time and effort you've expended. However, if you don't have enough money to do the entire upgrade right now, you'll have to do it in increments.

Upgrade timing also is important. When a particular increment is performed can be influenced heavily by the continuing advances of technology. Continuing technological advances produce options (and prices) that simply were not available earlier. Eighteen months ago, an 80486 processor was just a dream on a drawing board. Now they're available; but oh, what a price!

When new products are introduced, the prices of displaced products usually drop. With the knowledge that things are likely to improve if you will just wait long enough comes the question, can you afford to wait six months on the chance that some big improvement will make upgrading cost a lot less?

Money and Time

You should consider the time value of money. It's really a simple concept. You can do two things with money. You can spend it or you can save it. Once you spend it, it's gone. But if you save it, it'll be worth more later—the bank will pay interest to use it.

There's a conflicting factor—inflation. Given that inflation continues to be with us, in six months today's dollar is worth less than that. The intrinsic worth of a dollar is continually being eroded. So you have two factors working, interest and inflation. Interest is working for you and inflation against you. At today's inflation and interest rates, the net is a modest gain. It's not a big deal for a single PC upgrade, but if you are planning to upgrade all or most of your company's PCs, it becomes an issue. Defer the upgrade, put the money in the bank, and you get the upgrade and a profit. That's a super deal, right?

What do you expect to gain from the upgrade? If you expect that the productivity of the user(s) will be larger than any possible gains you might experience from investing the money elsewhere, then you should do the upgrade today.

Technology Shifts

Certainly, technology has been advancing at an accelerating pace. If there are parts of your upgrade that seem only marginally acceptable because the technology to do what you want isn't quite mature enough, then you should wait—at least for that element of the upgrade. Doing the upgrade in an incremental fashion allows time for technologies to develop. An example is the hard-disk controller with RAM cache.

Most of the upgrade motherboards on the market as 1990 begins feature either 80286 or 80386 CPUs. As you read this, there will be some 80486-based motherboards available. In this instance, you only need to wait a bit to take advantage of a large increase in computing power.

This sounds like a great case for putting off upgrades forever. Not so! We haven't said anything about prices. Most new technology items, like 80486 CPUs and boards, are very expensive. They may be well beyond the amounts you have set aside for the upgrade. Don't be discouraged if the latest and greatest costs too much. The prices for the older technology items will take a nosedive once the new ones are established.

If there are elements of your upgrade that seem only marginally acceptable because the technology to do what you want costs too much, then wait—at least for that part of the upgrade. Watch the computer magazines; if you see significant action developing in the technology of interest, wait it out. The older technologies usually end up costing less after the dust settles.

Now's the Time

Situations arise where cost can't be allowed to be the driver (it sounds like heresy, but it's true). If your sales staff is missing calls because their floppy-diskette-based PCs won't let them process data fast enough, you need an upgrade NOW. Maybe you have expensive professional staff sitting around waiting for their 8088-based PCs to crunch numbers. What a waste. You need an upgrade pronto.

These are cases in which failing to upgrade now is costing you money. In situations such as these, timing, not upgrade costs, is the concern. Get your PCs upgraded so your staff can perform their jobs efficiently. Do it now.

What to Leave Out

You have to do your upgrade in increments. How are you going to decide what to install first? Flip a coin. Throw darts at a list. You can't base it entirely on technical requirements. After all, you have budget constraints.

Upgrade for Word Processing

Let's look at some examples. First, we'll assume that you're going to upgrade a PC for word-processing use. Let's assume that the current PC is a floppy-diskette-based IBM PC or clone (two 360-kilobyte floppy-diskette drives) with a monochrome monitor and graphics adapter, a serial port, a separate parallel port, and a 150-watt power supply. Check the suggested upgrade configuration (Upgrade 1) for this system in chapter 8. The bottom line is $1460.85.

Suppose that you have $500 now to start the upgrade and you'll be able to get the remainder in four months. What's the best way to spend your money? We suggest that you get the 200-watt power supply first ($89.95). With it installed, you won't encounter any difficulties when adding the other components. The 150-watt supply in the example PC is too small for medium-size hard drives, several peripheral cards, and more than the absolute minimum amount of fast RAM.

Along with the new power supply, we would suggest that you get the enhanced keyboard ($69.95). It's different enough that you should give your troops as much time as possible to become proficient.

So far we've allocated only $159.90. The next item you should acquire is the 1.2-megabyte floppy-diskette drive ($119.95). You won't be able to format 1.2-megabyte diskettes, but you will be able to read from them and write to them if you have a recent ROM (read-only memory) BIOS (basic input-output system). If you've never upgraded your system ROM, check with your PC manufacturer for the most recent version. There are a number of BIOS suppliers out there, and generally their firmware is compatible with the popular PCs and clones. Talk to technical experts at some of the mail-order companies for help with your particular system.

Now we've reached $279.85 without shipping, taxes, or new ROM. The approximate shipping fee is 5% of the order for UPS Ground or about 11% of the order for Federal Express Standard. Usually, you pay sales tax only if you are buying from a vendor in your own state, but check to make sure. If you have to pay shipping and taxes, the upgrade to this point has probably cost you about $315.

At this point, we suggest that you halt the incremental upgrade until the rest of your money is available. You could go ahead and purchase either the 1.44-megabyte diskette drive or the 1:1 interleave controller, but you shouldn't attempt to install either one. You don't have a slot where the controller would fit; it requires a 16-bit bus slot. You need to maintain at least one 360-kilobyte floppy-disk drive to format diskettes as needed, so there's no place to put the 3.5-inch drive. The case of the example system has only two open half-height bays. The only rationale for buying one or the other component would be to assure its availability when it's time to continue the upgrade.

Upgrade for Medium-Size Data Bases (MS-DOS or PC-DOS)

Let's suppose that you want to upgrade an older PC for medium size data-base work and you'll be using either MS-DOS or PC-DOS. See details in Upgrade 4 in Chapter 8. The bottom line in this sample is $4435.65.

We suggest the 16-MHz 80286 rather than a 12-MHz version because it is able to keep up with the very rapid (10 megabits/second) data-transfer rate of the ESDI hard drive. Applications such as spreadsheets and data-base work that are typically I/O-bound benefit substantially from the faster data transfer rate and disk searches of the ESDI drives. In addition, the 16-MHz CPU will not have to be replaced if the user moves on to bigger data-base work running under PC-DOS or MS-DOS. You'll only need to upgrade memory and the hard-drive controller. (Get a caching controller with as much memory as possible.)

There is a caveat. Should you decide to go with data-base software that uses a DOS extender, you would do well to upgrade to an 80386- or 80486-based system at that time. Although DOS extenders can work with 80286-based systems, they perform much better with CPUs that are designed to swap between normal and protected mode.

We recommend upgrading to a 200-watt power supply to support larger hard-disk drive(s). We suggest scrapping the CGA adapter and color monitor because CGA characters are particularly difficult to read for extended periods. We suggest that you replace them with a 14-inch high-resolution color monitor and a VGA card.

Let's suppose that you have only $2000 available to begin the upgrade of this system. What do you buy with it? It's a very awkward amount. While it is about half the total cost before shipping and taxes, it's not enough to get the new hard disks, disk controller, and motherboard with memory. These items are the core of the upgrade. What are you supposed to do in a situation like this? Make the best of a bad situation.

The data-base work can't be done efficiently without the appreciably faster I/O, but the controller can't plug into the old motherboard (the controller needs a 16-bit expansion slot). That's a real Catch-22. To proceed as well as possible, go ahead and get:

(1)	The motherboard with memory	$766.15
(2)	The new power supply	$89.95
(3)	The enhanced keyboard	$69.95
(4)	The VGA monitor and graphics adapter	$649.90
(5)	The 5.25″ 1.2-Mbyte floppy-diskette drive	$119.95
	TOTAL	$1695.90

The argument for the new motherboard and memory is very straightforward. You can't plug in any of the new cards until you install the motherboard. With the new motherboard, you'll have a ROM BIOS that recognizes the 1.2-megabyte floppy-diskette drive. It'll be immediately useful. You'll be able to read, write, and format 1.2-megabyte diskettes. As we noted earlier, the enhanced keyboard is different enough so that your staff should have as much time as possible to become accustomed to it. The color monitor will provide crisp, clean, clear characters—a huge improvement over the CGA system.

This brings the total for the first element of the upgrade to $1695.90 before shipping and taxes. (We could have included the 3.5-inch 1.44-megabyte floppy-disk drive, but that would have pushed the total cost just over $2000 with shipping and taxes.) With a generous estimate for shipping and taxes, this preliminary configuration will set you back about $1900.

You may be wondering about the size of the suggested hard-disk drives. Why use two drives this big? You're probably thinking this is crazy. All your data-base work plus the program will easily fit on one drive. That may be true for now, but software and data bases have a way of proliferating. They expand to take up available space.

Admittedly, two 150-megabyte drives provide a lot of storage for PCs. After studying your current and future applications, you may decide that smaller drives would do. You can find ESDI drives and controllers in a wide range of capacities, but as we have mentioned before, buy more storage than you imagine you will need now. It is cheaper and easier to make the upgrade once rather than having to move to a larger drive within a year or so.

There's an even better reason for getting a second drive than just to keep from running out of application storage space. The second drive can be used as a high-speed backup medium. When your reputation and livelihood depend on always having access to current data, you can't afford to lose it because of an operator error or hard-disk failure. The probability is extremely small that both hard drives will crash simultaneously. You can't eliminate the possibility of operator error, but a backup copy on a second drive can give you reason to sleep better at night. Also, with the backup copy on the second drive, recovery of the data in the event of a failure can be fast enough that your customers may never notice a problem.

Of course, you could go with a tape backup, but that means you may lose one of your accessible half-height bays. (In that case, you'll have to give up the 3.5-inch diskette drive for now.) For the IBM PC/XT, there are four accessible half-height bays. But some clones may not provide that many. Tape drives are also notoriously slow. The ads in the Jameco catalog point to backing up 40 megabytes in 10 minutes. Naturally, you won't need to back up your entire disk each time, but that's a lot slower than a backup from one hard disk to another.

The Jameco catalog shows a QFA500 tape back-up drive with 150 megabyte capacity for $1049.95. The price includes one tape and an 8-bit adapter card that has to plug into an expansion slot. A spare 150-megabyte tape costs $39.95. They do have a smaller tape drive, but it only backs up 40 megabytes. Clearly, the QFA500 is not a cost- and performance-effective alternative to the second hard drive. The hard drive costs $1200, and you don't need spare parts lying around.

The CompuAdd catalog has an Irwin AccuTrak 80-megabyte tape backup for only $599. That's a good price. The spare 80-megabyte tapes cost only $29.95 each. So where's the catch? The tape drive has to attach to the diskette-drive controller. Our ESDI drive controller can handle only two floppy-diskette drives or one floppy-diskette drive and one tape-backup drive.

So we're back to losing the 3.5-inch 1.44-megabyte floppy diskette drive. That's not a very good option. The 3.5-inch medium may become the industry standard in the not-too-distant future. It is much sturdier than the 5.25-inch format, and it doesn't suffer from the incompatibilities found with the 360 kilobyte to 1.2-megabyte transition.

Upgrade for Large-Size Data Bases (Unix)

Let's consider one last incremental upgrade. We'll suppose that you want to upgrade from an 80286- to an 80386-based system. Now why would you want to do that? We just went through an exercise showing that an 80286 CPU could handle medium-size data bases. To get to bigger ones, you just need bigger hard drives, right?

Well, it's not that simple. The majority of data-base management software available for PCs comes from two basic sources—MS-DOS or PC-DOS applications and Unix applications. The MS-DOS and PC-DOS software seriously begins to run out of steam on medium-size data bases. The only viable options for handling large data bases are programs written to run under Unix.

Unix applications take up lots of hard-disk and RAM space. It's a very powerful operating system, but it requires lots of space. You'll probably need 70 megabytes of disk space just to accommodate the operating system and a few important utilities. If you want to use one of the windowing environments, you'll need over 100 megabytes. In addition, it takes at least 4 megabytes of RAM to run it.

Since we've pushed ourselves up against the performance wall as far as MS-DOS and PC-DOS operating systems are concerned, we will assume the PC that's being upgraded will use Unix as its operating system. The soon-to-be-modified PC is an IBM PC/AT or clone operating at 6, 8, or 10 MHz and equipped with a color monitor and extended graphics adapter (EGA), an I/O board containing both serial and parallel ports, a 5.25-inch 1.2 megabyte floppy-diskette drive, two 40-megabyte MFM hard disks, and a 200-watt power supply. Components for the upgrade are listed in Table 9–1.

Table 9–1. Components for Upgrade for Large-Size Data Bases

Part No.	Description	Cost
JE3525	25-MHz '386 Baby Motherboard with 32-kbyte Cache Controller	$1299.95
421000A9A-80	16 ea., 80-ns 1-Mbyte × 9 SIP (16-megabyte RAM)	$2719.20
356KU	Toshiba 3.5" 1.44-Mbyte Internal Floppy-Disk Drive	$109.95
46510	CompuAdd HardCache/ESDI Controller Card	$495.00
47476	CDC 630-Mbyte (14.5-ms) Full-Height Hard Drive	$2699.00
4210000A9B-10	4 ea., 1-megabyte × 9 SIMM (4 megabytes RAM for Hard Cache)	$639.80
JE1016	101-Key Enhanced Keyboard	$69.95
TM5156	Casper 14" VGA Monitor	$399.95
JE1057	Jameco 8/16-Bit VGA Card	$249.95
	TOTAL PRICE	$8682.75

This upgraded system is $3240 less than the very fast system specified in Chapter 8. This system is better prepared to store large amounts of data because it uses one very large (630 megabyte) hard drive. With 16 megabytes of system RAM, this PC can handle all but the very largest data bases. However, we have specified a slower CPU at a savings of $1300. If you estimate that the higher speed and having the very latest technology available in the 80386 arena are important, go for the 33-MHz board recommended in Upgrade 9 in Chapter 8.

We're going to operate under the assumption that you can't get the full $9600 to $9700 this system will cost including shipping and taxes. We'll assume that you have been allocated $5000 to initiate this upgrade.

What kind of system modifications can you put together with the money you have to spend? In truth, the answer is that you can't do much. You have enough money to get the motherboard with memory and some ancillary components, but you don't have enough to include sufficient memory for your operating system.

Unix files can be distributed across two disks, but that is generally accepted as poor practice. With just 80 megabytes when you combine the two existing disks, there's no room for a data base manager and a large data base. Since this is the reason for performing the upgrade, clearly you've reached an impasse.

Let's back up and ask the question, "What is the smallest amount of money that will leave us with an upgrade that will begin to operate in the desired mode?" It looks as though the answer is between $8800 and $8900. We could of course settle for a smaller hard-disk drive (330 megabytes) and reduce the costs between $900 and $1000. But then we would be reducing the capability of the upgraded system to handle very large data bases. Remember, you need as much as 100 megabytes for the operating system and utilities (including some form of windows). When you start thinking about taking 100-megabyte chunks out of the hard-disk storage space, it becomes clearer than ever that it is very important to hang the largest hard disk we can on the system.

It appears that this PC either will not function at all until you can get the entire funding package or it will have to operate without Unix. Operating under the DOS environment will severely curtail the size of the data bases that can be managed.

Assuming the DOS environment, you can use your $5000 of seed money to upgrade the motherboard and system RAM and install a 3.5-inch 1.44-megabyte floppy-diskette drive and an enhanced keyboard. This increment of the upgrade will cost $4199.05 before sales tax and shipping. With taxes and insurance, the total could be around $4700.

Here we have presented a case that is a partial redefinition to meet budget constraints. At least on a temporary basis, the system is neither fish nor fowl. After the first portion of the upgrade, it isn't ready to be a full-blown Unix machine, but it's lots more than the AT clone it once was.

Making Adjustments

You've just returned from a meeting with your boss, and you were told in no uncertain terms that you couldn't have $10,000 to upgrade your AT clone to a Unix machine. What are you going to do now? Fall back and punt? No, that's not the right answer. Let's consider what a minimum configuration will look like. Maybe you can get a request for $6500 or $7000 approved now that you have graciously—you did accept defeat graciously, didn't you?—accepted the decision to shoot your original request down in flames.

You can't have the system we specified above for large data base applications running under Unix. Let's revisit that system to see where we can trim to come up with a system that is still functional and can be upgraded a second time at a later date to get full performance.

The adjustments discussed in this paragraph are summarized in Table 9–2. We could get by with a 20-MHz '386 motherboard without a RAM cache. It's just slower. Along with the slower CPU, we could make do with a smaller amount of system RAM. Finally, it's possible to survive with a smaller hard drive.

Table 9–2. Example of Cost Reduction in an Upgrade

Part No.	Description		Cost
JE3525	25-MHz 386 Baby Motherboard With 32-kbyte Cache Controller		$1299.95
JE3025	20-MHz 386 Baby Motherboard		$649.95
		SAVINGS	$650.00
421000A9A-80	16 ea., 80-ns 1-megabyte × 9 SIP (16-Mbyte RAM)		$2719.20
421000A9A-10	8 ea., 100-ns 1-megabyte × 9 SIP (8-Mbyte RAM)		$1279.60
		SAVINGS	$1439.60
47476	CDC 630-Mbyte (14.5-ms) Full-Height Hard Drive		$2699.00
47453	CDC 320-Mbyte (14.5-ms) Full-Height ESDI Hard Drive		$1789.00
		SAVINGS	$910.00
		TOTAL PRICE	$5683.15
		TOTAL SAVINGS	$2999.60

We have clearly taken an ax to this upgrade. It has been emasculated; we've cut the total price by almost $3000. However, there is enough clout left to make a functional system. We retained the caching disk controller with 4 megabytes of RAM. That will allow for impressive improvements in I/O when compared with the old AT-clone system. The system will still be I/O bound, but, oh wow, it will scream!

The 20% decrease in CPU speed will be noticed in places where the computations are intensive, but it's still OK, if just barely. The reduction in system RAM is something you'll want to correct at the first opportunity. You may need to operate with the smaller hard disk until you can show your boss that it is getting too crowded to continue with it.

Following the tax and shipping-cost estimates we have used before, the top-end total for this sample system could be as high as $6365. This is probably a sufficient reduction below the $10,000 mark that you can get the bucks. You have to be careful about the way you present this reduction. If you go to your boss and show him the new reduced costs without explanation, you'll leave the impression that you didn't need the original system after all—you were just asking for the moon.

Be certain to write down the trade-offs you're making in CPU speed, data-storage capacity, and RAM capacity for super-fast data access and program-execution space. Explain that you can limp along with the reduced system, but you'll need to revisit funding for the entire upgrade in the near future.

Justification

Let's see, justification—that's word-processing parlance for whether your text lines up with the sides of the page. That's not quite right. Ah, now it's becoming clearer; it's the story you give your boss when your upgrade decisions are questioned.

Clearly you need to spend a considerable amount of money to upgrade one or more PCs. There has to be a rational basis for making the decision to stop or proceed. You must develop your rationale based on the tasks that have to be accomplished and the equipment necessary to accomplish the tasks.

New File Clerks

Unfortunately for you, you will frequently be called upon to support a decision that's been made by someone else without your input. You may be told that six new file clerks are going to be hired in the next two months and they will need access to PCs. What in the world does that mean to you? Should you buy a new PC for each of them? Upgrade an older PC or PC/XT clone to word processing status for each of them? How do you decide?

A good first step would be to prepare to upgrade three PC clones to word-processing status. A file clerk probably won't be spending as much time at the word processor as a secretary would. Based on the example upgrade given above, each system will require a little over $1600 in delivered parts. That would be a total cost around $4800.

You can prime the system by introducing a $5000 figure as needed to set up PCs so that there will be one for each two new file clerks. Ask questions of the person hiring the new clerks. Will each one need sole access to a PC? Is your assumption of two to one appropriate? Should it be more like four PCs for six clerks? In the extreme case, you'll have to provide six PCs. Be prepared for that eventuality. It'll cost roughly $9700. Don't hesitate to bring up that figure. It won't be cheap to provide each clerk with a PC.

Suppose a file clerk under ideal circumstances spends three hours per day filing and five hours typing. If two clerks must share a PC, that's two hours per day wasted. Assuming that a clerk plus overhead is $15 per hour, within one week there will be a waste of $150. For a 50-week work-year, that's a waste of $7500. For six file clerks, that's $22,500 wasted in a year. Whoa there! That $9700 total cost to provide each clerk a PC is beginning to look real good by comparison with the cost of having the clerks sitting around idle for an hour a day.

An analysis like this makes a very convincing case. To be able to pull it off, you have to have a realistic job description for the people who are to be getting the upgraded PCs. Go to the person responsible for the new users. Keep asking for data until you get what you need. Don't expect to get it the first time you ask. It's possible that the data doesn't exist and the supervisor will have to invent it or get it from another person. As long as you are using the same information as the supervisor, your estimate will be on fairly secure ground.

New Engineers

Let's return to an example from Chapter 8. We described a case where you are called upon to supply six new engineers with PCs. They were to be hired for 18 months. We suggested setting up six PCs for word processing and three macho PCs (33-MHz 80386s or 80486s) under the assumption that each engineer will need to be writing reports about current work and no one will be doing computations all the time.

Let's suppose that each engineer plus overhead costs $65 per hour. If each one needs to do five hours of computations a day on average, then we are wasting $130 per day, $650 per week, and $32,500 per 50-week work-year for each macho machine. Using this scenario, it clearly would be to your advantage to provide each engineer with a $15,000 (or less) macho machine.

Going in the opposite direction, an assumption of five hours of writing a day and three hours of calculations leads to two hours per day that each macho machine isn't used. In a week that's 10 hours. Over the course of a 50-week work-year that is 500 hours, or roughly one quarter of a work-year. That's not quite sufficient justification for reducing the number of hot PCs from three to two. With two PCs, there would be 16 hours of machine time available per day and 18 hours of engineer-PC interface time required. That would amount to $32,500 wasted in a year. So even in the situation where the PCs seem to be underutilized, you could wind up wasting a good deal of money if you don't provide at least three super-duper PCs.

Analyses such as these in which you provide estimates about PC use and costs are very powerful planning tools. They will assist you and your organization in deciding how to allocate PCs and the moneys needed to upgrade them.

Training

While you are busily estimating the appropriate amounts to set aside for upgrading your PCs, you should consider the costs of training. Newly upgraded PCs won't perform exactly as the old ones did. The people using them will be ill at ease or outright afraid for a period of time.

You know how it is when you're not quite sure of what you're doing. You're a little slower than you are when you're comfortable with what you're doing. With some people, it's worse than that. Some are afraid of doing something wrong, so they don't get their work done either quickly or effectively. In the worst case, some people are afraid of breaking the PC, so they don't do anything. It's up to you as the one most knowledgeable about the changes to recommend the amount of training needed to bring the new users up to speed.

Productivity

You're putting together this upgrade to improve productivity, right? How long are you willing to wait to begin seeing that improvement? There could be a long dry spell if you don't give the new users some help.

You know that there are all kinds of new users. There are the ones who have been complaining about their old machine and are ready to jump on the new one. They'll be up and running in no time at all if the transformation hasn't been too great. At the opposite extreme, there are the new users (really new) who haven't used a PC before. You may be reworking some older systems to provide upgraded entry-level PCs for these workers. For most of them, the learning curve is tall and steep. It's going to take the best of them quite a while to adapt to their PCs. These new users are going to need a lot of help. And, of course, there are lots of people in the middle; they can get up to speed mostly on their own with just a little help.

Certainly it's true that if you take someone away from the work that has to be done, the work doesn't do itself. This sounds like the argument some people give for not providing training. How do you feel about that? Can you make a good argument for training, even if it's going to take several days? We think that training is a very important productivity tool. In fact, most large corporations agree; many of them have either in-house training groups or consultants under continuing contract.

Let's look at some numbers to see if we can make a reasonable case for training. Suppose we take an $18-per-hour (including overhead) worker (a new user) away for training for three days. That's a cost of $432 plus the direct cost of the training. Let's suppose the training costs $400 per individual. That's a total cost of $832—not a small amount.

Let's be optimistic and assume that this person will lose only one hour per day (on the average) over a six-month period while slowly picking up informal training from coworkers. That's $90 per week and $2250 for half of a 50-week work-year. If the individual is a slow learner and loses 1.5 hours per day (as an average) for the same period, that's a cost of $3375. Even a very talented new user who might lose only 30 minutes per day (as an average) will cost you $1125 over six months. How about that! The cost of training is less in all three cases. You might argue with the six months figure, but it really takes a new user about that long to approach full productivity.

Have we convinced you that training is really cost effective? "Aha!" you say, "What about the work that wasn't done during the three days of training?" That's a good point. The work isn't going to go away. It has to be done. If it is a kind that can be delayed until your trainee returns, wait for it. The trainee will feel a bit swamped by the volume of material, but there will also be the understanding that you have confidence in this person's ability to apply what has been learned to getting the job done. In fact some organizations make certain that the trainee will only be receiving work that isn't critical for the first week following the training session. That provides enough time to get the work done while building confidence in the newly acquired skills.

What if the office is swamped with work and you need the extra hands just to bail? That's a bad situation, but it can't be improved a whole lot by someone who is intimidated by the equipment needed to do the job. It's tough to put off dragging in the first available help, but it is a much better long-term (here, long is more than the three-day training session) solution.

So now we've convinced you to train new workers. That probably wasn't too tough. It's easy to see them putter around with their machines. You know they aren't very productive until they get to know the equipment. But what about people who have had PCs for a long time and have just received an upgraded machine? It may even be the same case they had before with a new keyboard and new insides. Gosh, it looks the same; it probably even works almost the same. Why do they need training?

First let's be clear on one point. The experienced users don't need three days of training to learn how to turn on the PC with confidence. Clearly, they're a long way beyond that. Well, why do they need training? Ah yes, we're back to that question. The answer lies in the "almost."

You may have upgraded from a 360-kilobyte 5.25-inch floppy drive system to a mixed 1.2-megabyte 5.25-inch and 1.44-megabyte 3.5-inch system with one or more hard drives. That's a big change. There is a huge opportunity for time savings with good use of the hard drives. There is also a chance for time to be wasted by mistakes while trying to exchange 360-kilobyte (double density) diskettes with 1.2-megabyte (high density) ones and vice versa. You need to give these users information about setting up efficient subdirectories on their hard drives as well as cautions about exchanging diskettes.

Don't try to reformat a double-density diskette in a high density drive and expect the 360-kilobyte drive to read newly written data correctly. The read/write heads are smaller on the high-density drive. There is leftover extraneous information on the diskette. It'll be a real mess. For maximum efficiency, always format the double-density diskette in its own drive and then allow the high-density drive to write on that diskette.

It doesn't take long (maybe two or three hours) to give the experienced user as much of this kind of information as needed. It will be time well spent. Wasting time while trying to search through a root directory with a hundred entries is clearly unnecessary. Possibly even worse or at least more frustrating is having a diskette with information on it that you can read on your machine but you can't transfer to another PC. These problems should be addressed and fixed up front.

Another reason for training is new software. Along with the new hardware will typically arrive a new operating system. If you can make that transparent to the end user, there are still new application packages. You aren't likely to continue using all the old software for very long. After all, with the new hardware you have untapped resources. When the new software arrives, everyone is a new user.

A few of your techies will be positive that they don't need training—it's all in the manual. Leave them alone, or even better, leave them alone for a little while and then send them to school to become super users. Just make certain that they aren't the ones trying to help others until they achieve super user status. In the meantime, get some really qualified trainers to give one, two, or three short sessions on the new software. It'll bring your staff up to speed quickly. The longer they spend trying to figure out how to make the program do what they want it to do, the more it's going to cost you.

Benefits

There are many different reasons for upgrading a PC. What does the upgrade do for you? Do you need faster machines to process existing work more efficiently? You can get that. Do you need faster machines to take on work you couldn't do before? You can get that. Do you need more data storage so you don't have to sort through a stack of floppy diskettes? You can get that, too. Are you just tired of sitting around watching a monochrome display while your neighbors have color ones? That's another reason for an upgrade—keeping up with the Joneses.

Efficiency

One of the most telling arguments is reducing costs by improving efficiency. If you can save just one hour a day of an $18-per hour (including overhead) worker, you have saved $4500 in a 50 week work-year. Saving a comparable period for a $65-per-hour professional will result in savings of $16,250 in a year. That's not small potatoes. In either case, spending half or slightly more of the potential savings on an upgrade is well worth it. The upgrade will be paid for in roughly six months. After that, you have clear sailing. The benefits continue, and the costs don't.

Better Products

Your better product may not be in the form of a widget coming off a factory floor. It may be less waiting time for customers while the order clerks access the order/entry data base. Customers that get prompt, accurate information about their orders are very likely to come back again and again. Your product may be an engineering design that just couldn't be done on the old PC. That old machine was just a little bit flaky, and it wouldn't get verifiable answers on long calculations. Or maybe the old machine didn't have enough memory to handle the computations, so you had to make seat-of-the-pants decisions. With the new upgrade, those days are behind you (pun intended).

New Markets

Another benefit you can get from the upgrade is the opportunity to get into new markets. With your old PC, you may have been unable to sell data-base services to others outside your organization because you didn't have quite enough capacity to do your own work. Don't overlook this opportunity when you upgrade. Others in your company may need your services. Try selling within as well as outside your company. Of course, it may be easier to get along with the outsiders. They can't come around at odd times of the day to bug you about data for that report they just have to have out in 30 minutes.

You may even discover that your technical staff has become efficient enough to take on tougher jobs. Sometimes a new system will encourage a techie to dig in a little deeper to find out how it works. That can work to your advantage. Keep track of the new discoveries your staff makes—even the seemingly insignificant ones. There may be a pearl hiding in there that you can turn into a new market. There are lots of people working with PCs who aren't using them to full advantage. If you can help them work better, you'll be rewarded.

Upgrades can save you money in the long run. We've established that. The issue there is, how long is long? If you have to pay for the upgrade within 30 days, you'd better stick with the machines you have. But if you can write the upgrade off over six months to a year, we've shown that savings from less wasted time can do that for you.

Upgrades also cost money. We've looked at how to spread that cost by making incremental upgrades. We've also considered revising downward an upgrade that can't be paid for now.

Don't let the size of an upgrade deter you. If you have planned the upgrade to address a specific need, then the costs can be justified. You may not have been able to find everything you need in this chapter, but we hope that it has given you a foot up toward making sense of the dollars.

Conversion Tables

Powers of 2 and 16

16^n	n		2^n	n
		$16^0 = 2^0$		
		$16^1 = 2^4$		
		$16^2 = 2^8$		
1	0	$16^3 = 2^{12}$	256	8
16	1	$16^4 = 2^{16}$	512	9
256	2	$16^5 = 2^{20}$	1 024	10
4 096	3	$16^6 = 2^{24}$	2 048	11
65 536	4	$16^7 = 2^{28}$	4 096	12
1 048 576	5	$16^8 = 2^{32}$	8 192	13
16 777 216	6	$16^9 = 2^{36}$	16 384	14
268 435 456	7	$16^{10} = 2^{40}$	32 768	15
4 294 967 296	8	$16^{11} = 2^{44}$	65 536	16
68 719 476 736	9	$16^{12} = 2^{48}$	131 072	17
1 099 511 627 776	10	$16^{13} = 2^{52}$	262 144	18

Hexadecimal-Decimal Conversions

Hexadecimal	1	2	3	4	5	6	7	8	9	A	B	C	D	E	F
Decimal	1	2	3	4	5	6	7	8	9	10	11	12	13	14	15

Hex	Dec	Hex	Dec	Hex	Dec
100000	1048576	10000	65536	1000	4096
200000	2097152	20000	131072	2000	8192
300000	3145728	30000	196608	3000	12288
400000	4194304	40000	262144	4000	16384
500000	5242880	50000	327680	5000	20480
600000	6291456	60000	393216	6000	24576
700000	7340032	70000	458752	7000	28672
800000	8388608	80000	524288	8000	32768
900000	9437184	90000	589824	9000	36864
A00000	10485760	A0000	655360	A000	40960
B00000	11534336	B0000	720896	B000	45056
C00000	12582912	C0000	786432	C000	49152
D00000	13631488	D0000	851968	D000	53248
E00000	14680064	E0000	917504	E000	57344
F00000	15728640	F0000	983040	F000	61440

Hex	Dec	Hex	Dec
100	256	10	16
200	512	20	32
300	768	30	48
400	1024	40	64
500	1280	50	80
600	1536	60	96
700	1792	70	112
800	2048	80	128
900	2304	90	144
A00	2560	A0	160
B00	2816	B0	176
C00	3072	C0	192
D00	3328	D0	208
E00	3584	E0	224
F00	3840	F0	240

Printer Information

This appendix lists representative manufactures of daisy-wheel and ink-jet printers, as well as printer-support software that may be useful to you as you upgrade your system.

Daisy-Wheel-Printer Manufacturers

AEG Olympia, Inc.
Somerville, NJ

AT&T Data Systems Group
Morristown, NJ

Brother International Corp.
Information Systems & Peripheral Division
Somerset, NJ

Bull Worldwide Information Systems, Inc.
Billerica, MA

Citizen America Corp.
Santa Monica, CA

CPT Corp.
Eden Prairie, MN

Digital Equipment Corp.
Maynard, MA

Encore Computer Corp.
Ft. Lauderdale, FL

Fortis Information Systems
Commerce, CA

GENICOM Corp.
Waynesboro, VA

Harris Corp.
Melbourne, FL

Lanier Business Systems
Atlanta, GA

Olivetti USA
Office Products Division
Somerville, NJ

Panasonic Communications & Systems Co.
Office Automation Group
Secaucus, NJ

Primages, Inc.
Ronkonkoma, NY

Prime Computer, Inc.
Natick, MA

Qume Corp.
Milpitas, CA

Silver Reed (U.S.A.), Inc.
Ranch Dominguez, CA

Stratus Computer, Inc.
Marlboro, MA

Tandy Corp.
Ft. Worth, TX

UNISYS Corp.
Blue Bell, PA

Wang Laboratories, Inc.
Lowell, MA

Printer Software

The following list contains a random selection of printer control and enhancement software. Some companies have more than one product, although only one representative product is listed. All listed packages cost $100 or less, retail. In each listing, the first line identifies the product, and the remaining lines give the company name and location.

Fontware Installation Kits for Microsoft Windows
Bitstream, Inc.
Cambridge, MA

Disk Spool II
Budget Software Co.
Aurora, CO

Printbuff
CAPA Software Corp.
Saskatoon, SK

Laser Archivist
Cauzin Systems, Inc.
Waterbury, CT

Sideline
Connecticut Software Systems Corp.
Rowayton, CT

ConoFonts Manager
Conographic Corp.
Irvine, CA

Laser Fontpak vols. 1 and 2
Data Transforms, Inc.
Denver, CO

3-2-1 Liftoff
DP-Tek, Inc.
Wichita, KS

Fontcenter Fonts
FontCenter
Lynnwood, WA

9-to-24 Pin Printer Translator
Foresight Enterprises, Inc.
Escondido, CA

Print-Q-Assist
Fresh Technology Group
Mesa, AZ

Soft Font Manager
Human Touch Software
Sacramento, CA

Image Printing Utilities
Image Computer Systems
Avon, CT

JetPower Series
K & R Custom Software, Inc.
Newport News, VA

LaserFonts
KD Systems, Inc.
Raleigh, NC

PC Em-U-Print
Koch Software Industries, Inc.
Arlington Heights, IL

PopSet
Laser Connection
Mobile, AL

Printer Tool Kit
M.A.P. Systems, Inc.
Houston, TX

Printer Interfacer
MarcSoft Software
Lake Jackson, TX

Laser Library
The Mayflower Consulting Group
Burlington, MA

Freeze Frame
Michtron, Inc.
Pontiac, MI

Flipside!
Micro-Systems Software, Inc.
West Palm Beach, FL

SciFont
MicroGlyph Systems
Lexington, MA

LaserMenu
MicroLogic Software, Inc.
Emeryville, CA

PrintPlot
Microplot Systems
Columbus, OH

Font Tree
Nor Software, Inc.
New York, NY

E-Z-Set
Orbit Enterprises, Inc.
Glen Ellyn, IL

Personal Print Control
PDS, Inc.
Wallingford, CT

SideWinder
Personalized Software, Inc.
Fairfield, IA

Envelope Please
Quaid Software, Ltd.
Toronto, ON

PrintEase
SDG Innovations, Inc.
San Diego, CA

Jett-Set jr.
Sigma Data Systems, Inc.
Newark, DE

Side Step
SoftCorp, Inc.
Clearwater, FL

WYSIfonts!
SoftCraft, Inc.
Madison, WI

PrinScil
Software Consultants International
Kent, WA

Spool-Master
Software Masters (IN)
Indianapolis, IN

RSVP
Walker Richer and Quinn, Inc.
Seattle, WA

Sources of Accessory Hardware

The following is a list of sources of printer accessory hardware such as multi-plexers, buffers, and the like.

CPT Corp.
Eden Prairie, MN

Dickerson Enterprises, Inc.
Niles, IL

Johnathon Freeman Technologies
San Francisco, CA

Printer Pilot, Inc.
Santa Monica, CA

Sources of Ink-Jet Printers

The following companies offer ink-jet printers. Some of the companies listed have more than one model.

Canon U.S.A., Inc.
Lake Success, NY

Data General Corp.
Westboro, MA

Dataproducts Corp.
Woodland Hills, CA

Eastman Kodak Co.
Copy Products Division
Rochester, NY

GCC Technologies, Inc.
Waltham, MA

Hewlett-Packard Co.
Palo Alto, CA

Howtek, Inc.
Hudson, NH

IBM
Armonk, NY

Mannesmann Tally Corp.
Kent, WA

Sharp Electronics Corp.
Mahwah, NJ

Xerox Corp.
U.S. Marketing Group
Rochester, NY

Safety First

The basic rule for working with electricity is: Don't work with electricity. The sort of repairs and upgrades you'll find in this book should all be performed on a dead, or uncharged, machine. We say this for two reasons: First of all, although most of a PC is powered by low-voltage direct current, there is nevertheless dangerous electrical current at the incoming leads and within the power supply. Secondly, installing, removing, or adjusting electronic devices with the power on could subject them to short circuits or surges that will kill them, if not you.

Power Supply

The power supply in a PC is a sealed unit, and it is made that way for a reason. Wall current comes into the box, and as we've noted, you want to stay away from that. Inside the supply is another danger, one or more filter capacitors. A capacitor is a small can-shaped device that smooths out fluctuations in the current by storing some of the energy. Ordinarily, the power within the capacitors is dissipated very quickly after the unit is turned off, but this is something you do not want to test with your finger.

Power supplies are cheap, running from about $25 to $100, depending on the quality and wattage ratings. They are not worth repairing and therefore not worth opening. There is also no reasonable path to upgrading the power supply as part of a general upgrade to your system; you'll want to unplug your system and replace the old unit with a new one.

Turning Off and Unplugging

The proper way to deal with electricity in your PC is to get into the habit of first turning off the system, and then unplugging it from the wall outlet. Turning off the system gives you a visual check that the power has been shut off, and it should also give your system a bit of protection because of the clean on/off break made by a well-constructed switch.

But merely switching off the system does not remove all of the power from the system box. There is still power in the electrical cord to the system and to the on/off switch. A well designed switch will have its incoming power leads properly covered or shielded from an inadvertent touch. However, you may be putting a screwdriver into the system, or you may (although we wish you wouldn't) be wearing a dangling piece of jewelry as you lean over the machine, or you might end up dropping a tiny screw in the direction of the live leads.

Once again, our advice: Turn off and then unplug before doing any work under the covers. Then replug before you turn on the power switch.

Fuses

Most PCs have a fuse between the switch and the power supply. This device is in the line to prevent too much current from reaching the electronic circuits. A typical rating will be 2 amperes ("amps" for short). A printer can draw more current.

If the fuse blows, you will want to try to determine the reason for the excess current before you replace the fuse. We consider the blowing of a fuse in a machine to be a very serious situation, since we always place one or more surge protectors between our machines and the wall outlet, and these include their own first-line fuses.

Again, this is an area to stay away from if the system is powered. If you manage to connect across the fuse leads with your hand or a piece of metal you are holding, your hand or the screwdriver will become the new fuse, essentially allowing unlimited amperage into the system—possibly through your body on its way there.

Monitors

As some of the labels on the back say, there are no user replaceable parts in a monitor. We do not recommend that you open the case.

A cathode-ray tube (the display element of a monitor or television set) requires several thousand volts to produce a monochrome image, and as much as 25,000 volts for a typical color display. The amperage is low, but this is still something you don't want to be fooling around with yourself.

Printers

Repairing or upgrading the electronic circuitry of a printer is beyond the scope of this book. Instead, we will be talking about a few limited areas of upgrade: installing additional memory in a laser printer, installing additional font cards or cartridges in laser and impact devices, and installing or upgrading ROMs in certain classes of printers. In each of these cases, we will follow the same rules that apply to working with a PC: Turn off, then unplug the device before you perform any work on it.

Boards

Adding a new board or upgrading an old one is a relatively easy process. There are, though, some rules of safety—for you and for your machine—that you should follow.

Here is the procedure you should follow to remove an existing board from a PC:

1. Switch off the system and unplug it from the wall outlet.

2. Unplug any cables that may be connected to the board to be removed. The cables are usually connected at the rear of the board through openings at the back of the unit; some cables for internal devices such as disk drives may be connected to other parts of the board. You may want to make notes on what was plugged where to help you reinstall devices; it might prove handy to have a supply of small paper (not metallic) labels that you can attach to the cables to identify them as you remove them. (You may find that you will need to remove one or more other boards in order to get at the board you want. In this case, we especially recommend that you make notes on what was attached where.)

3. Remove the screw that locks down the peripheral board at the back of the unit. Be very careful in the handling of this small screw—try to avoid dropping it into the system unit.

   If a screw does fall in, be careful in your efforts to retrieve it; don't poke around with a screwdriver because this could damage some of the circuitry on the motherboard and other devices. (You did switch off and unplug the system first, right?) One of our favorite devices is a small wad of sticky tape attached to the eraser end of a pencil; plant the tape on the screw and gently retrieve it. Do spend the effort, though. A loose metal screw inside your PC is a short circuit waiting to happen.

4. Remove the board carefully, applying even upward pressure at both ends. You want to take care not to damage the connector at the bottom of the board and the receptacle into which it plugs.

5. Lay the board down on a soft, nonconductive, antistatic surface. Many boards come packed in a special pink foam sheet; hold onto some of this material for this purpose. In a pinch, a clean sheet of cardboard will suffice.

Working With Chips

You may be removing and installing memory chips, CPUs, and coprocessors. In doing so, you must guard against two types of damage that could destroy these tiny, sometimes expensive parts:

1. Physical damage. The chips plug into the circuitry of the motherboard or memory card through small metal prongs. You will have to guard against breaking these prongs off or inadvertently bending one in or out from the chip body and thereby blocking them from making proper electrical contact with the system.

2. Electrical damage. The chips are designed to work quickly with tiny amounts of electrical current within a properly managed circuit; a jolt of power beyond the rated specifications can destroy them. Here is where you must remember that the human body itself can function as a powerful reservoir of electricity. We'll explain in this appendix how to avoid buildup and discharge of static electricity.

A valuable tool for handling chips is an IC installer, which is a specialized holder for chips. An IC remover is a tweezer-like device that grips a chip under the front and back and allows a cautious retrieval. Either of these tools can be found at your local Radio Shack or other similar electronics store.

Static electricity isn't good for much of anything. It can't be used to operate your PC or electric pencil sharpener, but it surely can kill a sensitive electrical component. Your main job as it relates to static electricity is to avoid letting it build up on you.

Static electricity isn't much of a problem when the relative humidity is over 65 or 70%. Enough leaks off into the air (water vapor is a good conductor for static electricity) to keep you out of trouble. However, when the relative humidity is 30% or less, boy is static electricity a nuisance!

You may have noticed that whenever you scuff your feet across the carpet in winter (the relative humidity is usually low during the winter), you can send a little spark to the doorknob, light switch, or another person's ear. Well, that little spark is more than enough to blast a chip to oblivion. You can easily pick up a charge of several thousand volts. That's sudden death for a chip that's designed to operate on 5 volts, even if it has overvoltage protection.

Any time your clothing rubs across cloth or plastic, you will pick up a static charge. You can't help it; it just happens. The drier the weather, the bigger is the charge you collect, and the longer it takes to dissipate on its own.

You can prevent large amounts of static buildup by touching the metal parts of a plugged-in lamp when you first sit down to work. If you touch the lamp every few minutes while you are working, you will probably keep the static electricity down low enough that it won't be a problem.

It's a nuisance having to remember to touch some piece of metal every few minutes. Fortunately, there are commercial remedies. Antistatic wrist straps are sold by many electrical supply companies. One mail-order vendor, MCM Electronics of Centerville, Ohio, offers such a wrist strap for $10.95.

The antistatic strap is made of silver-plated monofilament fibers woven in an elastic strap. There is a 5-foot coil of cord connected through a 1-megohm (1 million ohm) resistor to a banana plug and alligator clip. The plug or clip should be used to connect the strap to ground (the *round* element of a 120 volt house receptacle or the metal frame of your PC power supply will do nicely).

The large-value resistor is in the device to prevent you from becoming the low-resistance path in case you accidentally connect the strap to a dangerous voltage.

With an antistatic strap in place, you can work without interruption. You needn't fear that static buildup will negate any of your careful work.

Company/Resource Lists

Removable Disk Drives

Model 1300/RIO (Qume Corp.): Has a capacity of 10 megabytes and is compatible with IBM PC, XT, and close clones. The list price is $1695.

> Qume Corporation
> 500 Yosemite Dr.
> Milpitas, CA 95035
> (408) 942-4000
> Fax: (408) 942-4052

Removable Megafile (44 MB) (Datastore Systems, Inc.): Has a capacity of 44 megabytes and is compatible with an IBM AT. It can operate through either SCSI or ST506 interfaces. The drive is a half-height, internal unit with an average access time of 22 milliseconds. The list price is $4,200.

> Datastore Systems, Inc.
> 10929 Franklin Ave.
> Franklin Park, IL 60131
> (312) 455-2227
> Fax: (312) 455-2251

Removable Megafile (129 MB) (Datastore Systems, Inc.): Has a capacity of 129 megabytes and is compatible with an IBM AT. It can operate through a SCSI interface. The drive is a half height, internal unit with an average access time of 18 milliseconds. The list price is $7,190. (For address, see above.)

Removable Megafile (244 MB) (Datastore Systems): Has a capacity of 199 megabytes and is compatible with an IBM AT. It can operate through a SCSI interface. The drive is a half height, internal unit with an average access time of 17 milliseconds. The list price is $10,545. (For address, see above.)

Removable Megafile (644 MB) (Datastore Systems, Inc.): Has a capacity of 645 megabytes and is compatible with an IBM AT. It can operate through a SCSI interface. The drive is available as either a half- or full-height, internal unit with an average access time of 18 milliseconds. The list price is $17,500. (For address, see above.)

Magneto-Optical Vendors

In optical media, the newest technology is *magneto optical*, really a magnetic drive with optical tracking mechanisms to make possible very dense data storage. Multigigabyte drives using this technology are available for PCs and minicomputers, providing an excellent data-exchange and backup medium. Some companies are using them for direct read/write for very large data-storage projects, such as laboratory data capture, drug testing, etc. Two current vendors of magneto-optical drives are:

See First Technology, Inc.
4655 Old Ironsides Drive, Suite 100
Santa Clara, CA 95054
(408) 748-7717
Fax: (408) 748-7621

Trimarchi, Inc.
P.O. Box 50
State College, PA 16804
(814) 234-5659

RAM/ROM Cards

A new form of permanent and read/write storage is a credit-card sized RAM/ROM card made by Sony. So far, it is in limited use, but it is expected to see wider distribution when memory prices come down. Right now, the cards are used in one PC-based network workstation and some terminals. These cards could be very useful additions to small computers, especially in the laptop market. Each card has enough storage to hold one or more applications, such as WordPerfect and Lotus 1-2-3, for example.

Sony Corporation of America
9 West 57th Street
New York, NY 10019
(212) 418-9427

Diagnostic Software

CheckIT (Performance Computer Diagnostics): Is designed for debugging and testing PCs running PC DOS and MS-DOS. It provides configuration reports, diagnostic tests, performance benchmarks, and repair tools. It tests the central processing unit, memory, hard disks, video subsystems, and communication ports. It includes floppy-disk, printer, keyboard, clock, mouse, and joystick tests. The list price for both 5¼-inch and 3½-inch diskettes and loopback plugs is $179.95.

Performance Computer Diagnostics
703 Grand Central Street
Clearwater, FL 34616
(813) 443-1331
Fax: (813) 443-6603

PC-Lint (Gimpel Software): Is designed for debugging and testing PCs running PC DOS, MS-DOS, or OS/2. It provides a diagnostic facility for the C programming language. It reports on bugs, glitches, and inconsistencies. It supports Kernighan and Ritchie (K & R) C and ANSI extensions. It includes a user modifiable library with definition files for most major compilers. It will work with any MS-DOS C compiler. It requires a minimum of 256 kilobytes of RAM. The list price for the single user version is $139. There is a network version available; this version is compatible with Novell, 3Com, and NetBIOS. Site licensing is available for the network version.

Gimpel Software
3207 Hogarth Lane
Collegeville, PA 19426
(215) 584-4261

R E D R (Realtime Error Detection & Recovery) (Delphi Data): Is designed for debugging and testing PCs running PC DOS, MS-DOS, or Unix. The source language is C. It has a library of C subroutines that are used to detect and recover from real-time errors. It runs in either diagnostic or recover mode. It requires a minimum of 10 kilobytes of RAM. The list price is $250 for single-user DOS systems and higher for multiuser systems.

Delphi Data (a Division of Sparks Industries, Inc.)
9069 Cajalco Rd.
Bldg. 1
Corona, CA 91719
(714) 279-7955
Fax: (714) 279-7957

System Sleuth (Dariana Technology Group, Inc.): Is designed for debugging and testing PCs running PC DOS or MS-DOS. The list price is $149.

Dariana Technology Group, Inc.
23704-5 El Toro Rd., Suite 348
El Toro, CA 92630
(800) 299-1557
(714) 587-2226
Fax: (714) 587-2221

Joysticks and Mice

Alphabetical Product List

Company addresses are listed in the second subsection of this section.

Artec Mouse AM-21 (Ultima Electronics Corp.): A three button mouse device that utilizes a rotary optical encoder. It has 356-dpi resolution. It is compatible with IBM PCs, XTs, ATs, and close clones. The list price is $18.

Artec Mouse AM-21 Plus (Ultima Electronics Corp.): A three-button mouse that uses a rotary optical encoder. It features 356-dpi resolution and Dr. Halo software. Compatible with IBM PCs, XTs, ATs, and close clones. The list price is $24.

Artec Optical Mouse A-20 (Ultima Electronics Corp.): A three-button mouse featuring an ergonomic design and 300-dpi resolution. Compatible with IBM PCs, XTs, ATs, and close clones. The list price is $28.

Artec Optical Mouse A-20 Plus (Ultima Electronics Corp.): A three-button mouse featuring an ergonomic design, 300-dpi resolution, and Dr. Halo software. Compatible with IBM PCs, XTs, ATs, and close clones. The list price is $33.

Bionic Mouse 800-A1, 800-A2, 800-A3 (Commax, Inc.): Mouse devices featuring a three-button action and compatibility with the Microsoft and PC mouse. Compatible with IBM PCs, XTs, ATs and close clones. The list price varies from $27 to $33.

C-820 (Commax, Inc.): A mouse featuring two-button action. The device is compatible with IBM PS/2 Models 30, 50, 60, 70, and 80. The list price is $20.

Cordless Manager Mouse (Numonics): A mouse device using infrared light to transmit data between the mouse and the CPU. Compatible with IBM PCs, XTs, ATs, and close clones. The list price is $175.

CPT Mouse (CPT Corporation): A three-button optomechanical mouse device featuring a nine-pin serial interface. Resolution is 200 cpi. The device is compatible with IBM PCs, XTs, ATs, and close clones. The list price is $110.

CPT Mouse-T (CPT Corporation): An optical mouse device featuring pop-up menus and 100-cpi resolution. The device is compatible with IBM PCs, XTs, ATs, and close clones.

DeltaGold Mouse (Delta Computer Corp.): A three-button mouse device featuring 200-cpi resolution. No pad or power supply is required for its operation. The device is compatible with IBM PCs, XTs, ATs, and close clones.

DMS-100 (Diamond Flower Electric Instruments Company, (U.S.A.) Inc.): A user-definable, two-button mouse device. It features an optical rotary encoder, an autorepeat key, and 200 cpi resolution. The device is compatible with IBM PCs, XTs, ATs, and close clones. The list price is $38.

DMS-200 (Diamond Flower Electric Instruments Company, (U.S.A.) Inc.): A three-button, optomechanical mouse device. The device features 200-dpi resolution and an RS-232C interface. The device is compatible with IBM PCs, XTs, ATs, and close clones.

E-Mouse (Mitsubishi International Corporation): A mouse device that emulates the Microsoft mouse. Included with the mouse are a D-9 connector and software. The resolution is 400 dpi, which is good enough for some engineering applications. Compatible with the IBM PC series and close clones. The list price is $130.

EasyStick (Interlock, Incorporated): A joystick that attaches to the keyboard. It works with programs using arrow keys. Using the knob like a joystick activates the arrow keys and moves the cursor. Compatible with the IBM PC series and close clones. The list price is $30.

Electronic Arts Mouse (Electronic Arts): A two-button mouse featuring tactile feedback, a silicone-coated ball, and a Microsoft-compatible driver with pop-up menus including the Deluxe Paint II program. The resolution is 200 dpi. The list price is $150.

Expert Mouse (Kensington Microware, Ltd.): A two-button mouse featuring optical technology, pop-up menus, and 200-dpi resolution. It is available in left- or right-hand models, and it is compatible with IBM PCs, XTs, ATs, and close clones. The list price is $169.

G80-2000 (The Cherry Corporation): A replacement keyboard featuring 123 keys of which 24 are programmable function keys, an integrated bar-code reader, a magnetic card reader, and a mouse. Compatible with IBM PCs, XTs, ATs, and close clones. The list price is $879.

Genius Mouse Model GM-6 Plus (KYE International, Inc.): A mouse featuring an RS-232C interface, a mouse pad, a mouse pocket, and software—Menu Maker, Dr. Halo III, and Slideshow. The resolution is 200-800 dpi, or 0.12mm/dot. The list price is $99. It is compatible with IBM PCs, XTs, ATs, and close clones.

Genius Mouse Model GM-6000 (KYE International, Inc.): A two- or three-button mouse, depending on the mode chosen by the user. Its resolution varies from 350 to 1050 dpi. It is compatible with IBM PCs, XTs, ATs, and close clones. The list price is $119.

Genius Mouse Model GM-U2 (KYE International, Inc.): A two button universal mouse with 350- to 1050-dpi resolution. Compatible with IBM PCs, XTs, ATs, and close clones. The list price is $129.

Genius Mouse Model GM-ST (KYE International, Inc.): A three-button mouse device featuring a resolution of 0.12 mm/dot, or 200 to 800 dpi. It has an RS-232C output. Compatible with IBM PCs, XTs, ATs, and close clones. The list price is $79.

Gravis Joystick (Advanced Gravis Computer Technology, Ltd.): A joystick with a pistol-grip handle with fire button. It has three microswitch fire buttons and an eight-position centering tension control. It is compatible with IBM PC series and close clones. The price varies from $50 to $170.

Gravis MKVI Analog and Switch (Advanced Gravis Computer Technology, Ltd.): A joystick with an eight-position variable tension switch and an analog joystick controller. It has three independent push buttons and a switch selector. The price ranges from $55 to $175. The device is compatible with the IBM PC series or close clones.

GT Mouse (GTCO Corporation): A three-button mouse device featuring a 900-mm/s tracking resolution for distortion-free drawing. The device is compatible with IBM PCs, XTs, ATs, and close clones. The list price is $109.

HiRez Mouse (Logitech, Inc.): A mouse featuring tactile feedback and 320-dpi resolution. Compatible with IBM PCs, XTs, ATs, and close clones. The list price is $149.

KB5153 (Key Tronic Corporation): An 87-key AT-style keyboard with a directly mounted touch pad. The touch pad operates as cursor, mouse, graphic, and function keys. There are 36 programmable areas on the touch pad. Compatible with IBM PCs, XTs, ATs, and close clones. The list price is $249.

Keycat (Power Source Computer Systems, Inc.): A combined enhanced (102-key) keyboard and supermouse. The mouse is a three button, optomechanical device. There is even a trackball on the right side of the keyboard. Compatible with IBM PCs, XTs, ATs, and close clones. The list price is $90.

KeyTrak (Octave Systems, Inc.): A keyboard that contains a trackball and mouse buttons. It has an XT- and AT-switchable y shaped cable for keyboard and serial ports. Compatible with Mouse Systems and MicroSoft serial mouse drivers and with IBM PCs, XTs, ATs, and close clones. The list price is $189.

Large Print Display Processor (VTEK): A display accessory that features a four-directional joystick and a reading-mode control. Size control is selectable from 2 × to 16 × in eight steps. Compatible with IBM PCs, XTs, ATs, and close clones. The list price is $2,695.

LG018 (3A Computer Corp.): A high-input-speed mouse compatible with the IBM PC series and close clones.

M-Mouse (Mitsubishi International Corp.): A two-button, optomechanical mouse featuring 200-dpi resolution. Compatible with IBM PCs, XTs, ATs, and close clones. The list price varies from $135 to $199.

Manager Mouse (Numonics): A mouse that does not require a special surface nor a separate power supply. No disassembly is required for maintenance. Compatible with IBM PCs, XTs, ATs, and close clones. The list price is $105.

Microsoft Mouse (Microsoft Corporation): A mouse featuring 200-dpi resolution as well as user-adjustable sensitivity and bundled software. Compatible with IBM PCs, XTs, ATs, and close clones. The list price varies between $150 and $200.

Microstick (CH Products): A joystick with eight modes of movement and PC mouse emulation. Serial communications can occur from 300 baud (bits per second) to 19.2 kilobaud. Compatible with the IBM PC series and close clones. The list price is $280.

Mini Mouse (CMS Enhancements, Inc.): A mouse device featuring 340-cpi resolution and Microsoft Mouse emulation. The device is compatible with IBM PCs, ATs, XTs, and close clones.

MitsiMouse (Mitsubishi International Corp.): A mouse featuring a silicone-coated ball and Teflon feet. Compatible with IBM PCs, XTs, ATs, and close clones.

Mouse (IMSI): A three-button, optomechanical mouse with a resolution of 200 dpi. The list price is $99.

Mouse-trak (ITAC Systems, Inc.): A trackball featuring an ergonomic design, user-definable keys, and a speed-control button. It requires no additional power supply; it gets its power from the host computer. Compatible with IBM PCs, XTs, ATs, and close clones.

MouseTouch (Elographics, Inc.): A touch screen that plugs into a serial mouse port. It emulates all mouse functions including single clicks, double clicks, drag, and cursor-move operations. The list price is $470.

MouseTouch (Information Strategies, Inc. (TX)): A resistive touch-screen device that emulates mouse functions using existing software. No special programming is required. Available with 12-, 14-, 19-, and 25-inch screens. The list price for the smallest device is $727. Compatible with the IBM PC series and close clones.

New Memory Pro (Maxi-Switch Company): A 125-key keyboard with 25 function keys and a mouse device. The keyboard has a very good tactile response and is DIN compatible. Compatible with IBM PCs, XTs, ATs, and close clones. The list price is $150.

OM-A1 (GVC/Chenel Corp.): A mouse featuring a three-speed switch for turbo (500 dpi), normal (250 dpi), and slow (200 dpi) operations. The device contains no moving parts. Compatible with IBM PCs, XTs, ATs, and close clones. The list price is $105.

OmniMouse (Mouse Systems Corp.): A two-button, optomechanical mouse featuring 200-dpi resolution and Designer Pop-up Menu software. Compatible with IBM PCs, XTs, ATs, and close clones. The list price is $89.

OPM-1 (SmarTEAM, Inc.): A three-button, optical mouse with 250-dpi resolution and no mechanical ball. Compatible with IBM PCs, XTs, ATs, and close clones. The list price is $79.

Optimouse (IMSI): A three-button mouse featuring pop-up software and a mouse driver. Compatible with IBM PCs, XTs, ATs, and close clones. The list price is $175.

PC Mouse (Mouse Systems Corp.): A three-button, optical mouse bundled with Designer Pop-up and PC Paint Plus software and Ultra-Res high-resolution software. It comes with a mouse pad. Compatible with IBM PCs, XTs, ATs, and close clones. The list price is $149.

PC Mouse II—Serial & Bus Version (Mouse Systems Corp.): A mouse device that is available in both serial and parallel versions. It is a two-button optical mouse featuring 400-dpi resolution and Microsoft compatibility. Software bundled with it includes MousePad, Designer Pop-up, PC Paint Plus, and Ultra Res. Compatible with the IBM PC series and close clones. The list price is $149.

Powermouse 100 (Prohance Technologies, Inc.): A two button, 40-key, programmable mouse device that uses predefined macro tables. Compatible with IBM PCs, XTs, ATs, and close clones. The list price is $195.

ProCorp Mouse (ProCorp): A contoured mouse with light touch keys. The resolution is 250 dpi. Compatible with IBM PCs, XTs, ATs, and close clones. The list price is $70.

Professional Series Mouse (Key Tronic Corporation): A two button mechanical mouse available in either serial or parallel verisons. It comes with menuing software for Lotus 1-2-3, WordPerfect, and dBASE III Plus. Compatible with IBM PCs, XTs, ATs, and close clones. The list price is $109.

RM-100 (RMK Systems): A three-button mouse featuring 300 dpi resolution and pop-up software. Compatible with the IBM PC series and close clones. The list price is $125.

Rollermouse (CH Products): A trackball device that uses an optomechanical design and features automatic acceleration and Microsoft Mouse compatibility. Compatibile with IBM PCs, XTs, ATs, and close clones. The list price is $170.

S-Mouse (Mitsubishi International Corp.): A two-button, optomechanical mouse that features a serial interface and resolution between 200 and 800 dpi. Compatible with IBM PCs, XTs, ATs, and close clones. The list price is $195.

Samurai Mouse (Qualitas Trading Company): A two-button mouse featuring 200-dpi resolution and pop-up menus. Compatible with IBM PCs, XTs, ATs, and close clones.

SunMouse (Suncom): A three-button mouse that comes with a test program and a mouse-driver program. Compatible with IBM PCs, XTs, ATs, and close clones. The list price is $70.

Super Mouse (Inmac Corp.): A mouse with a programmable baud rate up to 9600. Compatible with IBM PCs, XTs, ATs, and close clones. The list prices varies from $139 to $159.

SuperMouse SM (Penny & Giles Controls, Inc.): A three button mouse with the buttons user-definable. Compatible with IBM PCs, XTs, ATs, and close clones. The list price is $263.

Trackermouse (Penny & Giles Controls, Inc.): A two-button mouse that can function as either a mouse or a trackball. It features an adjustable tracking mechanism and a good tactile feel. Compatible with IBM PCs, XTs, ATs, and close clones. The list price is $169.

UDA Series (ALPS America): Mouse devices containing optical and mechanical encoders for CAD/CAM systems and PCs. Compatible with the IBM PC series and close clones.

Company Names and Addresses

3A Computer Corp.
45-56 Pearson Street
Long Island City, NY 11101
(718) 361-7878
(718) 361-7417

Advanced Gravis Computer Technology, Ltd.
7033 Antrim Ave.
Burnaby, BC V5J 4M5
(800) 663-8558
(604) 434-7274
Fax: (604) 434-7809

ALPS America
(Division of ALPS Electric (USA), Inc.)
3553 N. First St.
San Jose, CA 95134
(800) 828-2577
(800) 257-7872 (CA)
(408) 432-6000
Fax: (408) 432-6035

CH Products
1225 Stone Drive
San Marcos, CA 92069
(619) 744-8546
Fax: (619) 744-1669

The Cherry Corporation
3600 Sunset Avenue
Waukegan, IL 60087
(312) 360-3500
Fax: (312) 360-3566

CMS Enhancements, Inc.
1372 Valencia Avenue
Tustin, CA 92680
(714) 259-9555
Fax: (714) 549-4004

Commax, Inc.
15 Shire Way
Middletown, NJ 07748
(201) 671-0775
Fax: (201) 671-0804

CPT Corp.
8100 Mitchell Rd.
Eden Prairie, MN 55344
(612) 937-8000
Fax: (612) 937-1858

Delta Computer Corp.
300 N. Continental Blvd.
Suite 200
Segundo, CA 90245
(213) 322-4222
Fax: (213) 322-7878

Diamond Flower Electric Instruments Company (U.S.A.), Inc.
2544 Port Street
West Sacramento, CA 95691
(916) 373-1234
Fax: (916) 373-0221

Electronic Arts
1820 Gateway Drive
San Mateo, CA 94404
(415) 571-7171

Elographics, Inc.
105 Randolph Road
Oak Ridge, TN 37830
(615) 482-4100

GTCO Corp.
7125 Riverwood Drive
Columbia, MD 21046
(301) 381-6688
Fax: (301) 290-9065

GVC/Chenel Corp.
99 Demarest Rd.
Sparta, NJ 07871
(800) 243-6352
(201) 579-3630
Fax: (201) 579-2702

IMSI
1299 Fourth St., Penthouse
San Rafael, CA 94901
(800) 222-4723
(800) 562-4723 (CA)
(415) 454-7101
Fax: (415) 454-8901

Information Strategies, Inc. (TX)
888 S. Greenville Ave., Suite 121
Richardson, TX 75081
(214) 234-0176

Inmac Corp.
2465 Augustine Dr.
P.O. Box 58031
Santa Clara, CA 95052
(800) 547-5444
(408) 727-1970

Interlock, Inc.
P.O. Box 2160
Castro Valley, CA 94546
(800) 541-2429
(415) 357-6100

ITAC Systems, Inc.
3121 Benton St.
Garland, TX 7504
(800) 533-4822
(214) 494-3073
Fax: (214) 494-4159

Kensington Microware, Ltd.
251 Park Ave., South
New York, NY 10010
(800) 535-4242
(212) 475-5200
Fax: (212) 475-5996

Key Tronic Corp.
P.O. Box 14687
Spokane, WA 99214
(800) 262-6006
(509) 928-8000
Fax: (509) 927-5216

KYE International, Inc.
12675 Colony Street
Chino, CA 91710
(800) 456-7593
(714) 590-3940
Fax: (714) 590-1231

Logitech, Inc.
6505 Kaiser Drive
Fremont, CA 94555
(800) 231-7717
(800) 552-8885
(415) 795-8500
Fax: (415) 792-8901

Maxi-Switch Company
(Subsidiary of Eeco, Inc.)
6701 S. Midvale Park Road
Tucson, AZ 85746
(602) 294-5450
Fax: (602) 294-6890

Microsoft Corporation
16011 Northeast 36th Way
P.O. Box 97017
Redmond, WA 98073
(800) 426-9400
(206) 882-8080
Fax: (206) 883-8101

Mitsubishi International Corporation
701 Westchester Avenue
White Plains, NY 10604
(914) 997-4999
Fax: (914) 997-4976

Mouse Systems Corp.
47505 Seabridge Drive
Fremont, CA 94538
(415) 656-1117
Fax: (415) 770-1924

Numonics
101 Commerce Drive
Montgomeryville, PA 18936
(800) 247-4517
(215) 362-2766
Fax: (215) 361-0167

Octave Systems, Inc.
1715 Dell Avenue
Campbell, CA 95008
(408) 866-8424
Fax: (408) 866-4252

Penny & Giles Controls, Inc.
35 Reynolds St.
Attleboro, MA 02703
(508) 226-3008
Fax: (508) 226-5208

Power Source Computer Systems, Inc.
10020 San Pablo Avenue
El Cerrito, CA 94530
(415) 527-6908
Fax: (415) 527-3823

ProCorp
43-42 10th Street
Long Island City, NY 11101
(718) 784-2809

Prohance Technologies, Inc.
1558 Siesta Drive
Los Altos, CA 94022
(415) 967-5679

Qualitas Trading Company
6907 Norfolk Road
Berkeley, CA 94705
(415) 848-8080
Fax: (415) 848-8009

RMK Systems
132 Bellevue Avenue
West Collingswood Heights, NJ 08059

SmarTEAM, Inc.
19205 Parthenia St., Suite J
Northridge, CA 91324
(800) 233-7327
(818) 886-9726
Fax: (818) 886-6731

Suncom
290 Palatine Road
Wheeling, IL 60090
(312) 459-8000
Fax: (312) 459-8095

Ultima Electronics Corp.
1245 Reamwood Avenue
Sunnyvale, CA 94089
(408) 734-9208
Fax: (408) 734-9207

VTEK
1625 Olympic Boulevard
Santa Monica, CA 90404
(800) 345-2256
(800) 521-5605 (CA)
(213) 452-5966

Scanners Costing $1000 or Less

Alphabetical Product List

An alphabetical listing of company names and addresses is given in the second subsection of this section.

1374 Bar-Code Reader (Control Module, Inc.): A bar-code reader that uses a wand to pick up the desired bar code. The reader can distinguish different bar-code formats. It uses an RS-232C communications interface. Compatible with the IBM PC series and close clones. The list price is $445.

A-Scan (Auspicious Communications): A hand-held text and image scanner that supports the RS-232C interface. Capable of scanning old photographs. The conventional inputs are documents and pages. Compatible with the IBM PC series and close clones. The list price is $349.

Auto Slot Reader (Caere Corp.): An optical mark recognition device that supports both RS-232C and parallel interfaces. The input for this reader is a card-size document. Compatible with the IBM PC series and close clones. The list price is $965.

BC105 Fox and BC110 Fox (Bar/Code, Inc.): Bar-code readers that accept input from a bar-code wand. Compatible with IBM PCs, XTs, ATs, and close clones. The list price is $595 for the BC105 Fox and $695 for the BC110.

BCS-225 (Aedex Corp.): A bar-code reader that supports the RS-232C interface. The possible inputs are light wands and lasers. Compatible with IBM PCs, XTs, ATs, and close clones. The list price is $595.

BCS-225 and XP-300C (SIMS Software): Desktop bar-code readers. They can not read multiple bar-code formats. They operate with contact type bar codes. Compatible with the IBM PC series and close clones. The list price is $795.

BTC-100 (Behavior Tech Computer (USA) Corp.): A hand-held bar-code reader that derives its input from a wand. The reader supports the RS-232C interface. Compatible with the IBM PC series and close clones. The list price is $120.

BTC-102 (Behavior Tech Computer (USA) Corp.): A wand input bar-code reader that supports the RS-232C interface. It is not capable of multifont recognition. Compatible with the IBM PC series and close clones. The list price is $170.

BTC-202 (Behavior Tech Computer (USA) Corp.): A bar-code reader that supports the RS-232C interface. The reader gets its input from wands and codes. Compatible with the IBM PC series and close clones. The list price is $175.

CAT Image Scanner (Computer Aided Technology, Inc.): Used for scanning images at 300-dpi resolution. It can scan line art and halftone images. It uses a parallel communication interface. Software is included with the scanner. Compatible with the IBM PC series and close clones. The list price is $239.

CAT Image Scanner Model SI Plus (Computer Aided Technology, Inc.): Used for text and image scanning at resolutions from 50 to 400 dpi. The scanner will accept both document and page input. It is not capable of recognizing multiple fonts; software is included with the scanner. It is capable of scanning line art and halftone images. Compatible with the IBM PC series and close clones. The list price is $239.

CCD Bar Code Scanner (Opticon, Inc.): A bar-code reader that accepts input from scanners and wands. It uses the RS-232C communication interface. Compatible with the IBM PC series and close clones. The list price is $755.

CL 7 and F30 (Datalogic Optic Electronics, Inc.): Bar code readers that accept input from either a wand or a laser gun. Compatible with the IBM PC series and close clones. The list price varies from $245 to $745.

ClearScan (NCL America): A hand-held text and image scanner using either SCSI or parallel communication interfaces. The scan resolution is 400 dpi. It can scan line art and continuous-tone and halftone images. It does not possess multiple-font recognition capabilities. Compatible with the IBM PC series and close clones. The list price is $295.

CodeScan 2000 (Bear Rock Software Company, Inc.): A bar code reader that gets its input from a wand. Compatible with the IBM PC series and close clones. The list price is $495.

Complete Half-Page Scanner (The Complete PC): Configured to scan text and images. It cannot recognize multiple fonts. It is capable of scanning both line art and photographs. The scanner will accept both documents and individual pages as input. Compatible with the IBM PC series and close clones. The list price is $299.

Complete Hand Scanner 400 (The Complete PC): A hand-held text and image scanner. It can scan line art, photographs, and drawings at 200- to 400-dpi resolution. It is not capable of distinguishing multiple fonts. The input should be in page format. It can scan an 8½″ × 11″ page in 12 seconds. Compatible with the IBM PC series and close clones. The list price is $249.

Complete Page Scanner (The Complete PC): Used for scanning both text and images. The scanner is equipped with a flatbed and paper feeder. The resolution is 300 dpi. It is not capable of multiple-font recognition. Compatible with the IBM PC series and close clones. The list price is $899.

CYC Bar Code Series (KD Associates): Bar-code readers that support the RS-232C communication interface. Compatible with the IBM PC series and close clones. The list price is $495.

Datawand II (MSI Data Corp.): A bar-code reader that uses an RS-232C communication interface. Compatible with the IBM PC series and close clones. The list price is $450.

DL8000 (Datalogic Optic Electronics, Inc.): A hand-held bar-code reader that is compatible with the IBM PC series and close clones. The list price is $995.

DS-2000 (Chinon America, Inc.): A text and image scanner used primarily for scanning line art with 100- to 200-dpi resolution. Accepts both documents and individual pages. It can digitize an 8½″ × 11″ page in 16 seconds. The RS-232C interface is supported. Compatible with the IBM PC series and close clones. The list price is $545.

DS-3000 (Chinon America, Inc.): A text and image scanner used primarily for scanning line art with 300-dpi resolution. Font-recognition software is included. The scanner accepts both documents and individual pages. It can digitize an 8½″ × 11″ page in 24 seconds. The parallel interface is supported. Compatible with the IBM PC series and close clones. The list price is $745.

GeniScan GS-2000 (KYE International, Inc.): A hand-held text and image scanner that comes with software. The scanner operates with resolution that varies from 100 to 400 dpi. Compatible with the IBM PC series and close clones. The list price is $299.

Handy Scanner 3000 Plus (Diamond Flower Electric Instruments Company (U.S.A.), Inc.): A hand-held text and image scanner that operates with a resolution of 100 to 400 dpi. The scanner will accept both documents and individual pages as input. Software is included with the scanner. It is not able to distinguish multiple fonts. Compatible with the IBM PC series and close clones. The list price varies from $359 to $389.

HS-1000 and HS-2000 (Diamond Flower Electric Instruments Company (U.S.A.), Inc.): Hand-held text and image scanners that accept both document and page input. The resolution is 200 dpi. The scanners are capable of scanning halftone images, photographs, and logos. Compatible with the IBM PC series and close clones. The list prices are $169 and $189, respectively.

HS-3000 (Diamond Flower Electric Instruments Company (U.S.A.), Inc.): A hand-held text and image scanner with resolution from 100 to 400 dpi. It is able to scan halftone images, photographs, and logos. It accepts either documents or individual pages as input. One 8½″ × 11″ page can be scanned in 4 to 14 seconds. Software is included with the scanner. Compatible with the IBM PC series and close clones. The list price is $329.

IBM PC, XT, AT Series E-Z Reader (PERCON Peripheral Connections, Inc.): A bar-code reader that will accept input from a wand or slot reader. A wand is provided with the reader. Compatible with the IBM PC series and close clones. The list price is $635.

Image Scanner (Epson America, Inc.): An image scanner that operates with a resolution of 144 to 180 dpi. The imaging elements are silicon photodiodes. The scanner uses an RS-232C communications interface. Compatible with the IBM PC series and close clones. The list price is $300.

IX-8 and IX-12 (Canon U.S.A., Inc.): Text and image scanners. They scan a page at a time. The pages are processed in a normal sheet-fed mode. An RS-232C interface is standard. The resolution is 75 to 300 dpi. The scanners are able to scan both line art and photographs. Compatible with the IBM PC series and close clones. The list prices are $945 and $1190, respectively.

KB5152/B (Key Tronic Corp.): A bar-code reader that accepts input from a wand. Compatible with the IBM PC series and close clones. The list price is $795.

Loop Scan/400 (Focus Technology): A hand-held text and image scanner capable of accepting both documents and individual pages as input. The device resolution is 400 dpi. It is capable of scanning line art and photographs. Software is included with the scanner. Compatible with the IBM PC series and close clones. The list price is $249.

Mars 128 (Marstek): A hand-held text and image scanner that has multiple-font recognition capabilities. Its input may be documents, pages, badges, or cards. The device resolution is 400 dpi. It utilizes an SCSI communication interface. It can scan line art and halftone images. It takes the scanner 6 seconds to finish an 8½″ × 11″ page. Compatible with the IBM PC series and close clones. The list price is $299.

Micro-Scanner (Our Business Machines, Inc.): A hand-held text and image scanner that can scan halftone images. The device features a 200-dpi resolution and the ability to use both documents and individual pages for input. Compatible with the IBM PC series and close clones. The list price is $345.

MicroScanner 200 Series (American Microsystems): A bar code reader utilizing a light wand, a slot, or a charge-coupled device (CCD). There is no multifont recognition. The device supports the RS-232C interface. Compatible with the IBM PC series and close clones. The list price is between $395 and $1005.

Model 321 (GUIS America, Inc.): A desktop text and image scanner capable of scanning line art and halftone images at 200 dpi. The scanner is capable of multiple-font recognition. Parallel communications are supported. An 8½″ × 11″ page can be scanned in 10 seconds. Software is included with the scanner. Compatible with the IBM PC series and close clones. The list price is $895.

Model 521 (GUIS America, Inc.): A desktop, flatbed text and image scanner operating with a resolution of 75 to 300 dpi. It is able to scan line art and halftone images. The imaging speed is 15 seconds for an 8½″ × 11″ page. Software is included with the scanner; however, the scanner is not capable of multiple-font recognition. A parallel communication interface is supported. Compatible with the IBM PC series and close clones. The list price is $895.

Model 4002/4003 (Vertex Industries, Inc.): Hand-held bar code readers. The RS-232C communication interface is used. Compatible with the IBM PC series and close clones. The list prices are $495 and $595, respectively.

MR-23B (Barcode Industries, Inc.): A bar-code reader that takes its input from a badge, a card, or a keyboard emulation. Compatible with the IBM PC series and close clones. The list price varies from $315 to $595.

MSR-100 and MSR-150 (SIMS Software): Hand-held bar-code readers that can scan cards and magnetic stripes. Software is not included with the readers. Compatible with the IBM PC series and close clones. The list price varies from $695 to $995.

N-205 (Chinon America, Inc.): An image scanner. It accepts full pages as input. Both RS-232C and parallel interfaces are supported. The device resolution is 200 dpi. Compatible with the IBM PC series and close clones. The list price is $695.

NISCAN (NISCA, Inc.): A hand-held text and image scanner that can scan line art, continuous-tone images, and photographs. It can accept input from both documents and individual pages. It does not possess the ability to recognize multiple fonts. Compatible with the IBM PC series and close clones. The list price is $299.

PBPS-1000 Pocket Scanner (Packard Bell): A hand-held text and image scanner that has the capability to scan photographs. Software is included with the scanner. The device resolution is 200 dpi. Compatible with the IBM PC series and close clones. The list price is $295.

PC Barcode Processor Board (Input/Output Technology, Inc.): An expansion-board bar-code reader that uses a wand for input. It is not able to recognize multiple bar-code formats. Software is included with the reader. Compatible with the IBM PC series and close clones. The list price is $479.

PC Wand (Bear Rock Software Company, Inc.): A bar-code reader that supports the RS-232C interface and gets its input from a wand. Compatible with the IBM PC series and close clones. The list price varies from $395 to $899.

PC-Wand (International Technologies and Systems Corp.): A hand-held bar-code reader that uses a wand for input. Compatible with the IBM PC series and close clones. The list price is $495.

PC-Wand 100 (International Technologies and Systems Corp.): A hand-held bar-code reader that uses wands, lasers, and badges for input. Compatible with the IBM PC series and close clones. The list price is $399.

PC-Wand 200 "T Wedge" (International Technologies and Systems Corp.): A hand-held bar-code reader that accepts input from badges, wands, and lasers. It supports RS-232C communications. Compatible with the IBM PC series and close clones. The list price is $429.

PC-Wand 300 and PC-Wand 310 (International Technologies and Systems Corp.): Bar-code readers that accept input from wands and lasers. They support RS-232C, RS-449, and RS-485 communication interfaces. They do not possess multiple-font recognition capabilities. Compatible with the IBM PC series and close clones. The list price is $459.

PC-Wand 800 "WanderWand" (International Technologies and Systems Corp.): A hand-held bar-code reader that accepts input from a wand or a laser. The device can not recognize multiple fonts. It supports the RS-232C communication interface. Compatible with the IBM PC series and close clones. The list price is $889.

PC-Wedge (Time Keeping Systems, Inc.): A hand-held bar code reader that uses a wand for input. Software is included with the reader. Compatible with the IBM PC series and close clones. The list price is $289.

PCScanner III Model 645 (Caere Corp.): A bar-code reader. It will accept input from code pens, slot readers, and lasers. The supported interface is RS-232C. Compatible with the IBM PC series and close clones. The list price is $499.

PHD+ (Follett Software Company): A hand-held bar-code reader that comes with software. It is not capable of multiple font recognition. Compatible with the IBM PC series and close clones. The list price is $950.

Read Right CCD Scanner (Greywolf Technologies, Inc.): A hand-held bar-code reader that uses noncontact charge-coupled devices for input. Software is included with the reader. Compatible with the IBM PC series and close clones. The list price varies from $715 to $999.

Read Right Contact Scanner (Greywolf Technologies, Inc.): A hand-held bar-code reader that uses either a wand or hand-held pistol for input. The RS-232C communications interface is supported. Compatible with the IBM PC series and close clones. The list price varies from $275 to $399.

ScanMan (Logitech, Inc.): A hand-held text and image scanner with which software is included. The device resolution is 100 to 400 dpi. It can scan line art, halftone images, drawings, and logos. The input can be in the form of documents or individual pages. Compatible with the IBM PC series and close clones. The list price is $329.

Scanstar-PC II (Computer Identics): A bar-code reader. Compatible with the IBM PC series and close clones. The list price is $475.

Scanstar Wedge Series (Computer Identics): A bar-code reader. Compatible with the IBM PC series and close clones. The list price is $475.

Scanteam 2700 (Welch Allyn): A bar-code reader. Compatible with the IBM PC series and close clones. The list price is $458.

Scanteam 2800 (Welch Allyn): A bar-code reader that accepts input from lasers, wands, and charge-coupled devices. It uses the RS-232C communication interface. Compatible with the IBM PC series and close clones. The list price is $625.

Scanteam 2850 (Welch Allyn): A bar-code reader that uses a charge-coupled device for input. The reader uses the RS-232C communication interface. Compatible with the IBM PC series and close clones. The list price is $288.

Sceptre (Newer Technology): A desktop or internal-mount bar-code reader that uses a wand for input. Compatible with the IBM PC series and close clones. The list price is $450.

Series 10 IBM PC/XT/AT Model (PERCON (Peripheral Connections, Inc.)): A hand-held bar-code reader that accepts input from badges, wands, charge-coupled devices, lasers, and magnetic strips. A wand is provided with the reader. Compatible with the IBM PC series and close clones. The list price is $685.

ShapeScan SS-300; SS-300 Plus (Shape, Inc.): A flatbed image scanner that uses an SCSI communication interface. The scanning resolution is 300 dpi. It takes 18 seconds to scan an 8½″ × 11″ page. Individual pages are the only form accepted as input. Compatible with the IBM PC series and close clones. The list price varies from $979 to $1000.

SkyScan Model B-1 (Skyworld Technology): A hand-held text and image scanner that can scan photographs. The scanning resolution is 100 to 400 dpi, and it takes 9 seconds to scan an 8½″ × 11″ page. Either documents or individual pages can be utilized for input. Compatible with the IBM PC series and close clones. The list price is $289.

SkyScan Model D-120 Series (Skyworld Technology): Hand held text and image scanners that can scan photographs. The scanning resolution is 200 dpi. They do possess multiple-font recognition capabilities. The RS-232C communication interface is used. Compatible with the IBM PC series and close clones. The list price varies from $349 to $399.

Softstrip System Reader (Cauzin Systems, Inc.): Used for text scanning and character recognition. Input must come to the scanner in the form of strips. Compatible with the IBM PC series and close clones. The list price is $200.

SP MH 216 AF (Mitsubishi Electronics America, Inc.): A hand-held text and image scanner. The device has 200- to 400-dpi resolution. It can scan halftone images and photographs. Software is included with the scanner. It can scan an 8½″ × 11″ page in 10 seconds. It can scan either documents or individual pages. Compatible with the IBM PC series and close clones. The list price is $995.

TimeWand II (Videx, Inc.): A hand-held bar-code reader that uses the RS-232C communication interface. Compatible with the IBM PC series and close clones. The list price varies from $698 to $789.

Tricoder (Worthington Data Solutions): A bar-code reader that accepts its input from a wand. The communication interface is RS-232C. Compatible with the IBM PC series and close clones. The list price varies from $495 to $899.

WDP Reader (Worthington Data Solutions): A bar-code reader that accepts input from wands and lasers. Software is not included with the reader. Compatible with the IBM PC series and close clones. The list price is $399.

WDR (Worthington Data Solutions): A desktop bar-code reader that accepts its input from a wand. The communication interface is RS-232C. Compatible with the IBM PC series and close clones. The list price is $399.

XT-15A (MAXTRON): A hand-held bar-code reader that will accept a document as input. Compatible with the IBM PC series and close clones. The list price is $269.

Company Names and Addresses

Aedex Corp.
1070 Ortega Way
Placentia, CA 92670
(714) 632-7000
Fax: (714) 632-1334

American Microsystems
1110 S. Airport Circle, Suite 140
Euless, TX 76040
(800) 648-4452
(817) 571-9015
Fax: (817) 685-6232

Auspicious Communications
132 Bellevue Avenue
West Collingswood Heights, NJ 08059

Bar/Code, Incorporated
1104 Summit, Suite 106
Plano, TX 75074
(214) 424-9491

Barcode Industries, Inc.
12240 Indian Creek Court
Ammendale Technology Park
Beltsville, MD 20705
(301) 498-5400
Fax: (301) 498-6498

Bear Rock Software Company, Inc.
6069 Enterprise Drive
Placerville, CA 95667
(916) 622-4640
Fax: (916) 622-4775

Behavior Tech Computer (USA) Corp.
46177 Warm Spring Boulevard
Fremont, CA 94539
(415) 657-3956
Fax: (415) 657-3965

Caere Corp.
100 Cooper Court
Los Gatos, CA 95030
(408) 395-7000
Fax: (408) 354-2743

Canon U.S.A., Inc.
One Canon Plaza
Lake Success, NY 11042
(516) 488-6700
Fax: (516) 488-3623

Cauzin Systems, Inc.
835 S. Main St.
Waterbury, CT 06706
(800) 533-7323
(203) 573-0150
Fax: (203) 597-9762

Chinon America, Inc.
Information Equipment Division
660 Maple Avenue
Torrance, CA 90503
(213) 533-0274
Fax: (213) 533-1727

The Complete PC
521 Cottonwood Drive
Milpitas, CA 95035
(800) 634-5558
(408) 434-0145
Fax: (408) 434-1048

Computer Aided Technology, Inc.
7411 Hines Place, Suite 212
Dallas, TX 75235
(214) 631-6688
Fax: (214) 631-4059

Computer Identics
5 Shawmut Road
Canton, MA 02021
(800) 343-0846
(617) 821-0830
Fax: (617) 828-8942

Control Module, Inc.
380 Enfield Street
Enfield, CT 06082
(800) 722-6654
(203) 745-2433
Fax: (203) 741-6064

Datalogic Optic Electronics, Inc.
Bar Code Division
301 Gregson Dr.
MacGregor Park
Cary, NC 27511
(919) 481-1400
Fax: (919) 481-3654

Diamond Flower Electric Instruments Company (U.S.A.), Inc.
2544 Port Street
West Sacramento, CA 95691
(916) 373-1234
Fax: (916) 373-0221

Epson America, Inc.
23530 Hawthorne Boulevard
Torrance, CA 90505
(800) 922-8911
(213) 373-9511
(213) 539-9140

Focus Technology
18226 W. McDurmott
Irvine, CA 92714
(800) 852-0105
(714) 553-8626
Fax: (714) 553-8548

Follett Software Company
809 N. Front Street
McHenry, IL 60050
(800) 323-3397
(815) 344-8700
Fax: (815) 344-8774

Greywolf Technologies, Inc.
505 Main St.
P.O. Box 126
Willimantic, CT 06226
(203) 456-3322
Fax: (203) 456-4619

GUIS America, Inc.
9690 Telstar Ave., Suite 201
El Monte, CA 91731
(800) 888-8605
(818) 579-0047
Fax: (818) 579-7828

Input/Output Technology, Inc.
25327 Ave. Stanford
Valencia, CA 91355
(805) 257-1000
Fax: (805) 257-1015

International Technologies and Systems Corp.
635C N. Berry Street
Brea, CA 92621
(714) 990-1880
Fax: (714) 990-2503

KD Associates
13115 Washington Boulevard
Mar Vista, CA 90066
(213) 475-8545
Fax: (213) 827-8418

Key Tronic Corp.
P.O. Box 14687
Spokane, WA 99214
(800) 262-6006
(509) 928-8000
Fax: (509) 927-5216

KYE International, Inc.
12675 Colony Street
Chino, CA 91710
(800) 456-7593
(714) 590-3940
Fax: (714) 590-1231

Logitech, Inc.
6505 Kaiser Drive
Fremont, CA 94555
(800) 231-7717
(800) 552-8885 (CA)
(415) 795-8500
Fax: (415) 792-8901

Marstek
17785-A Skypark Circle
Irvine, CA 92714
(714) 833-7740
Fax: (714) 833-7813

MAXTRON
1825A Durfee Avenue
South El Monte, CA 91733
(818) 350-5706
Fax: (818) 350-4965

Mitsubishi Electronics America, Inc.
991 Knox Street
Torrance, CA 90502
(213) 217-5732
Fax: (213) 324-6578

MSI Data Corp.
(Subsidiary of Symbol Technologies, Inc.)
340 Fischer Avenue
Costa Mesa, CA 92626
(800) 854-3897
(714) 549-6000
Fax: (714) 641-5143

NCL America
1221 Innsbruck Drive
Sunnyvale, CA 94089
(408) 734-1006
Fax: (408) 744-0709

Newer Technology
1117 S. Rock Rd., Suite 4
Wichita, KS 67207
(800) 678-3726
(316) 685-4904
Fax: (316) 685-9368

NISCA, Inc.
1919 Old Denton Rd., Suite 104
Carrollton, TX 75006
(800) 245-7226

Opticon, Inc.
36 Ramland Road
Orangeburg, NY 10962
(914) 365-0090
Fax: (914) 365-1251

Our Business Machines, Inc.
12901 Ramona Blvd., Unit J
Irwindale, CA 91706
(818) 337-9614
Fax: (818) 960-1766

Packard Bell
9425 Canoga Avenue
Chatsworth, CA 91311
(818) 773-4400
Fax: (818) 773-9521

PERCON (Peripheral Connections, Inc.)
2190 West 11th Avenue
Eugene, OR 97402
(800) 873-7266
(503) 344-1189
Fax: (503) 344-1399

Shape, Inc.
Computer Products Divison
P.O. Box 366
Biddeford, ME 04005
(207) 282-6155
Fax: (207) 283-9130

SIMS Software
P.O. Box 607
Solana Beach, CA 92075
(619) 481-9292
Fax: (619) 481-3557

Skyworld Technology
1772 Lark Lane
Sunnyvale, CA 94087
(408) 446-9392
Fax: (408) 257-9337

Time Keeping Systems, Inc.
12434 Cedar Road
Cleveland, OH 44106
(216) 229-2579
Fax: (216) 229-2573

Vertex Industries, Inc.
23 Carol St.
P.O. Box 996
Clifton, NJ 07014
(201) 777-3500
Fax: (201) 472-0814

Videx, Inc.
1105 N.E. Circle Boulevard
Corvallis, OR 97330
(503) 758-0521
Fax: (503) 752-5285

Welch Allyn
Data Collection Division
Jordan Road
P.O. Box 187
Skaneateles Falls, NY 13153
(315) 685-8945
Fax: (315) 685-3172

Worthington Data Solutions
417 A Ingalls Street
Santa Cruz, CA 95060
(800) 345-4220
(408) 458-9938
Fax: (408) 458-9964

Mail-Order Firms and Others Mentioned in This Book

Parenthetical notes after the addresses indicate some of the products available from a particular source.

Alfa Power, Inc.
20311 Valley Blvd.
Suite L
Walnut, CA 91789
(714) 594-7171
Fax: (714) 595-4863
(Power supplies, clones)

Alywa Computer Corporation
831 E. Sandhill
Carson, CA 90746
(213) 604-9706
Fax: (213) 604-9707
(Clones)

American Research Corp.
1101 Monterey Pass Road
Monterey Park, CA 91754
(213) 265-0835
(800) 423-3877
(Clones (ARC))

Austin
10300 Metric Blvd.
Austin, TX 78758
(800) 752-1577
(512) 458-5106
Fax: (512) 454-1357
(Clones)

Bandy, Inc.
201 International Road
Garland, TX 75042
(214) 272-5455
Fax: (214) 272-5613
(Cases)

Black Box Corporation
P.O. Box 12800
Pittsburgh, PA 15241
(412) 746-5530
(Components)

Brier Technology
2363 Bering Drive
San Jose, CA 95131
(408) 435-8463
Fax: (408) 435-7921
(High-capacity floppy diskette systems)

Cable Depot
4487-B Park Drive
Norcross, GA 30093
(800) 343-4597
(404) 564-2323
Fax: (404) 381-2768
(Cables)

CompuAdd
12303 Technology Blvd.
Austin, TX 78727
(800) 333-3770
(512) 258-5575
Fax: (512) 335-6236
(Clones)

Computer Expert
1501 Broadway
Suite 2605
New York, NY 10036
(212) 840-2010
Fax: (212) 921-4172
(Clones)

Dalco Electronics
223 Pioneer Boulevard
Springboro, OH 45066
(800) 445-5342

DataStorm Technologies, Inc.
P.O. Box 1471
Columbia, MO 65205
(ProComm Plus Communications)

Focus Electronics Corp.
9080 Telestar Avenue
#302-304
El Monte, CA 91731
(818) 280-0416
Fax: (818) 280-4729
(Keyboards, cases, trackballs)

H.I.M.S. Technologies
368 Moontague Expressway
Milpitas, CA 95035
(800) 367-2924
(408) 946-9711
Fax: (408) 946-9744
(Clones)

Inmac
2465 Augustine Drive
Santa Clara, CA 95052

Innovative Technology Ltd.
P.O. Box 726
Elk City, OK 73648
(800) 253-4001
(Clones, LANs, printers)

InstaPlan
55 Redwood Hwy.
Suite 311
Mill Valley, CA 94941
(415) 389-1414
Fax: (415) 389-8046
(InstaPlan w/PERT project-management software)

Jade Computer
4901 W. Rosecrans Avenue
Box 5046
Hawthorne, CA 90251-5046
(800) 421-5500
(800) 262-1710 (CA)
(213) 973-7707
Fax: (213) 675-2522
(Components and systems)

Jameco Electronics
1355 Shoreway Road
Belmont, CA 94002
(415) 592-8097

Jensen Tools, Inc.
7815 46th Street
Phoenix, AZ 85044-5399
(602) 968-6231
Fax: (602) 438-1690
(Tools)

Legatech Computers
789 S. San Gabriel Blvd. #D
San Gabriel, CA 91776
(818) 309-2941
(Clones)

Lotus Development Corporation
55 Cambridge Parkway
Cambridge, MA 02142
(617) 577-8500
(Agenda project-management software)

Lyben Computer Systems
1050 East Maple Road
Troy MI 48083
(313) 589-3440

MCM Electronics
650 Congress Park Drive
Centerville, OH 45459
(513) 434-0031

Micro 1
557 Howard St.
San Francisco, CA 94105
(800) 338-4061
(415) 974-5439
Fax: (415) 974-6996
(Clones, disk controller)

MISCO
One MISCO Plaza
Holmdel, NJ 07733
(800) 876-4726
(Supplies, parts)

Northgate Computer Systems
P.O. Box 41000
Plymouth, MN 55441
(800) 548-1993

PC Designs
2500 North Hemlock Circle
Broken Arrow, OK 74012
(800) 627-4248
(918) 251-7503
Fax: (918) 251-7057
(Clones)

PC Exchange
7 Zel Plaza
Spring Valley, NY 10977
(800) 342-5729
(914) 426-2400
Fax: (914) 426-2600
(Components)

Software Partners
447 Old Boston Road
Topsfield, MA 01983
(617) 887-6409
(Time$heet Professional project-management software)

Supernet Computer, Inc.
1001 Baltimore Pike
Springfield, PA 19069
(215) 544-7722
(Clones)

Symantec
10201 Torre Avenue
Cupertino, CA 95014-2132
(408) 253-4092
Fax: (408) 253-4092
(Timeline project-management software)

Traveling Software
North Creek Corporate Center
19310 North Creek Parkway
Bothell, WA 98011
(206) 483-8088
Fax: (206) 487-1284

Tussy Computer Products
3075 Research Drive
State College, PA 16801
(800) 468-9044
(814) 234-2236
Fax: (814) 237-4450
(Swan clones)

UARCO Inc.
121 North Ninth Street
DeKalb, IL 60115
(800) 435-0713
(Supplies, parts)

Hardware Troubleshooting

The key to diagnosing and fixing most problems is to think of your computer as a gathering of small subsystems rather than as a single unit. By the time you've read this far into this book, this concept should be very apparent to you, since we have been concentrating on showing you how to upgrade or build a system one subsystem at a time.

For troubleshooting purposes, we'll divide the computer as follows:

Power Supply

System Board

Memory

Video Adapter

Video Display

Keyboard

I/O Ports

Printer

Modem

We'll also add, as a part of the computer, the operating system and applications software.

Before we proceed any further, let's establish a basic rule of troubleshooting: ASK THE QUESTION, "WHAT HAS CHANGED?"

1. Has the system ever worked before?

2. What is the most recent change that has been made to the system? Has a new part been installed? Has the equipment been moved? Has it been unplugged?

3. Can you restore the system to the way it was before any changes were made?

The process of troubleshooting is based on the application of human logic. If the computer comes to life, you don't need to spend time checking to see if it is receiving power. If the disk drives spin and load the operating system, you can skip over problem determination for the drives and controllers. Start by asking the question, "What is the apparent failure, and how is the failure related to the rest of the system?"

For example, if your video display is not working properly, you should concentrate first on the monitor itself. (Is it turned on? Is it plugged in? Are the controls for contrast, brightness, and color properly set? Are there any switches that might have been put in the wrong position? Is the cable properly connected at the monitor and computer?) You would move on from there to examining whether the video display adapter in the computer is functioning properly. (Is it installed? Is it properly seated in its socket on the bus? Have any switches or jumpers been changed?)

Because the computer is an intelligent system, in many instances it can help you in your troubleshooting by conducting its own internal tests (the *Power-On Start-up Tests*, or *POST*, that are included in the ROM BIOS of most PCs), and by cooperating with you in the conduct of a disk-based diagnostics program.

Obviously, though, there are situations in which the diagnostic programs will not help you. If, for example, your system is not getting power, then neither the POST nor the disk-based diagnostics will run. If the system is getting power, but the disk drives are malfunctioning, then the disk-based program cannot be used.

Power Symptom

As an example of the application of a logical approach to a troubleshooting problem, let's assume that the computer does not show any sign of life:

STOP SIGN: Do you smell something burning or hear electrical (not mechanical) noises? Quickly and carefully unplug the computer from the wall outlet. If there is a fire, you do not want to put water on the computer if you can at all avoid it, and you never want to put water on a device that is plugged into a live electrical outlet. You should have a dry chemical fire extinguisher in your home or office in any case. If you do have a fire, we strongly recommend that you take your system to a professional maintenance facility for diagnosis, repair, and a thorough cleaning.

1. BASIC QUESTION: Is the computer receiving power? Is the power-on light (if your system has one) illuminated? Can you hear the cooling fan in the power supply? If yes, then there is power from the wall to the system; skip to question 2. If no, continue below.

CHECK: Is the power cord plugged into a wall socket? Is the other end of the power cord firmly plugged into the computer?

SOLUTION: Reseat the power cord at both ends.

CHECK: Is the power cord cut or damaged in some way?

SOLUTION: Replace the power cord. You can obtain substitutes at most computer stores. Bring the old cord with you to be sure to get a properly shaped replacement part.

CHECK: Is the computer power switch turned on?

SOLUTION: Turn it on.

CHECK: Is the power cord plugged into a surge protector or multiple outlet power block?

SOLUTION: Determine if the device has its own on/off switch. Determine if the device has a fuse or circuit breaker. (If the fuse has blown or the breaker has tripped, it would be best to determine the reason for the outage before turning on the system again.) If you think the device itself may be at fault, remove it, and plug your computer directly into the outlet to see if it works.

CHECK: Is there power to the wall socket?

SOLUTION: Conduct a test. First of all, determine if the outlet is "live" by plugging in a radio or lamp that you know to be working. If it doesn't respond, the problem is not in your computer but instead in your electrical circuit. Is the outlet controlled by a wall switch? Turn the switch and see if power is restored. Check to see if the fuse or circuit breaker to the outlet has been blown or tripped. (If so, it would be best to determine the reason—a short or overload is most common—before you reset the circuit and turn your computer back on.)

2. BASIC QUESTION: Is the computer power supply functioning? The power light and the power supply fan are wired directly to the incoming line voltage, and the fact that they are functioning does not tell you whether the power supply itself is working properly.

CHECK: Determine the incoming voltage level.

SOLUTION: If you have an electrical multimeter, it would be valuable to examine the nature of the power being offered your system. Most "110-volt" PC power supplies are able to work properly in the range from 104 to 127 volts. Many such devices will shut down—or blow an internal fuse—if levels are outside this range. Your radio or lamp may operate over a wider range.

What if your power is outside the range? The problem may be a temporary one—a "brownout" by the power company at a time of very high demand, or a problem at the generating plant. Or you may have an ongoing problem with the power to your office or home. Start by calling the power company and asking if they are aware of a problem. Solutions to overvoltage situations include the use of a "power conditioner" device; such units also usually include surge-protection circuits.

Monitor

A common problem is a misadjustment of the controls on the front or back of the monitor. It is quite easy to turn down the contrast and brightness of the system so that your screen appears to be completely blank. Check for detents (clickstop positions) on the rotary dials that indicate the preferred position. The monitor might also have an "automatic" button that overrides any dial settings in favor of factory defaults; try switching it on and off.

Another possible area of fault is the cable from the computer to the monitor. The video signal is particularly sensitive to a loose connection or crimp in the cable.

Index

C

D